The Cultivator's Handbook of Marijuana

Ronin Publishing, Inc.   Berkeley CA 94701

The
Cultivator's
Handbook
by
Bill Drake

'uana

The material in this book is presented as
information and drug education available
to the public. The publisher does not
advocate breaking the law. However, we
urge readers to support N.O.R.M.L. (2001
S Street, N.W., Washington, D.C. 20009)
in its efforts to secure passage of fair
marijuana legislation.

ISBN 914171-53-4

Cover and text design by
Michael Patrick Cronan.

Typography by Robert Sibley; and
Ginger Ashworth, H. S. Dakin Company.

*Sections marked with the asterisk are new to
the 1986 revised edition.

W hen I wrote the first edition of the *Cultivator's Handbook* in 1969, only a few people in the country were growing seriously. There was no incentive to risk trouble for growing marijuana when anyone with $10 could find plenty of excellent quality Mexican around. Most of the folks I knew who grew in the late sixties did so for personal and political reasons, although some early commercial homegrowers were already well known in the West and East Coast undergrounds when this *Handbook* was first written.

Today the best estimates are that there are 200,000 people in the U.S. who grow marijuana for a living, and many more who simply grow a few plants as a hobby and for personal stash. Most of the small growers I know produce in the range of 10–30 pounds of high quality buds per year, because if you have many more plants than that in most places, you are asking for serious attention. This translates into annual production of between 2–6 million pounds of marijuana, or 2,000–6,000 tons. Most of this tonnage is top grade smoke, the well known Sinsemilla, bringing anywhere from $75–250 an ounce, depending on the time of year and the local market. This pricing range leaves the bottom and middle ranges of the market wide open for imported marijuana, largely Mexican, which sells from $35–100 an ounce, and has a lot of shake, stems and seeds.

Another reality of marijuana cultivation today is that it has gone mainstream in the American farm scene. Without marijuana as a cash crop, many of the remaining American family farms would be out of business. Sure there are still thousands of wild-man entrepreneurs with patches hidden in the hills, but there are a lot more regular-looking men and women who raise animals, fruit, vegetables, grain, or other conventional crops — and a small patch of high potency homegrown that pays all those bills that the hard work and conventional crops can't begin to touch. Marijuana has become an important part of the cash flow of a significant proportion of today's American small family farm. It is a prime example of what farm experts are talking about when they refer to high value cash crops as the salvation of the American small family farm — though of course, none of the current crop of experts is recommending marijuana specifically.

Several important new trends have emerged in America and the world since 1969, when this book was first written. Marijuana consciousness has made tremendous contributions to American society as those who learned from the insights of the drug experiences of the sixties and seventies have moved on into the middle levels of American institutions and society. While drugs like marijuana are popularly blamed for all that's wrong with society, the fact is that marijuana consciousness has already had a profound, revolutionary positive effect on the way Americans live and interact with each other.

Marijuana use has made millions of people more aware of themselves and others, more open as human beings, more willing to share the other person's perspectives. Marijuana use is no longer a revolutionary political or social act. Among those who have been using it for years, it is a normal part of life, in many cases simply an old habit. Among those new to the experience, it's still a great adventure in consciousness.

The contemporary drug scene has debased marijuana consciousness to some extent, since it is now often simply used as part of a wide range of simultaneous chemical highs. Marijuana used to be one of the few chemical adventures in town; now there are designer drugs being made and sold on every corner. Marijuana consciousness no longer encompasses the aspirations of a generation of young people — their rebelliousness, their beliefs and visions. Instead, marijuana consciousness has settled in for the long run in American society, and in each generation to come, there will be some who will use it and grow, and some who will abuse it and fail to grow.

The drug bureaucracy has settled in — as an acknowledged failure at its stated task. Thus it qualifies as a permanent fixture of government. The law continues to punish those who grow their own more severely than those who buy from a dealer, in effect protecting the territory of the organized drug producers and dealers. On the bright side, this web of semi-commando organizations provides an outlet for all those government guys in modified baseball caps who never got beyond Saturday morning cartoon mentality. Meanwhile, the international marijuana trade becomes steadily more corrupted and chemically contaminated.

Everything happening today in marijuana cultivation is a lot more sophisticated than the tools, techniques, knowledge, and marketing opportunities were in the late sixties when the first edition of *Cultivator's Handbook* appeared, but one thing hasn't changed — the law will still take away the property, freedom, and future of those caught growing marijuana. The reasons for this punitive situation have never had very much to do with the relative degree of danger presented by marijuana use in society. Still, armadas of attorneys, police, bureaucrats, counselors, officials of all kinds are kept afloat by the rising tide of anti-drug hysteria in America.

Not that widespread use of marijuana by increasingly younger people hasn't resulted in a lot of difficulty for plenty of people. With millions of people trying marijuana each year, and with many continuing to use and even abuse it, there are definitely health effects. Many of these negative health effects have to do with deliberate contamination of marijuana by government agencies which spray the fields with herbicides, but fail to prevent the harvesting and selling of this chemicalized trash. There is also a serious problem created by the use of insecticides by marijuana growers in Third World countries. In addition, any time you have millions of people using a substance — drug or food — there are going to be health problems which arise in some of them. At the same time, it is clear that marijuana use, by and large, has failed to create the degenerative havoc which its scapegoaters used to erect vast legal, police and bureaucratic structures.

These structures are now firmly in place, and they wield power over all citizens, drug users and non-users alike. For instance, drug enforcers are now seriously proposing, with strong support from industry technocrats and many others, that all workers and employees in America submit to testing of their blood and urine for evidence of drug use. Once government agencies and our private bosses acquire the power to force people to pee into a jar or give a blood sample at their command, does anyone suppose they will fail to progress from there to mandatory genetic coding and other human engineering programs?

Drug laws have acted in general to advance police and other potentially tyrannical state powers into areas of personal privilege and liberty where they could not have gone, without the license to pursue bad guys no matter what the cost to society.

Observant readers will note that the same government which uses drugs as an excuse to take away our fundamental liberties, fails to regulate cigarettes, snuff, and other "tobacco" products in any way, and thrives on the taxes created by all those millions smoking and dipping their way into chemical death. (The story is far worse — for a taste of what the government, and the cigarette industry is really doing to smokers, check the Appendix in the back of this book.)

It is clear that society as a whole is not worried about drugs in the same way that our leaders and our institutions are. Our leaders and institutions see some very real problems, and associate them with drugs. They see lack of productivity and drugs, low job performance and drugs, school problems and drugs, emotional traumas and drugs, joblessness and drugs — and they all say "Aha! It must be the drugs!" Thus enlightened, they are easy prey for the guys in the suits and the high tech helmets and choppers. "Yes," they say, "it is the drugs. Give us enough manpower, enough machinery, and enough money, and we will stop the drugs."

Next come the host of professionals serving the interests of the drug police, the institutions, and our leaders. Oh yes, say the counselors, the social workers, and other laborers in the field of the distressed psyche — it is definitely the drugs which are causing the problem. Along come the scientists, hard and soft varieties, who make magic in the name of research and announce things like "One marijuana joint is as harmful as a pack of cigarettes," and add their editorial endorsement to the notion that drugs are the problem. Then too, there have been thousands of people who got entangled with drugs, had a bad life experience, and are now thoroughly convinced that if they hadn't done drugs, they would have lived a better life.

These reformed sinners do what such folks have always done — which is to become fanatical about saving others from what they believe caused their own downfall. The assumption is always "I couldn't handle this particular problem, so you certainly can't handle it either. I am going to save you by preventing you from having the original experience, which is so terrible that you must take it on my authority rather than experiencing it yourself."

The anti-drug crusades have gathered in millions of bewildered souls longing to hear that it's drugs and the devil to blame for what's wrong with America. They are right, of course, but for all the wrong reasons, and the delusion system which supports their reasoning is as dangerous as the drugs they fear. The fact is that some drugs do have an evil spirit, a demon in residence, and these demons can do awful, inhuman damage. Many westerners laugh when they look at Buddhist drawings of demons, grotesque creatures with fangs, claws, tongues of fire, and giant red eyes, adorned with necklaces of human skulls. How unsophisticated, many think, to believe in creatures like this in a modern world of computers, cars, and designer drugs. The fact is, the Buddhists are just drawing what they see when they look at the world through eyes which see reality from a different perspective than we do. What they draw is real, and anyone who thinks differently and proceeds to do drugs with a contempt for the reality of demons is offering himself as a charmingly naïve snack for some very nasty psychic entities.

A recent corollary development is that a strong consciousness has grown among young people who do not use drugs — they no longer consider themselves the unadventurous, the nerds. They've seen a lot of their fellow kids crash and burn on drugs, and the halls of their schools are littered with the ghosts of young people from classes gone before who got into drugs, got lost and died or were destroyed. The young people today who reject drugs are growing up free of many potential problems. Those who do use drugs, but who stick with the natural drugs, and use them with intelligent moderation, are the winners in today's drug scene, where so many true demons lurk in brightly colored pills and innocent crystal powders.

(Left) Polyploid leaf.
See photographs pages 71 & 143.

The marijuana plant is a great force in the evolution of human consciousness. It is central to the liberation of feelings and ideas, the development of sensory awareness, and the appreciation of life as it is lived each moment. The study and cultivation of marijuana is an act of joy.

I have loved this plant for years. So this book will be about the Cultivation of Marijuana, not just the growing of it. One cultivates marijuana and, by marijuana, one is cultivated.

The marijuana plant is a being of a high order. It will thrive on whatever planet it finds itself. Its sexuality is fully developed. A fine degree of awareness shows in its adaptability. Its potent life force manifests itself in its energy of growth and form. Its creativity as a chemical sorcerer is unsurpassed. This magical chemistry of the marijuana plant has brought much of civilization to its present locus: poised on the edge of flight into inner space.

Marijuana has been one of humanity's most deliberate companions for over 20,000 years. It has made its home with us wherever we have wandered — in our dung heaps and garbage piles, alongside our trails and roads, on our rooftops, beside our graves, and, lately, in our homes. The marijuana plant has been the delight of several high civilizations. Ours is the most recent, and the inheritor of the whole of the past.

This hardy being doesn't need our hand in its life in order to grow well. You can toss a few seeds on the ground, rake them under, and wait for the rain and sun to work together. A plant will usually grow. But these plants have a relationship with us which goes beyond need. It borders on choice. It is easy enough to realize we have chosen this plant. It takes more thought to realize that this plant has chosen us.

Marijuana and the People

Cannabis serves several purposes for man. As a source of fiber, this plant has long served to clothe people, make tents for them, and hang them. The fiber of the hemp plant is long, strong and durable, wearing as well as flax or cotton, and it is more easily processed. The seeds provide an oil with a number of industrial uses, primarily in paint and soap manufacture, and the residues from the oil extraction are pressed into a cake which makes excellent animal feed. In a number of places the seeds are roasted and eaten by connoisseurs. Smoked, they can give you a bad headache. The resin contains the substances responsible for the magical, visionary and euphoric properties of the drugs derived from this plant.

Marijuana is one of our oldest cultivars. Written records of humanity's involvement with *Cannabis sativa* go back almost 5,500 years and it is certain that the relationship preceded writing by thousands of years.

The Chinese have a long association with hemp (*ma*). Their main use of the plant has always been for its excellent fiber. But all parts of the plant find some place in the Chinese herbal medicine system. The flowers (*ma-p'o*) are used in treating sores, wounds, burns and ulcers. The seed coat, or bract (*ma-len*), with its strong resin content is used in treatments for nervous disorders. The seeds themselves (*ma-jen*), when applied as a paste, are used to counteract inflammation, local swelling, or puffiness of the skin. Seeds are also considered a good laxative and diuretic compound and are excellent for worming infants and animals. The oil extract of the seed (*ma-yo*) is used as a hair tonic and to combat stomach problems. Fresh leaves, crushed and used as a warm poultice, are perfect for scorpion bites according to this system, while the ash obtained by completely burning the plant is most useful in making sky rockets.

Evidence of early hemp culture has turned up all over the world. In the region of the Volga River, the Sythians grew hemp for its fiber, but did not neglect its other properties. They developed a technique of throwing the flower tops into a smoldering fire and gathering around the fire underneath a blanket or skin. Then they inhaled the vapors rising from the coals. An inefficient and wasteful way to smoke marijuana, one might criticize, but the Sythians had plenty of flowers, and papers were rare on the banks of the Volga 3,000 years ago.

Hemp fabrics have been found in Egyptian sites dating from 2,000 B.C. and in Turkish sites from around 800 B.C. The early Romans knew of hemp cultivation in their eastern Mediterranean colonies and the Mesopotamian valley, where it certainly had long been known.

Hemp cloth has turned up at sites in Europe estimated to be 6,000 years old and at many other sites of more recent origin. Researchers who have taken core samples of lake beds in England report that the pollen count curve for Cannabis shows continuous and increasing cultivation beginning with early Anglo-Saxon settlement of the British Isles. King Arthur knew what he was doing in the fields of Camelot.

There is much interesting debate on exactly where Cannabis originated. Most experts agree that the plant comes from Asia, but there is little agreement on where in Asia it first attached itself to the human community. There seems to be some good evidence that the origins of Cannabis lie to the north of the Himalayas, to the east of the Caspian Sea, and to the south of Lake Baikal — in other words, Central Asia. Most scholars agree that Cannabis entered Europe from Russia rather than the Mediterranean, and many date its arrival from the invasion of the Sythians around 1,500 B.C. The westward spread of the plant

the plant most desirable for fiber was pulled early in its life. In the course of history, hundreds of variants of Cannabis have been produced by the fine finger of human intent. Then, too, Cannabis is a plant with a mind of its own. It grows where it pleases and changes itself to suit conditions. It is even capable of spontaneous metamorphosis during growth to adapt to environmental conditions, with no human help or interference at all.

In its migration with human beings across the face of the planet, the marijuana plant has experienced many

followed the fortunes of the Teutonic peoples. At this point in the plant's history confusion develops.

One of the primary reasons for the confusion over Cannabis' origin is its long intense involvement with people. From the first, humanity's relationship with the plant has been manipulative.

In areas where man was primarily interested in it as a source of fiber, he selected the long tall spindly plants at the expense of the flowery leafy ones. In areas where the drug properties were preferred,

struggles. All else being equal, the determining factor in a plant's spread is competition. All plants compete in a given area for that neighborhood's water, nutrition, space, and light. The competition among plants can be physical — faster growing plants crowd out others. It can be toxic — one plant's juices poison the soil so others can't grow nearby. It can be sneaky — one plant's roots extend deeper, it gets better nutrition and *then* crowds the others out. It can get pretty nasty in the plant world in its own slow-motion way.

Cannabis in its natural state — leaves and flowering tops — is known by many names. India knows it as Bhang and Ganja, in Turkey it is Kabak, in Tunisia it is Takrouri, and in Algeria and Morocco it is Kif. The marijuana of Lebanon and Syria is called Hashish el Keif. In southern Africa it is Dagga while further north in Africa, near the equator, it is called Djamba. In Brazil, it is known as Maconha. In Madagascar the flowering tops are called Rongony while in Mozambique this most smokable of herbs is Suruma. In each case, these names designate the unprocessed flowering tops and leaves.

sweetened milk or water. On occassion, it is mixed instead with alcohol, in which case it is called Lutki. Lutki is often fortified with either opium or Datura. Then it is called Mudra.

Ganja comes in three basic forms. It is always prepared from the mature flowering tops of usually unfertilized plants.

Flat Ganja is prepared by cutting away all large stalks and lower leaves. The remaining spikes are placed on mats. Barefooted workmen then trample on the cross-layered piles in the heat of the day

The ways in which flowering tops of Cannabis are prepared vary considerably, but the products of India are, by and large, representative.

Bhang is prepared from leaves plucked from the growing plant, generally the lower leaves of the male plant. These leaves are usually ground or finely chopped while still green and are prepared as a drink or sherbet. Bhang is regarded as a low grade drug or, in many places, as something other than a drug — as a tonic or simple refreshment. Bhang is pounded and mixed with spiced and

and, as each layer is flattened, another layer of fresh spikes is added. The flattened spikes are then separated, packed flat and graded according to size, as either *Large Flat* or *Ewig Flat*.

Round Ganja is produced by rolling the large mature flowering spikes of Cannabis between the hands until they become smooth, round, and tapered. These tapered spikes are then packed 24 to a bundle.

Chur-Ganja is the waste from processing either flat or round Ganja. It consists of broken pieces of flowering tops, powder, leaf fragments, small twigs, etc. It is often dried, chopped, powdered and bagged and is considered the lowest grade of Ganja.

In most countries, no such ceremony of preparation exists. Usually, the flowering tops are simply harvested, dried, crushed, occasionally mixed with tobacco or datura, and smoked.

Charas, or Hashish, is the crude resin obtained from the flowering tops of unfertilized female Cannabis grown in very hot dry regions of the world. Generally speaking, the hotter and dryer the climate, the more pronounced the little droplets of resin on the flowers will be. This is because the resin serves, among other things, as a means of conserving moisture in the leaves and flowers. This is especially true when the plant is approaching maturity and the small flowers are in delicate condition.

Crude resin products, known as Charas in much of the Far East and Hashish in the Middle East, are an ancient trade item. For many centuries, Charas was produced at Yarkand, now Soche, in China. To the market at Yarkand was brought the Charas grown on the slopes of the great mountain ranges of that region — on the northern spurs of the Chung-Kyr Mountains, the arid slopes of the Parnir, and the sweeping southern slopes of the Tianshan range.

Hash merchants from the south made their way to the Yarkand market each year in great trade caravans and, having made their purchases, followed the Black Jade Road down to the Indus River Valley, crossing the formidable Kara-Koram pass at a height of 5,562 meters. Other traders came to Yarkand from Persia and the West and would return home by way of the ancient Silk Road through the broad trench of the Red Waters River Valley. There are two great rivers intertwined here, running between the magnificent Trans-Alai range and its sister range, the Alai, in modern day USSR.

Charas is processed differently in different places. In some countries, when the plants reach maturity, cultivators move through the fields dressed in leather jackets rubbing against and embracing the plants. The resin is then scraped from their jackets with blunt-edged, curved knives. Other places, strips of rough leather are drawn over the flowering plants in the heat of the day

and the strips are scraped after they accumulate a coat of the sun-warmed resin. Elsewhere, the cultivators go into the field with a bowl slung at their waists, rolling and kneading the flowering tops with their hands. The resin extracted is scraped from their hands into the bowl. The resin collected by any of these methods is first quality, very potent and very clean.

This premier quality resin is most often marketed in small sticks or cakes, rarely weighing more than 250 grams. They are slightly plastic in consistency, become brown with age, and often show distinct signs of hand-processing. Fresh resin has a minty odor, with an underlying heady sweetness.

Methods of secondary collection vary but share certain characteristics. In all cases, the plant is harvested and dried. The dried plants are gently beaten and the powder obtained is collected on mats or cloth set beneath the beating bench.

In other places, the dried plants are rubbed between cotton sheets which are then scraped and the produce set aside as best quality. Subsequent, rougher rubbings take place, until the dried plant will no longer yield resin to the cloth. Each successive stage results in less and less commercially valuable resin.

The resin obtained from secondary collection methods is usually treated in one of two ways. In the first case, the resin is kneaded with a little water and formed into a rough mass of plastic consistency. This mass is left to air-dry and finally cut into sheets which age to a dark brown on the outside.

In the second instance, the resin collected by beating or rubbing is put into linen, skin, or other sorts of bags and is steamed. After a bit of steaming, the dough-like resin is pressed into various shapes, often imprinted with a commercial emblem.

Most hashish reaching the U.S. is processed from secondary collection resin and is rarely worth its premium price. In an extensive series of assays, hashish on the streets in the U.S. averaged lower in THC content than good home-grown marijuana. When you're buying instead of growing your own, fresh potent hash oil is usually a far better buy than hashish.

Over the centuries of cultivating and observing Cannabis, people have noticed the relationships that either hurt or help the plant. Marijuana does particularly poorly in competition with spinach, garden cress and rye. (Maybe the narcs will unleash deputized spinach upon Nebraska!) But if Cannabis is grown in association with Beetroot (*Beta vulgaris*) or a certain species of turnip (*Branica oleracca*), all members of the cabbage family, or (as many cultivators in the corn belt of America already know) that wonderful sweet garden corn, it grows marvelously well.

While Cannabis has struggled with other plants and usually prevailed, and gotten together with humanity, it has also developed a relationship with the animal world. Birds love the oil-rich seeds of this fruitful plant and in their ecstasies of eating have swallowed many seeds whole. Throughout the ages Cannabis has flown here and there in the bellies of the birds and then found itself plopped down on the earth in a pile of poop, ready to go.

Some ancient Italian in a proverb-making mood observed "Hemp will grow anywhere, but without manure, though it were planted in heaven itself, it will be of no use at all." How lucky it is for Hemp to find Heaven in a pile of birdshit. How fortunate for the birds to find themselves high. How fortunate for the first men and women to notice how the little singing creatures became euphoric after eating the seeds of the tall, strong-smelling plant. The planet is tight.

Myths—
Fact
and Fiction

There are a number of persistent myths about Cannabis in circulation and this seems like a good time to lay them aside.

One of the hardiest myths is that the potency of such strains as Panama Red, Acapulco Gold, Colombian, etc., is due to a felicitous combination of growing conditions. In fact, growing conditions have nothing to do with a plant's *potency*. There is a relationship between soil quality and the overall health of the plant and certain mineral deficiencies cut way down on resin production (p. 58). Also, climate affects such aspects of a plant's growth as foliage, resin secretion, and number and size of flowers.

But potency itself is strictly genetics. The strength of any given plant as drug material is a combination of resin quantity and potency. Quantity is environmentally determined to a substantial degree. Potency is genetically fixed.

There are usually significant variations, however, between different parts of the plant. In general, the higher up on the plant, the higher the potency; and the further out toward the growing tips of branches, the more potent the leaves. The gradient of potency is such that the top flowers on a mature female can have as much as 1000% more THC by weight than the innermost bottom leaves.

There are ways to manipulate the genetics of the growing plant to enable it to produce a more potent resin (p. 158). But the idea that you have to live in the tropics to grow good marijuana just isn't so, as thousands of successful cultivators know. Plants as potent as any from Oaxaca or Colombia can be grown in Fairbanks and Minneapolis as easily as in Maui.

There is another persistent myth which holds that male plants are useless for smoking, that they are weak in potency, low in resin, and generally ought to be depised and discarded. This is totally false (pp. 40-43).

One growing myth holds that very high nitrogen fertilizer is always best for Cannabis. The fact is, the closer the soil is to natural the better. Too heavy a dose of nitrogen in early life will kill a little plant while a nitrogen surplus in later life will cut way down on resin secretion. Most often, marijuana plants in natural settings don't need a lot of fiddling around with nutrients; however, there are a few very productive things cultivators can do to feed their plants for optimum growth. We'll cover these later on.

Many people believe all that is needed for an artificial light source to grow Cannabis is an ordinary lightbulb, but such bulbs emit an overabundance of red and infrared rays, starving the plants of essential full-spectrum energy. This causes them to stretch toward the light source in an agony of deprivation. Some people might mistake this fast growth as a positive sign but the plants soon just lay down and die. The relationship between Cannabis and light is covered extensively in a later chapter.

It is also not true that Sinsemilla is anything mysterious. Sinsemilla is a lovely and poetic Mexican name for the unfertilized mature female of proper genetic background grown during long hot days. Anyone can grow Sinsemilla as long as they learn to recognize and pull the males in time and meet ordinary environmental conditions.

Many people believe that Cannabis is more potent in very alkaline soils. It is true that when soil pH drops, young plants, in particular, suffer. But the relationship between plant health and soil environment is complex and the discussion on pp. 60-63 should dispel any myths about alkalinity as a factor in potency.

High temperatures are not necessarily conducive to production of an optimum plant either, though the relationship between high temperatures and resin production is considerable. This does not mean, however, that a cultivator must have high temperatures in order to grow premier marijuana. As for creating high humidity situations — don't do it. Cannabis does not do well indoors with high humidity. Such conditions can cause an accumulation of plant poisons in the leaves which can kill the plant in short order. Or it can result in a crop of plants great for weaving but poor for smoking.

Detailed discussions of these myths and the realities which confront them will be handled in the appropriate places in the body of the book. Over the years the number of dead plants and ruined efforts resulting from the circulation of the many myths, half-truths and simple errors is a shame. I have done my best to check out all the information which appears in this revised edition. There has been a great deal of growing experience and research in the last decade. Much of it is very useful, confirming earlier conclusions about optimal growing methods, and elaborating upon knowledge of the subtle life processes of Cannabis. Again, any cultivators who feel they have information to add or dispute what they find here, please communicate. If changes are called for, I will make them.

It's easy to forget that there is no reasonable basis for marijuana's illegal status. The laws which have made criminals of millions of us were conceived by a conspiracy of frustrated repressed males, fifty years ago, in an atmosphere of petty venal backroom politicking. All it took to create the Marijuana Menace was a few self-aggrandizing cops, afraid they were about to lose their jobs because prohibition was ending, a few congressmen who knew a good bad thing when they heard about it, and a paranoid newspaper publisher who fawned over the police, hated the non-rich and non-white, and who knew that his style of hate was what was needed daily by millions of anger addicts.

The motivation of this loose conspiracy was fear: fear of loss of control over the poor and the uneducated, and fear of the renegade. It was easy to make marijuana illegal: nobody with any influence smoked it. Those who did — poor people, creative people, black people and brown people and yellow people, free-floating street entrepreneurs, hustlers and schemers — were the classic victims of social paranoids, the natural prey of the corrupt law and the sensationalizing press.

This seamy state of affairs stood in some contrast to 19th century America's experience with marijuana. From 1860 to 1900, semi-secret, very discreet but often very luxurious hashish-houses sprang up in most major American cities. The houses were frequented by society and the artistic-intellectual community, who were mimicking the avant-garde of Europe, where hashish was the rage.

France was, in this period, an exporter of avant-garde cultural styles much as California is today. Sophisticated young French heads were commonplace in many American cities, so the discovery of marijuana and hashish by young Americans was not long in coming.

With condescending amusement, a London writer describes the marijuana scene of the 1860's:

"Young America is beginning to use 'the Bang', so popular among the Hindoos, though in a rather different manner. It is not a 'drink' but a mixture of bruised hemp tops and the powder of the betel, rolled up like a quid of tobacco. It turns the lips and gums a deep red, and if indulged in largely, produces violent intoxication. Lager beer and schnapps will give way for 'Bang' and red lips, instead of red noses, become the style."

From red noses in 1760 to red lips in 1860 to red eyes in the 1970's. It has long been part of our American heritage; an aspect of the Bicentennial stolidly ignored.

But by the first decade of this century, the anti-drug forces were becoming strong and marijuana, along with other popular and folk drugs, was coming under increasingly effective attack. It was soon driven underground.

In 1915, California enacted the first legislation against marijuana and classed it with the hard narcotics. By the late 20's, marijuana was illegal in such places as Texas, Colorado and Louisiana — all states where there was significant use of the drug by large numbers of non-white people against whom the enforcement of any prohibition law was both easy and popular.

In 1930, the Bureau of Narcotics was established and from then until 1937, when the first marijuana laws went into effect, America was treated to a propaganda campaign which was both absurd and very effective. This entire effort stemmed from the attempt to prevent marijuana from making inroads into the white middle class.

A sampling of the crude but effective mentality which energized the Marijuana Menace reveals the racist thrust of much of the propaganda. Ethnic minorities had no voice and could be slandered, scapegoated and exploited by anyone with authority. The narcotics police did just that.

Harry Anslinger — first commissioner and just about founder of the Bureau of Narcotics — was moved to warn his countrymen in 1929 that "abuse of this drug consists principally in the smoking thereof, in the form of cigarettes for the narcotic effect. This abuse is noted particularly among the Latin-American or Spanish-speaking population. The sale of Cannabis cigarettes occurs wherever there are settlements of Latin Americans."

Medical opinion was similarly unenlightened. In 1931, the New Orleans Medical and Surgical Journal informed its readership that "the debasing and baneful influence of hashish and opium is not restricted to individuals, but has manifested itself in nations and races as well. The dominant race and most enlightened countries are alcoholic, whilst the nations and races addicted to hemp and opium, some of which once attained the heights of culture and civilization, have deteriorated both mentally and physically."

In 1928, Winnifred Black, an anti-drug polemicist, said in her book, *Dope*, a classic tract, that "you can grow enough marijuana in a windowbox to drive the whole population of the United States stark, staring, raving mad." No small thinker, Winnifred. Wonder where she got her seeds?

With this nonsense being thrown about and with no effective voice raised in

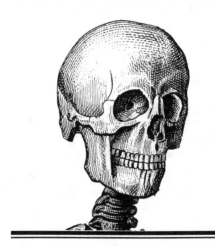

support of marijuana and its use as a drug of choice, it's no wonder it was made illegal. The interests of a small effectively placed group were served. The people affected by the laws were in no position to make any fuss. In 1937, the busts began.

Grateful acknowledgement to Michael Aldridge for inspiration for "Creation of the Marijuana Menace".

For many years there has been a great debate among botanists and marijuana connoisseurs over whether or not Cannabis Sativa and Cannabis Indica are two species, or two varieties of a single species. Without attempting to get between advocates of either point of view, I would simply like to point out that there are plenty of distinctions between the two Cannabis types, beginning with their historical origins. Cannabis Sativa has a European history going back many centuries, during which time it was cultivated almost exclusively as hemp, a fiber-producing plant with no known psychoactive properties. Wild Sativa plants make a bit more resin than their domestic cousins, but not enough to interest anyone but the most dedicated rope smoker. The only appreciators of wild hemp are the birds, and when escaped Cannabis goes to seed, there's always a mellow little chorus of chirps and whistles coming from the center of the thicket. Few early Europeans noticed these little birdy parties, and when they did, they probably tried eating the seeds too — with predictably dull results. Nobody in Europe, or the rest of the Old World, knew anything about smoking — it took the discovery of the New World to introduce this practice to the rest of us, and the first tobacco was a lot more psychoactive than any of the hemp then being grown.

Sativa didn't really come into its own until it was brought from Europe to the New World by colonists hoping to establish a fiber trade in the early Americas. The first Sativa fields established in Cuba were no doubt suitable only for shirtmaking, but by the end of the first season the birds had probably given the whole act away. Let's not forget that this Sativa hemp was now being grown in an area of the world where everybody smoked anything within reach. As soon as the first campesinos saw warblers collapsing onto the warm tropical earth with sleepy smiles on their stiff little beaks, they must have grabbed a handful of cornhusks and fired up. Enter the grandfather of Acapulco Gold.

On the other side of the world, in the Himalayas and the rainforests of Asia, another Cannabis had been known and revered for centuries. This plant grew as a squat, intensely green bush in the mountains, and grew to impressive heights in the lowland forests and on the Indian plain. Cannabis Indica was known across Asia as a holy vessel, an earthly manifestation of Shiva, transmuted from the ocean waters in the earliest times by this great God, and given to a weary mankind as a balm for all worldly cares.

For thousands of years, Cannabis Indica has been valued as a medicinal and spiritual plant, as a source of visions, a reliever of misery, and a giver of mental, physical and ethereal pleasures. Once again, this Asian Cannabis was never smoked until the discovery of tobacco in the Americas brought this curious practice to light. Many people have the mistaken notion that people in Asia have been smoking forever, but the fact is that no evidence of smoking pre-dates the landings of the Europeans in their New World.

European botanists exploring Asia for new species during the 18th and 19th centuries were confused by the squat,

angular, aromatic plants which they discovered growing around shrines and the places of holy men, obviously carefully tended and cared for as part of the spiritual presence of the place. These plants were clearly related to the Cannabis of Europe which they had known for centuries, but equally clearly they were different. To further cloud the issue, the Asian plants were clearly being smoked for their effect, and these botanists had no knowledge of the practice of smoking anything but tobacco. (They had no way of knowing what we can also only surmise — that by the 18th century, the practice of smoking Sativa was probably well-established in the Americas.)

Thus began the debate which rages to this day — are Sativa and Indica the variations within the same species, or are they two altogether different plants. There are very clear differences. Indica plants are vigorous growers whose virtue lies in squat, angular mass. On the other hand, Sativa plants aren't happy unless they achieve that perfect Christmas Tree look. While Indica responds readily to pruning and training, Sativa resists the hand of the willful cultivator.

Indica can easily be trained into what amounts to a vine by pruning each set of sun and fan leaves as they appear, leaving only the topknot. The pure, woody stem of such a plant, totally without leaves, climbing along a wall to a rooftop where it blossoms into a solid head of flowers, is as thick and knotty as the grape vines of the California valley where I first saw it growing.

When Sativa comes into flower, she produces long, slim colas, or flowering spikes, which arch from the base of the plant to the tip. Her flowers make a continuous sweep from bottom to top, blending into one another along the stem, rarely breaking profile. Indica is squat by comparison, more horizontal than vertical in profile. Sativa produces light, tight flower clusters which cling along the stem; Indica produces clusters at clearly spaced intervals along the stem, rising from elbows where the stem makes a 15–20 degree bend. The Indica cluster is erect, dense, and solitary, and an ounce of Indica bud will be considerably smaller than an ounce of Sativa, so great is the difference in mass.

Indica plants go through several flushes, building their buds in a bloom-and-pause rhythm, while Sativa blooms in one long, continuous flush. The Indica plant thrives even in sparse environments; Sativa responds best when it is pampered.

Choosing which type of Cannabis to grow is a matter of personal taste, because either Sativa or Indica will do equally well in the hands of a dedicated grower. These matters of taste have to do with the type of high enjoyed, which is a genetically-linked but environmentally influenced trait in Cannabis.

The basic distinction is between two types of marijuana experience — being stoned, and being high. Being stoned is like being hit on the head with a big rock, where the "light flight" is is what being high is all about. When heavy stone is smoked a person stays in one place and the exper-ience takes him or her over; with the light high the person soars, and never touches the ground, and the heavens are explored. Getting high, and getting stoned, are the two basic faces of the marijuana experience, and every person has their own preference.

Heavy, stony marijuana is typified by good Colombian Sativa and by Hawaiian Indica, grown at 1000–2000' in the tropical foothills. The light, intense high is typified by Oaxacan Green, or by Nepali Indica, grown at high altitudes in the intense ultraviolet light of the great Mexican highlands or the California Sierra.

If seed is chosen which came from high country plants, no matter where it is growing the Light Flight is likely to be achieved, and if plants with a sea level heritage are chosen, the Heavy Stone effect will be reached— again, regardless of where the current generation is being grown. If a person has a strong preference for one type of marijuana experience over another, they should try to select their seed by the criteria above.

For Indica cultivation, the only route available to most folks is to score some Hawaiian bud or a genuine Thai stick. There are lots of make-believe Thai sticks around, but the giveaway with these is that they are usually tied onto broom straw rather than real bamboo. They are also usually skinny, and are often green instead of the typical rich brown of the genuine Thai. Another clue is that false Thai sticks are often tied with thread, or even dental floss, rather than the plant filaments used by true country Thai stick makers. From any good Indica bud or stick, a half-dozen or so good viable seeds should be available — all anyone needs for a fine, personal crop.

Nobody will have any trouble getting Sativa seed. Most of the marijuana on the streets at moderate prices is Sativa, usually Central or South American in origin. These seeds will be more genetically mixed than most Indica, due to the massive commercial growing taking place in the countries of origin. The best clue as to how the Sativa plants will turn out is the quality of the parent materials which have been smoked. If the parent is liked, with a little care and attention, the child will be loved. There is nothing like individual attention to bring out the best in a Cannabis plant.

Use of opiates on a large scale is not a new phenomenon in Western societies, nor is wholesale addiction. The current epidemic has yet to reach the proportions of the narcotic plague which persisted for generations in this country during the late 19th and early 20th Centuries. Conservative estimates of the addicted population of the United States at the turn of the century place the number at between one and two million living persons. This does not take into account the large number of people, namely children, who succumbed to toxic dosages of opiates. Given the population of this country during these years — around 75-100 million people — the chances are quite good that one of your grandparents was a junkie, or that one of your great uncles or aunts never survived beyond infancy to produce cousins for you.

One of the largest markets for opiates in the country was the soothing syrup trade, aimed primarily at infants who were giving their parents a hard time by crying and carrying on, or who made the mistake of appearing sickly. This genre of medicines included preparations which were known as baby syrups, colic cures,

infants' friends, teething concoctions and so forth. Parents were put at ease by labels which assured that the preparation "Contains nothing injurious to the youngest babe" and that "Mother need not fear giving this medicine to the youngest babe, as no bad effects come from the use of it." Laws were passed to prevent such claims appearing on preparations which did, in fact, contain addictive and toxic dosages of opiates, but then, as now, the laws were quickly circumvented by quick-thinking entrepreneurs. A representative list of products offered to distraught parents of uptight infants looks something like this:

Dr. James' Soothing Syrup Cordial	HEROIN
Children's Comfort	MORPHINE SULPHATE
Dr. Fahey's Pepsin Anodyne Compound	MORPHINE SULPHATE
Dr. Fahrney's Teething Syrup	MORPHINE AND CHLOROFORM
Dr. Miller's Anodyne for Babies	MORPHINE SULPHATE AND CHLORAL HYDRATE
Dr. Fowler's Strawberry and Peppermint Mixture	MORPHINE

Gadway's Elixir for Infants	CODEINE
Dr. Grove's Anodyne for Infants	MORPHINE SULPHATE
Kopp's Baby Friend	MORPHINE SULPHATE
Dr. Moffett's Teething (Teething Compound)	POWDERED OPIUM
Victor Infant Relief	CHLOROFORM AND CANNABIS INDICA
Hooper's Anodyne (The Infant's Friend)	MORPHINE SULFATE
Mrs. Winslow's Soothing Syrup	MORPHINE SULPHATE

There are numerous cases on record in the medical journals of this period of infant drug addictions; but very few of infants who died of liberal doses of these friendly snake oils. The addicted child syndrome was quite common — as soon as the effects of one dose of the soothing syrup wore off, the child became irritable and raised a fuss which led to a quick mouthful of the medicine to quiet the ruckus. Infant addicts appeared plump and healthy and, except for their periodic tantrums when mama was late with the elixir, they appeared on the surface to be pink and pacific. As a matter of fact, however, their metabolism was very poor, they withstood illness very badly and their musculoskeletal development was seriously impaired.

Shortly after several of the more restrictive laws had been passed, some manufacturers of these soothing syrups began putting out products which were, in all respects, the same except that the syrups no longer contained the opiates and other narcotics. These new products apparently did not give satisfaction to the harried motherhood of the country, for there were immediate and vocal demands that the "old kinds" of preparations be once more put on the market.

In the tradition of free enterprise, which holds that it is imperative that a consumer consume from the cradle to the grave, regardless of the quality or length of that span, the entrepreneurs of America did not neglect other markets for their products. One ready-made market for the imaginative manufacturer was a result of our preference for anything but water. Soft drinks were a national institution by the early 1800's, and when the flood of narcotics began in the latter part of that century, the fizzy drinks were a national pool into which the opiates began to flow. A marvellous new technique for assuring consumer brand loyalty — the ideal equilibrium state in a free capitalist society — presented itself in the form of addictive drugs.

The primary addictive agents found in the soft drinks of this period were cocaine and caffein. In the initial stages of this developing industry, the kola nut played a prominent role due to its reputed tonic and stimulant qualities. Most of the contemporary soft drinks with some variation of the word kola in their name grew out of this initial belief. After several years of manufacturing soft drinks from extract of kola nuts, however, it was discovered that kola nuts didn't really contain any significant active ingredient except caffein. Kola nuts were expensive to process, and the supplies were somewhat limited, so naturally the soft drink manufacturers began to look around for ways to cut their expenses and increase their profits. They found their answer right in their own backyard — it turned out that waste tea leaves could be easily processed to get the caffein they needed, and this, of course, represented a tremendous savings because they were then able to use the waste products of one drug industry to support the growth of a second drug industry. A triumph of ingenuity.

Of course the competitive aspects of the soft drink industry made it inevitable that no one was going to be fully satisfied with simple caffein extracts, and many foresighted pioneers turned to cocaine as a natural additive. Cocaine had a long folkloric history, full of accounts of its tonic virtues. People were not generally negative toward cocaine, which somehow seemed more natural and healthy than opium and its derivatives.

During the days of the industrial revolution, when millions of people were being subjected to tedium and boredom in the name of economic expansion, destined to create the good life for all, tonic drinks had a ready-made market among the pick-me-up crowd. The problem quickly became so serious in this country that life insurance companies, those bellweather institutions of practical capitalism, began to raise the rates on people who drank more than a certain number of soft drinks in the course of a long day in the factory. Among the brands viewed askance by the insurance folks were Koca Nola, Celery Cola, Wiseda, Pillsbury's Koke, Kola-Ade, Kos-Kola, Cafe-Cola, and Koke. These brands were, of course, the favorites of the swinging Kola generations of the 80's and 90's.

The opiates do enjoy a wide range of useful application in the treatment of diseases, and they are particularly effective in mucous disorders of the breathing system. Opiate drugs have been used for over two-hundred years, both by legitimate physicians and by people who for one reason or another chose to treat themselves for disease and organic disorder. Taking advantage of the latter group, which numbered in the millions in this country before the advent of large scale medicine, many manufacturers of asthma and catarrah remedies liberally dosed their customers with cocaine, codeine, chloral hydrate, heroin, morphine, opium, belladonna, stramonium, lobelia, potassium iodide, potassium nitrate and so forth. Most commonly these curatives relied upon the opiates.

One of the many asthma remedies available to sufferers was, "Davis Asthma Remedy," the brainchild of an enterprising realtor. This curative contained a primary active ingredient of chloral hydrate, and each dose at the recommended level consisted of from one to eight grains of the stuff. Quality control was pretty much lacking in those days. The directions and the label read "Dose can be increased or diminished or taken as often as needed. Adults can repeat it as many as eight times in succession. If necessary, take as many as three doses all within fifteen minutes. Tell others how it benefits you after using it." Chloral hydrate is, naturally, addictive and holds a firm place in American folklore as the notorious knockout drug.

Asthma remedies such as that of Davis' were commonly sold as cures for catarrah — the common chest cold — but there were also several specific catarrah cures on the market. Most of these specifics contained cocaine in liberal doses. One of the biggest sellers was a brand known as Dr. Agnew's Catarrah Powder, out of Baltimore, Maryland and, after the Food and Drug Acts were passed, out of Toronto, Canada. The mutual food and drug laws made it an offense to ship cocaine-laden drugs interstate, or to trade in them in any area under Federal jurisdiction, but that did not deter the most aggressive of the dealers. Dr. Agnew, for one, proved particularly hard to stop. A USDA agent reported in 1907 that "A clergyman (from Washington, D.C.) interviewed the writer some time ago as to the possibility of taking action against a certain firm supplying his communicants with a catarrah powder formerly under the name of Dr. Agnew's Catarrah Powder; and if so, what the

charges would be. The firm was also advised that the reason for making the application was that the laws of the District of Columbia were so stringent and so rigidly enforced that it was exceedingly difficult, if not impossible, to purchase any cocaine or cocaine preparation in this jurisdiction. The firm in question responded to the effect that the desired article would be sent at a certain price. The amount named for three packages was transmitted by postal order and three packages of Dr. Agnew's Catarrah Powder were duly received."

Dr. Agnew's Catarrah Powder contained 10 grains of pure cocaine to the ounce. This was an exceptionally generous portion, no doubt designed to promote return customers; but there were quite a few remedies in competition with Agnew for the market. Several of these competitors took the route of advertising their remedies as cough and cold specifics, leaving catarrah and asthma to the big boys. Examples of these medicaments, aimed chiefly at the youth market, are:

Acker's English Remedy	CHLOROFORM
Adamson's Botanic Cough Balsam	HEROIN HYDROCHLORIDE
Dr. A. Boschee's German Syrup	MORPHINE
Dr. Bull's Cough Syrup	MORPHINE AND CODEINE
Dr. Femer's Cough-Cold Syrup	MORPHINE

Jackson's Magic Balsam	CHLOROFORM AND MORPHINE
Von Totta's Cough Pectoral	CHLOROFORM AND MORPHINE
Pastilles Paneraj	CHLOROFORM AND MORPHINE
Kohler's One-Night Cough Cure	MORPHINE SULPHATE CHLOROFORM AND CANNABIS INDICA
Chlorodyne Pastilles	MORPHINE CHLOROFORM AND ETHER

Many cold and cough sufferers in those days did not have colds or coughs — they had tuberculosis. Who could then blame the quick thinking businessman for cashing in on the ready market of consumption cures? These remedies did, in fact, allay that coughing, tickling sensation and other distressing symptoms of deep chest disease. Many folks had their symptoms so effectively suppressed by the heavy doses of narcotics in those narcotic cures that they died, true enough, of terminal lung disease; but they died without so much as a tiny wheeze. Some of the well-known and widely used consumption cures were:

Tuberculozyne	HEROIN
Prof. Hoff's Consumption Cure	OPIUM
Gooch's Mexican Consumption Cure	MORPHINE SULFATE
Dr. Brutus Shiloh's Cure for Consumption	HEROIN AND CHLOROFORM

Along with the ills of TB and chest ailments in general, things weren't going so well with the heads of the population. Headache mixtures in those days commonly contained codeine and morphine, along with acetanilid, acetphenetidin, antipyrin, and caffein. Epilepsy cures were also highly touted, usually containing one or more of the bromides in addition to the run-of-the-mill opium and morphine.

One of the most interesting aspects of this whole drug scene was the very large business which grew out of drug addiction treatments and cures, largely of the home-remedy type, which were advertised as "mail order express treatments." If you were on the mailing list of the patent medicine promoters, after a period of time you could count on receiving literature on these cures for narcotics addiction. Response was, naturally, quite heavy.

The only catch to the cure was the nature of the treatment. In most cases the addiction cure was presented as a highly secret and profoundly respectable compound known only to the agent offering this miraculous substance. The true nature of these addiction treatments were, however, much closer to the mundane. Mail order physicians commonly prescribed formulae such as: "alcohol 12.5%; morphine 22.0 grains per fluid ounce; *Cannabis indica* extract four minims to the fluid ounce."

The "James Mixture for the Gradual Reductive Treatment of Narcotic Drug Addictions" contained 24 grains of morphine to the fluid ounce. Habitina, product of the Delta Chemical Company, contained 16 grains of morphine sulphate and eight grains of heroin to the fluid ounce. Such treatments characteristically bore the solicitous injunction, "When you open this bottle, order your next month's treatment in order to avoid any break."

Heroin was the most common ingredient in these express treatments, and for good reason. Heroin had just been developed as a cure for morphine addiction. It was considered a positive turn of events when an addict switched from morphine to heroin, just as today methadone is lauded for its benign narcosis.

(Below) Worden McDonald author of An Old Guy Who Feels Good

Marijuana:
An Herb
for the Aging

One of the groups most deprived by marijuana's illegal status is the aged because this fine herb has so many qualities which would improve the quality of life of so many old people. This is an invitation to the old to allow themselves to grow and experience marijuana.

It is an herb with gentle, usually positive body consequences. Body problems with marijuana, such as a mild nausea or discomfort, are most often the result of nervousness and unfamiliarity rather than of the herb itself. Marijuana encourages both social impulses and introspective urges. Thus a more tranquil, and a more active life as well can derive from use of the herb. Marijuana facilitates a coming to terms with one's self, a project which is particularly important as age increases. The herb promotes a sense of well-being, it opens people up to each other. Loneliness is a major problem with many people, especially the old.

The herb's effects are easily learned, and easily controlled, by the person who uses marijuana. In marijuana, the old will find an herbal aid to relaxation, as well as a mental and sensory stimulant. Marijuana encourages appetite in many people, and appetite is a problem with many elderly people. Morale definitely improves. Grumpiness indices like national Ex-Lax sales would probably decline rapidly as the people discovered marijuana.

Marijuana is cheaply and easily grown anywhere — even the bedridden can grow a fine crop. Growing the plant is an interesting, involving thing to do. The marijuana experience is a link with the young. Turning on together with Grandma and her homegrown Sinsemilla would appeal to countless grandchildren. The marijuana experience could link generations of Americans as no other contemporary or historical experience yet has.

Some old people probably shouldn't use marijuana. Some will have bad initial experiences, some will simply not allow themselves to let go and experience their high mind. But introspective marijuana experience can provide many keys to mental health, and with marijuana many old people would begin to heal themselves in deep ways.

Old people don't live on because they're afraid of death, though many are. Old people live on because life is interesting. It may be totally made up of routines, and those routines may be painful and depressing; but they are life to us and therefore they are interesting.

Marijuana could be an economic boon to many old people. Many could grow it well enough to develop a small clientele, and the use of it would no doubt replace a lot of expensive medicines having to do with nerves, digestion, sleep and so forth. Characteristically, Cannabis experience is accompanied by a lowering of the materialistic drive and concern — though there may also be a heightened appreciation of the physical world and of the artistry of the natural realm. Many old people face fears which arise out of materialist myths and perceptions, which trap them in fearing loss of material possessions. Old people will be better able to enjoy life with few possessions when their mind is at peace and they are able to seek and find love for themselves in the world. Marijuana can bring about conditions where this seemingly utopian, but actually quite simple, set of possibilities may prevail.

Marijuana might also awaken an interest in sexuality in the old, as it will surely reawaken people in other aspects of their sensory life, their imagination, their physical being and body, and their creativity. Old people are not as likely as the young to get distracted by the trivial, once their attention is focused, and marijuana is a great liberator of attention to focus upon deep places in Being.

If, as it may be, you have an old person in mind who might be open to discovering marijuana, why not consider providing that person with at least a few seeds and some simple instructions, even if the gift is best made anonymously, or perhaps it can be made in person, with feeling.

There have been a number of serious, heavily-funded attempts on the part of government supported botanists to breed strains of the marijuana plant that would have no resin-producing properties. These experiments have been taking place over the past ten years or so, contemporary with many other memorable government experiments: the spraying of Mexican fields with deadly poisons, launching a marijuana satellite to detect criminal horticulture, and developing killer weeds which attack Cannabis on their own. Predictably, such keystone cop antics have employed a lot of otherwise unemployable types, but they have not done much to make life hard on the marijuana plant. Similarly, the attempt to produce the resinless plant has failed. The scientists working on this project discovered that the funny Cannabis reverted to its old resin-making habits as soon as it was let loose in the fields. The plot has been halted, frustrated by the innate nature of this great plant.

(Below) Young female
flower with resin
glands appearing

the Marijuana Plant

Both male and female marijuana plants have a great many botannical characteristics in common.

The stalk is fluted and hexagonal and often hollow with a pithy central cavity. It is covered with fine hairs which run vertically along the stalk often lying flat against its surface. Each of these hairs is a single cell. They are located all over the plant, not just on the stalk.

The points where branches diverge from the stalk are called nodes. They appear along the mature stalk at intervals varying from two to ten inches depending on the variety and growing conditions. The mature Cannabis stalk is very tough and fibrous and becomes practically rock-hard near the base. Early in life, the branches on Cannabis are opposite each other. As growth continues, the branches become staggered on opposite sides of the stem.

I have seen plants 25 feet tall with stalks as big around as my arm. Mature females, however, rarely exceed six to eight feet under temperate growing conditions. Many are considerably shorter, particularly the plants whose ancestors come from very hot and dry environments where the plants tend to be squat and bushy.

The leaf of the marijuana plant is one of its most beautiful features. It is shaped like a tapered spearhead with sawtooth edges, four to sixteen teeth per side. The leaves are a delicate shading of greens and green-blues, especially noticeable in the early morning and late evening. At these times the plants take on a silvery glow, like beings from other worlds; shadowy, mysterious creatures whose purpose among us is obscure, though welcome.

In the normally developed plant, leaf clusters will have from three to eleven leaves per cluster, while the most common count is seven or nine. The leaves are darker in color on the top, and along the bottom are covered with a fine silver down.

The root system of the plant consists of a main tap root about a foot deep for every six to eight feet of above ground height and a mass of thin lateral roots which spreads in a halo from five to ten inches on all sides of the tap root. In rich organic soils this lateral system is more developed and the tap root is shorter than in poor sparse soils.

Each cluster of leaves has a little stem, sometimes hollow, which is angular rather than rounded. It has a characteristic groove along its upper side and is often covered with fine hairs lying along its length.

The marijuana plant requires adequate elbow room in order to develop its full foliage. Where this is given, the female in particular can become extremely bushy. Where the plants are crowded together, they may grow quite tall with only the most spindly top knots of leaves. All things being equal, crowding favors development of males. Spacing promotes growth of females.

Cannabis has been a source of fascination to people involved in the study of reality structures at the molecular level. Cannabis is a master chemist, manufacturing elusive molecules which behave in strange wonderful ways. Not the least of these is the effect upon the observer's relationship with his own thoughts and senses.

Cannabis is known to manufacture over 40 different specialized compounds. There is much confusion among scientists over what to call these many compounds, over what they look like, and what they do. Cannabis produces certain molecules when it lives in Colombia which it does not produce when it lives in Sweden. The compounds continually change as the plant is living and dying and after it's dead. Depending on the heat and day length of its environment, the plant will produce more or less resin, with a different combination of molecular compounds, at each location.

A strong theory is that trace elements in the soil, which vary widely from one acre of soil to another, have a drastic effect upon the enzymatic balance in Cannabis. This balance is tied to the resin chemistry in ways as yet only dimly understood.

Day length may also affect the balance of molecular compounds in the resin. The idea is that the more sun a plant gets, up to a point, the more psychoactive compounds it produces in its resin.

That makes good sense to me. Cannabis is a sun-drinking plant, a hardy desert and mountain race. It is in its nature to seek out the hot, dry places and the high

mountain valleys. There she sings her
songs of joy in living. Her songs are the
molecules she creates under the rich sun.
With care from the people who tend this
high plant, Cannabis in all its forms can
respond with great chemical magic.

Cannabis is an intricately-wrought
being: a high form in the order of
things. Unlike simpler, more primitive
flora, Cannabis does not carry its male
and female sex organs on a single plant.
Cannabis is dioecious, that is, males and
females are separate distinct individuals.
This is of special note for the cultivator
since the female of the species has more
abundant leaves, tightly clustered flower
spikes and a heavier resin content.

Both sexes exhibit a host of behavioral
and physical variations through a wide
range of environmental conditions. In a
field of Cannabis one normally finds a sex
ratio of 1:1, with slightly fewer males
than females in many instances. Under
severe conditions, the sex ratio of a given
population can change from 1:1 to 9:1,
female, in a single generation. Under
certain conditions of stress, Cannabis is
capable of changing its sexual nature
during the life cycle of a single plant,
sometimes becoming hermaphroditic and
sometimes undergoing a full switch —
usually male to female.

The survival instinct in Cannabis is
powerful, and in an environment which
threatens its reproductive capacity, it can
change even its gender to accommodate
new circumstances. It is crucial to
appreciate the complex nature of the
potent life forces of Cannabis,
particularly if you attempt some of the
manipulations of sex covered in later
chapters.

Many people are still confused about how
to tell a male plant from a female. This is
especially difficult when the plants are
very young. There is only one method I
know of that will give a good indication,

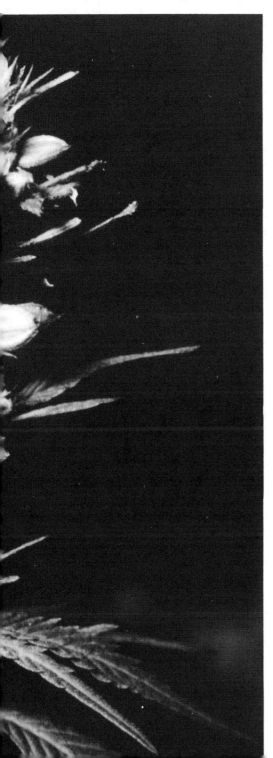

(Below) Hermaphrodite (male and female flowers on same shoot)

of which plants are going to be male and which will be female before the sexual organs develop. This method is called the Leaf Mass Index Calculation.

To calculate the leaf mass index of a plant, count the number of points on the three central leaves in the cluster, divide by three, and arrive at an average number of points. Then count the number of leaves per cluster on several clusters, and, again, find the average. Multiply these two averages. This is the leaf mass index. The higher the leaf mass index, the greater the likelihood that the plant is going to be a female. (The LMI is not a surefire way of determining the sex of your plants. Still, it's the best I know.) Be sure to choose leaf clusters from comparable locations when comparing plants' LMI.

Other than this indicator, there are no consistent physiological differences between the sexes before flowering. After flowering, the most striking differences are in growth rate, leaf size, pigment content, and longevity after completion of the reproductive act.

The first sign that flowering is beginning will be the appearance of little buds called primordia where the branches join the main stem. When these buds first appear there are no visible differences between male and female. However, usually within 72 hours of their appearance, the buds on the male plants will take on a rounded shape. The buds on the females will develop a little point: the bract, which will extend to enfold the flower as it develops.

It will be important to remember when you are dealing with sex-related phenomena in Cannabis, that each plant bears within itself the potential for becoming either male or female, whatever its sexual identity at the moment. Cannabis holds on to its sexual identity very strongly under some conditions, abandons it readily under others. Too much intervention in your plants' life processes can kill them as surely as any hostile environmental forces. Keep in mind that it is appreciation which marks the difference between a cultivator and a mere exploiter. Understanding the marijuana plant requires appreciation, sensitivity, and close encounters.

The resins of the marijuana plant are almost entirely insoluble in water. (They *are* soluble in alcohol.) This fits the natural scheme of growth and protection. The sudden rains of the plant's desert home cannot, with one swift passing shower, wash away the resin and lay the plant bare to the ruinous sun for the rest of the day. The dew, which comes before dawn in all but the most parched locales, cannot moisten and lift the resin as it boils away in the first rays of morning. The water held in the cells of the plant is urged outward and away by the heat of the sun. It is the resin, which the escaping water moistens but cannot dissolve, that keeps the liquid life of the plant contained.

Of course, this description is somewhat overplayed. The plant does breathe. The resin secreted by the plant does vaporize to a degree and it does gradually get washed away when the rain falls and the dew lifts. But the point is there is an intelligence here.

The chemistry of the resin of the marijuana plant does not have to be as complex as it is in order to do the job of protecting the plant from water loss. It is quite possible for plants to make substances which protect them well from heat and water loss without making a substance which fits in so well with the evolution of human consciousness. Remember, please: this plant has been following humans around for thousands of years, making itself always useful for fiber when needed and opening the doors of perception when called upon to do so.

The slender graceful male marijuana plant has been misunderstood by cultivators of many countries, almost as long as the plant has been grown for drug purposes.

For centuries it has been assumed that the resin produced by the male plant is less potent than that of the female. Lord knows how many million plants have been pulled and discarded by growers laboring under this misconception. The reality of the situation, now well established, is that plants from the same community of seed (genetically comparable backgrounds) will produce resin of equivalent potency regardless of sex.

The origin of the idea that males are useless for drug purposes lies in the fact that Eastern cultivators pulled male plants as soon as they were identifiable to prevent fertilization of the females. For if the female is fertilized, her resin production drops drastically.

Whatever the function of resin — and there is some debate on this, most believing resin helps prevent ultra-violet light damage and excessive water loss — it makes sense that the female, once fertilized, would switch emphasis from her own survival to the survival of her seed. At the point of fertilization she has, after all, fulfilled her purpose to bear fruit. What is a plant, after all, but one seed becoming many?

So, that is why the male is pulled. It is a trade-off, actually. If you don't pull the males, you get more leaf mass at harvest, the leaves and flowers of both male and female plants. However, there will be less resin production on the parts of the females. Male resin production remains fairly constant.

If you pull your males as soon as they can be identified, you will harvest less green weight. What is harvested, however, will be higher in resin content though not higher in potency. Potency remains constant unless the genetics of the plant have been manipulated during its lifetime.

Identification plays a big part in a cultivator's decision to pull all or some of the males in a field or growing bed. Once the sexual organs are formed, it is easy to identify the male flower.

The male flowers develop in loosely arranged bundles, appearing on the ends and margins of many small branches, distant from the leaf clusters of the plant. The branches with flowers directly attach to the stem of the plant, usually sharing a node with one or more small branches which support a leaf cluster. At the top of a mature male plant, however, there are rarely any branches supporting leaf clusters. There tend to be only branches supporting flower clusters.

The male flowers have no petals as such, though the sepals enclosing the flower

pod are often mistaken for petals. There are five of these sepals, or sheaths, and their color is usually a light white or a yellow-green, with a red tinge. The sepals are covered with minute hairs, giving them a downy look and feel.

In a mature male plant these sepals tend to be about ⅛ inch, 3.5 mm, long. The sepals enclose five tightly packed stamens, which pop apart after the sepals open, and dangle little anthers from thin silky threads in the breeze. It is these anthers which produce and disperse the pollen when fertilization time draws near. It is pretty easy to gauge the onset of the divine moment by looking closely at the anthers. Note whether they are swollen and eager looking. Note, too, whether their surfaces are dusted with pollen.

This pollen is carrier of half of the coded life message of the plant. When a single grain of pollen reaches a single female flower, tightly curled tubes inside the pollen grain burst forth, and penetrate the depths of the flower. An amalgam occurs which completes the life message. A fertile seed is created.

The sepals on the male flower will unzip and the anthers will dangle forth about 12 hours before actual pollen release. If you have been waiting until the last possible moment to harvest your males before they fertilize the females, you don't have a very large time window. Under average circumstances, it will pay to examine your male plants several times every 24 hours from the time sex-organ development begins.

Male plants produce less chlorophyll than the females and are able to thrive on less intense light. This explains why a group of marijuana plants will turn out predominantly male under conditions of short day length. Cannabis is a survivor and will do what it must to make it.

Male plants also produce less auxins in their tissue fluids. Auxins are growth regulators manufactured within the cells of the plant. They are vital to the plant's development of leaves and flowers and to its vigor and health. The various techniques for altering the sexual expression of Cannabis often call for chemical intervention in the manufacture of these auxins.

The tissue fluids of male Cannabis plants test slightly acid with litmus paper. So, if the soil is acid, a plant growing there will tend to become a male in order to keep a balance between its internal state and this environmental determinant. Female cannabis, by contrast, is slightly alkaline in her tissue fluid balance. Alkaline soils tend to favor the development of females — all other factors being equal (which, of course, they rarely are).

Male plants often follow a unique pattern in blooming. It is one of the great symphonies played out by life in nature.

At dawn the process begins with a single flower, close to the stem, almost invariably about two-thirds of the way up the plant. As the sun rises, the blooming moves outward from this first flower until, at last, all the flowers have opened. The anthers are exposed.

Between the seventh and the twelfth hours after the process has begun, the flowers will be opened, sepals unzipped, anthers in readiness. Then, one by one, the anthers pop out of their bundled clusters and dangle down, suspended upon their glistening threads, waiting to catch the breeze.

Upon their surfaces the tiny pollen grains appear as if by magic. One minute the surfaces of the anther seem smooth and barren of pollen and the next minute they are lightly dusted with white or yellow pollen. The motes of life lie waiting for a breeze to carry them to the females standing patiently downwind, receptive and extended.

In some fields of plants this process is a highly coordinated one. The males do not swell into readiness before the females have reached their peak of receptivity. In whatever language, by whatever means, there is communication here between plants, an exchange of information on the highest level.

Just as two humans can communicate sexual excitement without words, whether they are strangers or familiar lovers, so communications like "Over Here!" and "Don't Stop!" radiate between the Cannabis males and females in a field. The messages upon which life depends for continuity are not restricted to words or gestures. In this, as in all things, nature is quite sly. What species would survive if dependent upon ordinary conscious initiative and their own ordinary faculties? The process of creation is always extraordinary, as it is with Cannabis in the fields in the first light of dawn.

Soon after the release of pollen, the male plants begin to die. The signs of their passing first appear near the base of the plant, where their green color starts to dull and fade. The lower leaves shrivel. The plant will give off a dry rustle and release its last puff of pollen if shaken by the wind. The completion of the life cycle of the male is at hand, usually a month or more before the female has completed her work.

Females outlive the males by three to five weeks, or even more, depending upon the variety. Tropical strain females tend to be much longer lived than temperate zone plants. The cycles of temperate zone plants are responsive to the growing season, to the fact that a plant grown too early will be killed by a frost, and the plant too late in starting will be cut down by chill autumn winds. The greater life span of females also reflects their greater health and vigor. This is due to the fact that the females have more complex life processes to support than males and therefore require a broader base of vital energy.

The flower of the female does not look as complex as that of the male. However, the internal structure of the female flower and the operations within this inner structure are elaborate and marvelous.

The external flower structure begins with the downy green sheath which surrounds the seed. This is called the bract. The bract is what we smokers use when we have smoked all our stash and have nothing left but seeds. We pick through the seeds to find the ones still wearing those thin jackets. Popping the seeds out

(Left)
Female Sinsemilla flower
(Right)
Single female flower magnified: two pistils emerging from single bract. Bract has glandular and non-glandular trichomes

(Below) Seed coat and bract
(forms from bract
of young female flower)

Thai seeds

Colombian seeds

Afghani seeds

of their coats, we hope to collect enough of these little green cups to roll a decent joint. Ironically, the bract is that part of the plant highest in THC. Think of spending all those years squeezing seeds, feeling put upon by life, when we were actually smoking a premium part of the plant.

The bract forms a cup with overlapping edges. This cup surrounds the seed-to-be as the flower of the female develops. As the female approaches maturity, two fuzzy hairs poke forth from the tip of the pod. These are the stigmas, the pollen-snagging instruments of the seed. If you pull back the protective cup of leaves, the immature seed within the bract will look like a glistening, white, slightly oval egg. After pollination, it develops its hard seed coat and the stigmas, their purpose served, drop away. The base of the pod begins to swell, preparatory to forcing the seed out of its cup and onto the ground.

There are three types of glands responsible for secreting resin. They are found in the greatest concentration on the bract covering the seed.

As we said, there is debate over the function of resin in the plant's processes. Of course, from the human point of view, there is no such debate. For us, the function of resin is clear.

While there are a number of shielding and resin-secreting cell structures on the surfaces of the Cannabis leaves, these three types predominate.

The stalked glandular trichome rises from the undulating surface of the marijuana leaf on a stalk composed of strong, interwoven, flexible cells. At its crown is a broad space filled with tissue in which resin is manufactured. The resin oozes out around the crest and base of the crown and flows down the stalk onto the surface of the leaf. Wandering in a forest

of stalked glandular trichomes would be similar to roaming through a dense pine wood on a hot day when the sap fairly flows from the trees. These resin factories stick way up from the leaf's surface; they often huddle beneath the protection of giant cystolithic trichomes, great glands containing no resin-producing structures, but whose strong arched canopy affords protection to the resin glands below.

Another resin gland is the sessile gland discovered and described by Prof. J. W. Fairbairn of the University of London, who is the scientist behind the photos in Chapter Nine. The sessile gland is a sphere of magnificent size, as size goes in this microscopic world. It lies in small depressions of the leaf surface protected from crushing by the great cystolithic hairs which dominate the horizon. This sessile gland needs protection. Except for resin, it has no insides. Unlike the stalked gland it is essentially hollow, a living storage container, a resin-filled bag snagged to the leaf surface by the merest of filaments. These glands burst easily and break loose easily. One can image them set rolling by the slight shrivelling of the leaf surface when exposed to drying heat. The surface twitches, the sessile glands break loose and roll along until they contact something solid or pointed. There they burst and spill their resin, quickly slowing down evaporation on that part of the leaf's surface.

Meanwhile the stalked glands, immune to all but a great buckling of the leaf surface, continue creating and secreting resin, uninterrupted by the rolling and splashing at the foot of their stalk. It is remarkable how much sense this plant makes at the microscopic level, as at all levels.

The embryo plant develops within the hardening seed coat soon after fertilization. Within a week, a fully formed embryo can be detected, though dropping of the seed does not normally occur until much later. The two embryo leaves are packed together along one side of the inner wall of the seed and the root precursor is packed up along the opposite wall. Between these two primitive plant parts is packed the endosperm, or food supply, rich with the oils so prized by industrial man and the birds.

Compared with the males, female plants produce large amounts of chlorophyll and produce large amounts of the auxins associated with vigorous growth, such as in height, leaf mass, and root structure. The tissue fluids of the female plant are neutral to slightly alkaline in pH, which may have something to do with their ability to produce more of the protective resin than males. However, as has been pointed out, sex is associated only with resin quantity, not potency. In any case, it is true that a plant which starts its life as a male and switches to female never seems able to attain the leafiness and vigor of a true female. Neither will it produce resin at the same rate as a true female.

Largely because of their greater leaf mass, but also because of their vigorous water uptake, female plants will outweigh male plants at least 2:1 at maturity. Often the ratio is much higher. They will have more leaves per cluster and more leaf clusters than the male. Due to their heavier bodies, females will have greater energy requirements and exert greater draw upon the nutrients of their growing medium.

While the males are reaching maturity and preparing to release their pollen, the females are entering their fertile period and undergoing developmental changes in preparation for reproduction. The bracts enclosing the eggs are spreading slightly apart so that the tiny stigmas can protrude. The leaf clusters around the flower show a marked drooping so they won't interfere with the circulation of pollen-bearing breezes. Water intake, which has been declining slightly since the peak of the growth period several weeks before, shoots up again. It becomes critical that the plant have plenty of sunlight. A week of cloudy weather at this fertile time can throw off the biological clocks of the plants so radically that sexual abnormalities in the next generation will tremendously increase. Marked temperature changes can shrivel the exposed sexual organs, which do not adapt well to any changes in environment at this point. Nutrient requirements alter. The female plant experiences a strong need for calcium and potassium, in particular — the equivalent of the human mother's mythified craving for ice cream and pickles.

If good seed is desired from the female, she should not be harvested for at least ten days after pollination. Otherwise, the seed will be weak and immature. If it does manage to germinate, the plant produced will be spindly, low in vigor, and a disappointment in terms of resin yield. There is no need to rush. If seed is what you want, the female will show her readiness by dropping the seed when a flower cluster is lightly shaken.

Leaving the female in the ground after fertilization does cut way back on resin production since the plant is turning her energy to producing viable seed. The decision on when to harvest, then, is an individual one. For maximum resin, the plant should never have been allowed to become fertilized. For maximum seed production, the plant should be allowed to grow until the seeds drop when the plant is shaken.

The incredible survival drives and mechanisms of Cannabis sometimes manifest themselves as sex anomalies on the flowers of both males and females. These sex anomalies appear whenever normal growth pathways are blocked or threatened by hostile conditions. If such sex anomalies appear on your plants, even if they are in all other respects healthy, you can be certain they are being threatened by some form of environmental pressure. A review of such matters as nutrient balance of the soil, photoperiod conditions, or atmospheric conditions (cigarette or marijuana smoke in an indoors environment?) may provide a clue to the plant's problem. Of course, if you are experimenting with sex change techniques, expect and accept abnormal sexual development as part of Cannabis' survival drive.

Cannabis carries her seeds proudly, massed at the heads of her flowering tops. This means that, while developing, her seeds are exposed to relatively intense radiation. High intensity UV radiation is particularly dangerous and damaging to fast-dividing tissue, as in the growing tip and the embryo seed. Shielding of the delicate parts with tissue is ineffective, since UV rays can penetrate many layers of cells. Chemical absorption of high-energy light, the weaving of molecular traps so subtle that they can snare the very high energy of ultra-violet light, is the only option available to plants.

In the complexity of Cannabis resins, it looks as if provision has been made for the manufacture of sun-screening elements. Legend, observation and science concur. There is a complex relationship between sunlight intensity, and resin production in Cannabis. Many people, including me, speculate further. It seems clear, in my experience, that what Cannabis creates in response to intense sunlight is the source of the intensity of my own experience with the plant.

The light makes the difference. This makes sense when we remember that life grew on this planet in response to the light of a certain star, which we call Sol, the Sun. It is known that as far out as our instruments reach, all stars are

essentially similar in chemical make-up.
The extreme variations between stars in
radiation output, including light spectra,
are due to differences in pressure,
temperature, and surface gravity and not
to different chemical compositions. On
the planets circling those stars, life, as we
know it, will evolve only if the star emits
a kindly light. Within five parsecs of
earth, only Tau Ceti and E-Eridani have
our criteria for the evolution of life:

*(1) They are stars with a long stable
maturity;*
(2) Their light is of moderate intensity;
*(3) There is a temperate zone in the space
around the star;*
*(4) They have stable planetary orbits
(ruling out almost all dual-star systems.)*

As life has evolved on worlds circling
moderate, gently beaming stars, it has
done so in response to the particular
radiation spectrum of each star. Where
life has evolved, it has probably followed
the earth pattern in most cases, the deep
earth pattern, not the superficial. So it
has probably evolved plant, animal, mind,
and other forms of life. As mind has
evolved, it has no doubt encountered
psychoactive compounds in the natural
order which have triggered new
perceptions and awareness. This is the
history of earth under our sun and it
seems reasonable that, under other stars,
interactions among beings would proceed
along similar pathways: always guided
and formed by the light of the particular
star.

The linkage between life and light is
intimate, touching at all possible
interfaces. In the manufacture of
compounds to screen its developing seeds
and other developing parts from the uv
rays of Sol, Cannabis has taken her place
in Earth's design as an instrument of
enlightenment.

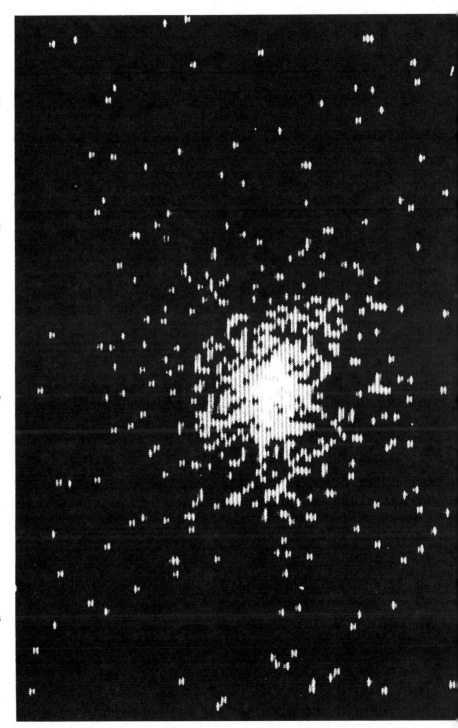

(Below) Over-mature female flower
(note abundance of large
glandular resin structures)

Marijuana and the Land

Cannabis is a tough, versatile plant which adapts readily to most environments. That does not mean it has no preferences. As noted earlier, the marijuana plant first met man through living on his dung and garbage heaps. To this traveller from the harsh lands of Central Asia, the rich piles of nutrient laying around man's habitats must have looked awfully good. Cannabis probably sighed with relief — no more scrambling through the thin soil for food; no more seeing her seeds bounce off hard, dusty soil; no more exposure to the little creatures of field and forest who nibble and destroy young plants. Also, it was the beginning of some special attention. Cannabis has carried with it an inherent toughness, bred into its ancestors, characteristic of all races which dwell in the hard places of earth. Still, it responds beautifully to the attention of cultivation.

There is tremendous variability in soils from region to region, and within regions, down to the smallest parcel of land. Within the same field it is not uncommon to find three or more types of soils. Plant cover also plays a part in determining its composition since plants differ markedly in the minerals they take up, transform, and return to the soil. Likewise, there are conditions of exposure, drainage and pollution which affect soil composition. The physical appearance of land is not a good guide to its productivity. A gravel soil can be very fertile. Desert soil can make Cannabis bloom. Black soils that look rich can kill or starve Cannabis. To determine which would make good places to grow your crop, a lot of factors have to be taken into consideration. This chapter represents the best research I have been able to uncover plus the discoveries of a number of dedicated farmers and gardeners who have been growing Cannabis under a variety of conditions for a number of years.

We'll look at a synthesis of the best of this information. This is an area in which the experiences of successful cultivators will be invaluable to others. I'd like to again encourage interested parties to contribute to the publication of this information. Send it to me for editing and possible inclusion in our first, or some subsequent, *Journal of Marijuana Cultivation.*

Outdoor cultivation in soil is the most appealing way of raising potent marijuana plants primarily because sunshine is free and there are few limits to plant growth. Indoor cultivation, however, is becoming more necessary as available growing space near cities and towns becomes limited and ripoffs of outdoor marijuana becomes more prevalent. And while indoor cultivation has the disadvantage of initial expenses, that expense is quickly absorbed with the first crop of high quality marijuana.

Still, as marijuana comes closer and closer to legalization, outdoor planting is bound to become more feasible. In this spirit, we will now look at some of your cultivation options.

The soil which is to be used should be of as uniform quality as possible. The importance of this fact becomes apparent when you begin to modify certain characteristics of your crop, particularly with indoor growing, and are counting on a consistent sort of outcome. Non-uniform soil quality can jeopardize even the most sophisticated experimental efforts. For indoor work, this means that all soils used should be thoroughly mixed, and for outdoor planting it means you should stick to areas where the soil has been deposited in uniform depth from the same general source, and has been adequately prepared.

Uniformity of the soil also is desirable if you contemplate re-using it. Cannabis soaks up a great deal of the nutrients in any soil, and when you re-fertilize you want to be certain that you aren't going to burn some of your plants and starve others because the nutrient level wasn't even to begin with. We have calculated that Cannabis absorbs the equivalent of 1500 kilos of fertilizer for every 100 kilos of fiber obtained from the mature plant. Since fiber yield is about 6.5% of the weight of the mature plant, this means that Cannabis absorbs around one kilo of nutrient per kilo of vegetable mass. This gives an idea of the importance of adequate nutrition.

In a mature plant, the proportions of plant products break down in the following way:

Loss in drying	±30%
Leaves, roots and tops	±25%
Extraneous stem material	±15%
Sticks	±15%
Seed and miscellaneous	±10%
Fiber	± 5%

This means that one can count on leaves and flowers to constitute from ten to twenty percent of the harvested weight of a crop.

Outdoor soils which are particularly well-suited to cultivation of the marijuana plant are the sandy loams, especially those with low clay content and plenty of sand, even fine gravel. Soils of sedimentary rock origin are usually excellent. They are stable, aerate easily, and usually provide a good balance of trace nutrients.

The generalization about sandy loams need not cause anxiety if you live in an area with another type of soil. Cannabis will thrive in most soils. It will give excellent resin yield in many soil conditions, provided other environmental factors harmonize well. A truly limiting element is the compaction factor of the soil, which is directly proportional to clay content. High-clay soils will resist generation of the lateral root systems. Cannabis depends upon these roots to extract raw materials from the soil, with the exception of carbon which she gets from the air. Also, clay soils are often poor in organic matter because little grows there and dies, becoming food for later plant generations. Worst of all, clay soils promote pooling of water around the roots. Water does not soak into clay soils, even when it works its way below the surface. Instead, the water, running off the slick plates of clay, finds the shafts burrowed by the plant's roots, quickly fills them up, and drowns the plant. The roots of the plant take up oxygen from the soil and when they are immersed, the plant drowns as certainly as do humans. Plants, of course, can hold their breath for long periods of time while the soil around them is thoroughly soaked, provided there is good drainage afterwards. When watering marijuana, the soil should be soaked through and through. Good drainage should be immediate, leaving the soil soaked, but not water logged.

You can make a pretty good guess at the clay content of soils by squeezing a few handfuls from the area under consideration. The topsoil should ball together with a two-handed squeeze, but should crumble easily into fine particles. If it breaks apart in pronounced chunks, or if it resists breaking, it is either too wet or it has too much clay. In either case, it is not a good idea to plant there. Another test is to ball up a little soil, wet it, and rub it on the palm of one hand with the thumb of the other hand. Note if it is slick or grainy. Slick is not good; grainy is good. That's a general but useful rule.

The topsoil should allow good root penetration. Twelve inches is ideal. Check this by pulling a variety of plants native to the field. Note their root structure. Are they plants with significant taproots, some six to eight inches or better? Does a great variety of growth occur in the field? Look at the soil clinging to the roots of the pulled plants. Does it cling tenaciously or crumble away easily? Probe down into the holes made by pulling plants. Does the tip of the stick come out slightly moist or dry?

Certain sorts of plants are indicators of wetness. Cattails, sedge, blue-green moss, marsh marigold, willows, rushes, many of the worts, and skunk cabbage are all moisture loving plants and indicate ground far too wet for Cannabis. Bluegrass, clover, walnut trees, burdock, pigweed, purselain, and lambsquarter all grow in well drained areas with good organic content. Broomsedge, chamomile, fennel, and sorrel indicate poor soils, lacking in moisture and fertility.

Keeping in mind that Cannabis thrives in well-drained land, you may want to modify your land with a simple drainage system. If your ground stays wet for more than a day or two after a one inch rain, if your ground stays cold and moist well into the warm weather, or if

| soil classes | limits in the proportions of the soil separates | | |
	sand, %	silt, %	clay, %
sand	80-100	0- 20	0- 20
sandy loam	50- 80	0- 50	0- 20
silt loam	0- 50	50-100	0- 20
loam	30- 50	30- 50	0- 20
silty clay loam	0- 30	50- 80	20- 30
sandy clay loam	50- 80	0- 30	20- 30
clay loam	20- 50	20- 50	20- 30
silty clay	0- 20	50- 70	30- 50
sandy clay	50- 70	0- 20	30- 50
clay	0- 50	0- 50	30-100

Source: Davis, R. O. E., and H. H. Bennett, *USDA Bur. Soils Cir.* 319, Table 1.

the ground buckles and heaves quite a bit in hard winter freezes, chances are that your soil is retaining too much water.

To install a line of drainage tiles, first locate the slope of the land. You will want to run the tile line from a high point to a low point where the water can drain away instead of pooling — preferably a ditch, creek bed or some other watercourse — though the drainage line can simply terminate in a low spot that you don't mind turning into a bog. Don't lay a drainage line high on a slope or against the natural drainage of the land. Lay the line so it draws from higher ground.

You can dig the trench by hand or hire a machine. One line of four inch drain will draw water from all the land 25 feet on either side, so you will need 50 feet between drainage lines, if you are going to install more than one. The trench should be dug from two to three feet deep. Keep it narrow. Pile the dirt up at one edge so it can easily be pushed back. Lay the drainage tiles evenly in the bottom of the trench. If you use modern perforated tile or continuous gutter, fine. But if you use clay tile, leave a gap between tiles of about ¼ inch. Be sure that the slope of your tiles is continuous in the direction you want the water to go. When all the tiles are laid, toss in about six inches of straw, hay or the like on top of the tiles and fill in the ditch with dirt. On land that needs it, the addition of just one tile line can produce dramatic results. The addition of drainage is often all that is needed to convert an ordinary spot of land into a garden.

Drainage problems are often interpreted as nutrient deficiencies. So, if your plants aren't doing well, look for drainage problems too.

*Average physical
composition of
common soils*

soils	percentage of separate present						
	fine gravel	coarse sand	medium sand	fine sand	very fine sand	silt	clay
coarse sand	5.0	13.0	27.0	30.0	11.0	8.5	5.5
medium sand	5.0	13.0	20.0	32.5	14.0	9.0	6.5
sandy loam	5.0	10.0	11.0	26.0	11.0	22.0	15.0
fine sandy loam	2.0	2.5	5.0	20.0	27.5	32.0	11.0
silt loam	1.0	1.5	2.5	6.0	11.0	56.0	22.0
clay loam	3.0	5.0	5.0	12.0	10.0	28.0	37.0
clay	0.0	2.0	2.5	5.5	7.0	37.0	46.0

Source: Compiled from data given in *The Principles of Soil Management*, by Lyon and Fippin, The Macmillan Company, New York, 1911.

The spread of marijuana cultivation has carried the fine herb into every geographical area of North America. It is no longer an escaped fiber plant, thriving but yielding little in the way of its prized psychoactive resin. When left alone in nature, Cannabis is often wise in choosing well-drained fertile soil. It particularly likes the banks of streams, the ditches and gullies along roadside, all the formations which follow the natural drainage patterns of the land. The spread of marijuana under natural circumstances is largely in the hands (or rather the paws, beaks and hoofs) of the creatures who prize its leaves and shoots. These creatures tend to stay within their own environment. This assures Cannabis that it will not be transported from a supportive environment to one less suited for growth.

When people cultivate marijuana, there is no such assurance of consistency in the environment. In the hands of people, marijuana must adapt to a range of outdoor environments, some natural, some highly prepared, some supremely beneficial, some bordering on hostile. This is due primarily to the rapidly shrinking number of good, protected, growing sites on public land within reasonable reach of towns and cities. As the number of people cultivating marijuana outdoors increases, the competition for excellent outdoor sites will get more and more fierce. Many people are finding that their only real option is either private ownership of some land or indoor growing at home.

This situation, I feel, is temporary. Very soon, it should become clear that personal cultivation of this ancient herb can no longer be prohibited. The marijuana plant will move freely into the outdoors under cultivation by friendly concerned hands. Small farm life will be substantially revived with the legalization of marijuana; so long as the government limits acreage and prohibits the dealing, at any level, in both tobacco products and marijuana.

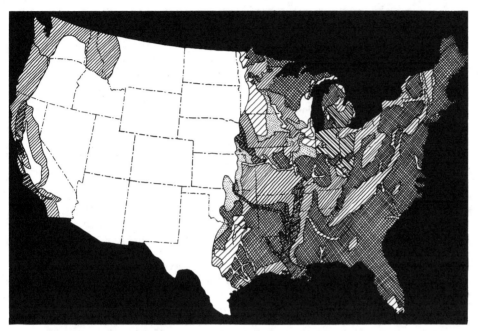

☐	Very rich in lime
▨	Dominantly rich in lime with some areas more acidic
▦	Acid with lime or calcium available in subsurface
▩	Acid poor in lime or calcium
▨	Mixed areas of high and medium lime (calcium)
▨	Mixed areas of medium and low lime
▧	Mixed areas of high, medium and low lime

So, with the coming legalization of marijuana in mind, I would like to take a look at the soils of North America — not to instruct anyone living on the land as to the dirt underfoot — but merely to paint a picture, however simplified, of the kind of soils we will be dealing with in this country.

The prairie soils centered in Iowa, eastern Kansas, Oklahoma, and Texas are generally excellent in the nutrient qualities needed for marijuana. Dark brown in the north to red in the south, this vast, rolling basin is high in organic content, due to the ancient sediments which have settled in the basin much as dirt settles in the bottom of a bathtub. These prairie soils can be very fertile, but, of course, the white man has been upon them for a hundred years and more, so in some places the soil is rich, natural or cultivated, while in other places it is acid and leached of natural energy. Even naturally occurring prairie

soils are subject to drainage problems since there is little relief to the flatness of the land. Some prairie areas have hardpan right under the surface.

In cultivated parts throughout the great sunbowl of the Midwest, there are many rich gardens of sunflowers, corn, and Cannabis. People living in small towns throughout this region often discover that their backyard was once a garden and the topsoil is deep and fundamentally complete. Many a backyard in the Midwest has already seen marijuana cultivation, either as an ornamental plant around the turn of the century or as a homegrown medicinal herb of the 19th century. More than a few grandmothers, throughout this fertile region of the country, are longtime Cannabis cultivators.

The grey and red desert soils of eastern Oregon and Washington, Idaho, Nevada, Utah, and the western slope — the great Rocky mountain and inter-mountain basin region — are often poor in organic content. But the yards of many homes have been gardens in the past and can be revived to surprising fertility with some effort. The desert soils will also support lush growth, if supplied with water in good amounts and if other growth conditions are met. Many of these soils have accumulated salts on top, which must be flushed away, or hardpan underneath, which must be broken up with deep working. When you find that you are limited to such difficult soils, it makes sense to create fertile plugs rather than to wrestle with the earth. A fertile plug is simply a hole filled with a prepared growing medium. As long as you have good drainage, which is no problem in areas free of hardpan, a fertile plug will grow good marijuana in all but the worst alkaline soils. To create a fertile plug in the desert, the hole should be dug, and then flushed heavily with water several times before filling. This will leach the salts from the earth surrounding the hole and show whether or not there is good subsoil drainage. As for the composition of the plug material and the size of the hole itself, ideas abound, varying from region to region. Whatever variations on the basic requirements (good drainage, aeration, fertility, and a depth of at least 18 inches) you try, there should be good results.

The major problem with inter-mountain soils is that root temperature can fluctuate wildly, having as much as a 50° rise and fall in a single day. Wild Asiatic Cannabis was adapted to these extremes in her original mountain and desert homes, but her New World cousins are not so hardy. Protected environments are desirable. Spots not exposed to winds, south-facing hillsides, canyons and valleys with rock faces which store and radiate heat — all of these will make for a good location. Some form of ground cover, a three inch layer of straw is the easiest, will often make the difference between intolerable root fluctuations and a livable range for the marijuana plant.

The red clay and dark humus soils of the southeastern and central coastal states, often with heavy mineralization, support fine marijuana when drainage is adequate and pH is balanced. The gray clay soils are very poor in nutrients and will not support marijuana without more effort than is worthwhile. Quite often in the southern Atlantic and Gulf states a simple green manuring is all that is needed, i.e., the ploughing under of clover or vetch that was planted in the fall.

Some of the dark, rich-looking southern soils are actually not very fertile, since their nutrients are bound and are not available to plants. Many southern soils can benefit from the addition of sand, perlite, or vermiculite, to improve drainage. In many places, cultivators build up mounds on which they plant, rather than attemping to cultivate a whole area. If you use composted materials to build up your clay soil, remember to add lime to bring the compost's natural acidity into line. A few spoonfuls for every cubic foot of soil will usually do. Additionally, the fertile plug method works very well in southern areas of poor soil, as long as there is good drainage.

There are professional cultivators all over the southern and southeastern portions of this country. Many local authorities have come to see the absurdity of arresting marijuana farmers, despite law in the South, which in most places is still repressive. Some of the finest undisturbed marijuana cultivation in America takes place where once poor southern planters were lucky to realize $50 an acre after a season of brute labor and sweat.

The fine brown and reddish-brown dry grassland soils of the western states are found everywhere that spring wheat is planted. Lower than prairie soils in organic matter, they have many of the same characteristics. They are usually found with a rocky subsoil layer. A combination of the fertile plug and the mound planting approach is used with success in the more unworkable areas of western soils. The primary problem with western soils is that they usually need extensive working in order to bring them up to marijuana quality.

This will require that a ground cover be planted and worked in for a season or two before any serious, large-scale planting is attempted. Water is another problem with western grassland soils and it often has to be imported. If the planting site is near a town, water can be supplied by a variety of drip irrigation devices — usually, large containers with drip hoses running from them to the crop, or individual plastic containers with small holes poked in the bottom and set out around the plants. In most places, large five gallon plastic buckets are not hard to find in the trash. These buckets, when a few very small holes are poked in the bottom, will water an area six feet in diameter for five to seven days when protected from evaporation. Experiment with pins and plastic cups until you get a slow-drip size hole.

The other problem with outdoor growing in the West is that it is becoming increasingly likely that marijuana will be ripped off before it reaches maturity. And, even if your outdoor plants make it to maturity, it is altogether too possible that, when harvest time comes, you will find a small army camped around your plants.

The principal nutrient problems with New England soils are created by leaching, due to the ample rainfall throughout the year in this region. Magnesium and calcium are usually the principal deficiencies — treatment with dolomitic limestone is an easy remedy. In much of the East, acidity is a problem, even in gardens which have been worked for a long time. So, if you have moved into a home with a garden in the back, don't assume just because it grows vegetables that it will grow marijuana. Check the pH. Drainage is a common problem in New England and the whole Northeast in general, since the water, in the valleys and floodplains, runs off slowly and soaks in deep. Mound planting is practiced with effectiveness all over New England, though drainage through the subsoil remains a requirement even with this technique. Strains of marijuana adjusted to the short growing season, or brought to flowering by artificial means, do well in New England.

The adobe soils of the Southwest often look like intermountain desert soils to the north, but they are normally much higher in clay content, cracking into characteristic squares when dry. They are much more fertile when worked with organic materials, when watering is minimized to prevent compaction, and when the soil around the base of each plant is worked by hand several times through the season to keep it loose. In the late fall, adobe soils should be turned and green manure, lawn clippings, straw, gypsum or sand added, and a cover of vetch or clover sown. In the early spring, the cover will be turned under and, just before planting, the large clods of soil will need to be broken up. Within a couple of years, adobe soils which have never been worked before become so fertile and yielding with this routine, that all you need from then on is to sow a yearly cover in the fall and turn it over in the spring.

58

Regional
Soil
Deficiencies

The
Outdoor
Environment

Throughout the country there are regions of bog soils, but they are particularly prevalent in the Midwest and Northwest, across Canada, and through the Atlantic states and South. These areas are usually acidic and poorly drained. Planting in such areas is usually easiest if a mound is used, trenched on two sides for drainage. Orient the trenches with the slope of the land if it is discernible. Soil in boglands is usually poor in a number of nutrients, notably phosphorus, and the addition of nutrients often will not help. They are quickly bound by the acidic bog soil. For mound planting in such areas, it's easier to import the soil for the mounds rather than try to work with the soil already there.

Zinc deficiencies are widespread in the western and southeastern U.S. Notable zinc deficiencies occur in the interior valleys of California, parts of eastern Washington, most of southern Arizona, central Texas and southern Oklahoma, portions of Mississippi, Alabama, and Georgia, all of South Carolina and eastern North Carolina, and central Wisconsin. The use of manure in preparing the soil almost always overcomes any deficiency of this trace material.

Soils with iron deficiencies are concentrated in the West. The eastern slope of the Rockies, and western Kansas, Nebraska, Oklahoma, Texas, and New Mexico are deficient, as is south Texas, much of Idaho and Utah, and the Los Angeles and San Francisco areas. Greensand is an excellent remedy.

Copper deficiencies are major in the Florida panhandle, southern Michigan, and northern Indiana. Copper deficiencies often occur in peat soils. The conventional remedy is application of copper sulphate, but hardwood sawdust will also do the job if used in a compost.

Boron deficiencies, like zinc, are widespread in the U.S. Most of New England and Appalachia, most of the South excluding Florida, the Midwest to the Mississippi River, much of Washington, and the Willamette Valley in Oregon are all areas where boron problems are common. Household borax or boric acid are remedies. Use only 1 to 1½ ounces on a plot 10 meters by 10 meters. Work it in months before planting. Be careful not to breathe it.

Magnesium and manganese problems are not widespread. Any soil which has been treated with dolomitic limestone should not show any deficiency. Problems do occur in North and South Carolina, Georgia, Florida, Maryland, Delaware, New Jersey, Maine, and parts of the dairy belt in the Midwest.

Cobalt is widely deficient in the Northwest, the Northeast, the northern Midwest, Arkansas, and Florida. Plowing under vetch or most any legume will help.

While Cannabis is one of the hardiest of plants once it is established, there are a surprising number of environmental concerns. The soil in which Cannabis grows must have a neutral ionization. Soils in which there is a sodium concentrate should be avoided. In many parts of the West, this is a serious handicap, but it can be remedied. Plants grown in unmodified soils of this kind will be short, high in cellulose, very sparsely leafed, low on the starches and sugars of high health, and will yield a very low concentration resin.

Drainage is important for Cannabis. Look around when you are choosing a site. If you were water and fell where you are standing where would you go, seeking the lowest levels? Stay away from low meadows next to streams at the base of sloping hills. Avoid fertile low spots in the prairie with lots of big, wide-blade grasses, cottonwood trees, and so forth. Avoid, too, meadows in the valleys of slow-running streams. Do not plant down terrain from a large body of water. The general rule is: avoid those places where water will pool, no matter how far underground. Also, watch out for places where water traverses slowly.

The soil should be loose enough to facilitate the penetration of roots. If you are serious about planting in hardpan, it will have to be broken up with a shovel or plow. Be sure to work in enough humus when breaking up hardpan. This will prevent drying and blowing of soil in areas subject to heat and winds.

Check the kind of plant growth naturally occurring in the area. Look at the health of both the ground-level and the knee-height weeds. Do they crowd together as though there is a feast for all? Or are they separate, each jealously astride its own little territory of meager subsistence?

A lot of animal trails through the area could spell trouble for your seedlings in their first four weeks. The sugars of sprouting diminish rapidly with age and soon the seedling loses its appeal to hungry critters and is safe. Except from its ultimate fate.

Poke around and check the depth of the topsoil by pulling a few plants. Do the roots go down deep or are they stunted? Are the plants hardy? Is the ground springy like a mat or hard like a pavement? Is there direct access to the sun from first light to last? If not, for how long is the sun obscured?

Marijuana plants thrive in light and airy soil in which water and air move easily, with moderately low moisture levels, good drainage, a good supply of organic matter, the proper pH balance, and an absence of leaf eating pests and critters.

Most soils, especially backyards, can benefit from having organic matter worked in. Soils are improved by the addition of rotted leaves, old musty hay, straw, compost, manure, peat moss, kitchen garbage (food only), sawdust from hardwoods, and other organic materials. Avoid pine needles, the bark of most trees, and untreated human waste.

Activated sludge is a good commercially available source of organic matter. Another good conditioner, in many cases, is peat moss. Mixing a three-inch layer of peat and fertilizer together and then working this layer in to a depth of 12 inches will give a good basic growing bed. Peat has one drawback. It rapidly acidifies the soil, so 2 cups of lime for every 10 lbs. of peat is needed to keep the pH in line.

Avoid ammonium sulfate when buying chemical fertilizer. It kills earthworms. There are often over a million earthworms per acre. The churning they give the soil, the nutrients released through their bodies, their very bodies as they endlessly die (a thousand pounds of them each year per acre), make these little creatures an irreplaceable and priceless part of the natural soil.

If killed by chemicals, worms can gradually grow back in from the surrounding territory. The web of worms surrounding the world six inches under the ground knits itself together in time, so long as the web is not torn in too many places at the same time. But why wound the web in the first place? There are viable alternatives to ammonium sulfate.

The get-rich-quick scheme of the 1950's was chinchilla ranching. In the 1970's, hopeful players of the "Life's Little Follies Sweepstakes" are betting on worm farming. A worm ranch is not a place of sidewalks and warm spring rains where wormboys ride herd on beetleback, scanning the sky for robins. It's a bunch of bins, chockful of the kind of garbage worms love most. The bins are stuffed with worms gulping plain old dirt at one end and turning out the world's most potent dirt at the other. This earth is called worm castings and it is a great addition to your growing soil. Also, folks with eczema report that the skin on the hands and forearms clear up after working with worm castings; a side-benefit for anyone afflicted by this uncomfortable condition. And even if you choose not to use pure worm castings in your growing bed, the potency of this material should convince you to have a healthy worm population in your soil.

Flat, wet soils are often impossible to drain, due to the lack of a slope. In addition, many such areas are quite acid, which severely limits the uptake of the three major nutrients — nitrogen, potassium, and phosphorus — as well as other water soluble nutrients which easily leach out. The alternative is to build up small mounds of soil. Then, treat the mounded soil to bring the pH into line; fertilize it to restore an adequate nutrient balance; and add organic materials to increase aeration and resist compaction. Make the mounds about six feet in diameter with an elevation of two to three feet. Run a ditch about a foot deep outside the mount to further promote drainage. Sow your seeds so that you get maximum coverage without crowding and, if available sunlight is a problem, be sure to orient the mound so that the southern face receives maximum exposure. Plant more heavily on that side.

Cultivators in India use mound-planting almost exclusively in certain areas and New World Indians used this sensible device for a number of their important crops, including tobacco and corn.

To raise the pH of acid soil, you will need to spread dolomitic limestone. Don't use quicklime as it easily destroys the humus in the soil. On every 10 meter by 10 meter plot, spread 30 lbs. of dolomitic limestone to raise the pH a full point in sandy soil. On a sandy loam, use 50 lbs. per 10 meter square. For rich loams, use 70 lbs. Spread the limestone on top of the soil after the soil has been worked. You won't have to plow or rototill it under. Just let it sit on the surface and leach down into the soil. So that you don't burn your plants spread the dolomite on the soil in the late fall or early spring, at least one month before you sow seed.

*Approximate amounts of finely
ground limestone needed to raise
the pH of a 7-inch layer
of soil as indicated**

soils of warm-temperate and tropical regions†	from pH 3.5 to pH 4.5 limestone tons per acre	from pH 4.5 to pH 5.5 limestone tons per acre	from pH 5.5 to pH 6.5 limestone tons per acre
sand and loamy sand	0.3	0.3	0.4
sandy loam		0.5	0.7
loam		0.8	1.0
silt loam		1.2	1.4
clay loam		1.5	2.0
muck	2.5**	3.3	3.8
soils of cool-temperate and temperate regions‡			
sand and loamy sand	0.4	0.5	0.6
sandy loam		0.8	1.3
loam		1.2	1.7
silt loam		1.5	2.0
clay loam		1.9	2.3
muck	2.9**	3.8	4.3

*All limestone goes through a 2-mm. mesh screen and at least ½ through a 0.15-mm. mesh screen. With coarser materials, applications need to be greater. For burned lime about ½ the amounts given are used; for hydrated lime about ¾. Source: USDA Handbook No. 18, p. 237.
**The suggestions for muck soils are for those essentially free of sand and clay. For those containing much sand or clay the amounts should be reduced to values midway between those given for muck and the corresponding class of mineral soil. If the mineral soils are unusually low in organic matter, the recommendations should be reduced about 25%; if unusually high, increased by about 25%, or even more.
†Red-Yellow Podzol, Red Latosol, etc.
‡Podzol, Gray-Brown Podzol, Brown Forest, Brown Podzol, etc.

Approximate amounts of sulphur or aluminum sulphate per 100 square feet necessary to increase the acidity of a silt loam

pH	sulphur, pounds	aluminum sulphate, pounds	pH	sulphur, pounds	aluminum sulphate, pounds
8.0-7.0	2.0	4.5	7.0-6.5	1.5	2.5
8.0-6.5	3.0	7.0	7.0-6.0	2.0	5.5
8.0-6.0	4.0	10.0	7.0-5.5	3.5	9.0
8.0-5.5	5.5	13.5	7.0-5.0	5.0	13.0
8.0-5.0	7.0	17.5	6.5-6.0	1.5	3.0
7.5-7.0	1.75	3.5	6.5-5.5	2.5	6.5
7.5-6.5	2.0	5.0	6.5-5.0	4.0	10.5
7.5-6.0	3.5	7.5	6.0-5.5	1.5	3.5
7.5-5.5	5.0	11.5	6.0-5.0	3.0	7.5
7.5-5.0	6.5	15.5	5.5-5.0	1.5	4.0

Source: Laurie, Alex, *Soilless Culture Simplified*, McGraw-Hill Book Company, New York, 1940, p 79.

Available major nutrients in chemical fertilizers

	N	P	K
ammonium sulphate	20.6	0	0
urea	46	0	0
muriate of potash	0	0	20
nitrate of soda	16	0	0
sulphate of ammonia	20	0	0
potassium nitrate	14	0	46
triple super phosphate	0	47	0
urea-formaldehyde	38	0	0

Source: Cherry, E., *Fluorescent Light Gardening*, D. Van Nostrand & Co., Princeton, N.J., 1965, p 113.

N = Nitrogen, P = Phosphorus, K = Potassium

To lower the pH of alkaline soil, work in two lbs. of sulphur on a 10 foot by 10 foot plot. This will lower the pH about one point. Sulphur is readily available at nurseries and pharmacies.

An excellent way to determine if your soil needs lime is to spread dolomite on one half of a test plot. Leave the other half natural. In a month, plant a crop of sweet clover. If the half of the plot with the lime grows noticeably better clover, you know that you need to lime the whole garden. Clover is especially sensitive to soil acidity. You will find it a good indicator of neutral areas. Signs of soil acidity are wild berries and many of the ferns. They thrive in acid soil, as do oak trees, black spruce, white pine, hemlock, and red spruce. Indicators of an alkaline soil are the white spruce and white cedar. Alfalfa and apple trees can also indicate alkalinity. Since far more plants thrive in slightly acid soils than in even slightly alkaline soils, there are fewer natural indicators.

Always perform working-in operations at least one month before planting. Above all, soil needs time. There is no such thing as instant soil or instant nutrition.

It is essential that organic matter is worked thoroughly into the soil. Organic matter which is not mixed well will tend to form a matted subsurface layer which can block the flow of water to the subsoil.

The pH scale measures concentration of hydrogen ions. When water breaks down in soil, different components have different electric charges. When there is a perfect balance of negative and positive ions in the soil, the pH reading is 7 — a neutral reading. When there are more positive ions than negative, the soil becomes acid, and the pH reading is lower than 7. When there are more negative ions the pH reading is higher than 7, and the soil is called alkaline.

The pH scale is like the Richter scale, which measures earthquakes. Each step up or down the scale represents a geometrical increase in the ion concentration. From pH 7 to pH 6 represents a tenfold increase in positive ions; but from pH 6 to pH 5 represents a hundredfold increase, and pH 5 to pH 4 represents a thousandfold increase in concentration, compared with the pH 7 level.

City water varies in pH. Hard water, or mineralized water is alkaline. Heavily chlorinated water or water smelling of sulphur (rotten eggs) is highly acid.

It is a good idea to test the pH of your city water. If its acidity or alkalinity is too far beyond the range of 6.5 to 7.5, use distilled water to freshen your plants.

Most water treatments result in a salty water which is worse for plants than the untreated water. If your water is no good, use distilled water.

If you don't want to buy distilled water, allow your tap water to stand in a shallow container for 48 hours. Many of the volatile chemicals will disappear, moving the pH of the water toward neutral.

There is no reason why superior marijuana cannot be grown indoors, and there is no reason why anyone should feel they can't do it.

Soil cultivation of marijuana indoors will often require that you either locate, dig and transport enough high quality sandy loam or other soil to fill your growing beds, or that you buy a commercial nursery soil. There is really no problem with commercially prepared soils if they are not treated with herbicides or pesticides, and if they are completely pH balanced. Long-chain by-products occur in the combustion of the herbicides used in nursery soils to prolong shelf-life. The gas-byproducts in the combustion of dry Cannabis are grim enough (perhaps worse than tobacco). There is no need to add a soup of long-chain nerve toxins to our bloodstreams because agribusiness finds it convenient to use herbicides to control pesky growths.

Commercial soils for the cultivation of marijuana should (1) be neutral to slightly alkaline in pH, (2) contain at least 15% fine sand and be grainy, (3) be heat sterilized, and (4) be manufactured locally if at all possible. Most commercial soils will benefit from the addition of 10-15% by weight of vermiculite and perlite.

The marijuana plant grows in some pretty barren soils where it does fine and produces a great deal of resin. But when it is in good soil and gets plenty of powerful, unfiltered sunlight, it will do even better. On the other hand, too rich a diet may send this slightly spartan plant into permanent shock. It can grow dumpy with circulation problems and go barren from too much of a good thing.

It is not a bad idea to routinely add one cup of lime to each 50 lb. bag of commercial soil and whenever fertilizing outdoor soils, lime can be usefully added at the rate of one cup for each five pounds of fertilizer.

If you have dug your soil, it will have to be sterilized. Do this *before* you add any supplements to it. Bake it in an oven at 350° F. for one hour in containers approximately one quart each so that the heat can penetrate. Moisten the soil before heating so that the steam can help sterilize. Be prepared for a smelly kitchen as the stuff cooks.

An alternative to indoor sterilization is to take large cans like coffee cans and poke a few nail holes in the bottom. Fill these with your choice dirt and set them upright in an outdoor fire with a good hot bed of coals. Be sure to have the dirt thoroughly moist before setting the can on the fire. Moisten a couple of times, a half cup of water per can. When the coals have cooled, your dirt will be nicely sterile and your home will be spared an ordeal by odor.

Indoor soils should hold moisture but not allow pooling of water. To test for this quality, poke a small hole a few inches deep in freshly watered soil. If, after a few minutes, standing water appears at the bottom of the hole, the soil is probably too compact (if you haven't gone too heavy on the water). A pint per cubic foot shouldn't produce pooling in the hole. The same crumbly quality is required of indoor soils as outdoor soils and the same test will do.

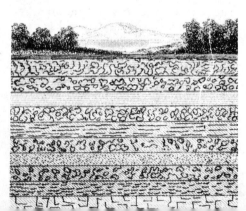

	N	P	K
Asgrow soluble fertilizer	20	20	20
Atlas Fish Emulsion	5	1	1
Bio-Gro Liquid Fish Fertilizer	10	5	5
Black Magic Liquid Fertilizer	10	15	5
Black Magic Blossom Booster Liquid	4	10	10
Blue Whale Soluble Plant Food	6	2	1
Corenco Liquid Fertilizer Concentrate	5	10	10
Du Pont Soluble Plant Food	19	22	16
Gro-Stuf	20	20	20
Hyponex Plant Food	7	6	19
Hy-Trous	4	8	4
Instant Vigoro	19	28	14
Miracle-Gro	15	30	15
Ortho-Gro Liquid Plant Food	10	5	5
Plant Marvel	12	31	14
Ra-Pid-Gro	28	21	17
Spoonit Flower Food	18	20	16
Take-Hold Starter Solution	10	52	17

Source: Cherry, E., *Fluorescent Light Gardening*, D. Van Nostrand & Co., Princeton, N.J., 1965, p 112.

Agrico Rose Food	5	9	6
Agrinite	8	25	0
Armour's Sheep Manure	1¼	1	2
Asgrow Plant Food	5	10	5
Black Magic Tablets	2	3	2
Bone meal (typical)	2	22	0
Bovung	2	1	1
Driconure	3	2	1

*Available major nutrients
in soil incorporated fertilizers*

*Nitrogenous
carriers*

material	nitrogen, per cent	relative availability on basis of 100	acidifying effect on soil	retention by soil
urea	46	90	acid	medium
ammonium nitrate	35	95	acid	low
ammonium sulphate	21	90	acid	medium
cyanamid	22	90	alkaline	medium
calcium nitrate	17	100	alkaline	low
sodium nitrate	16	100	alkaline	low
ammonium phosphate	11	90	acid	medium
blood	10	80	acid	high
tankage	6	70	neutral	high
cottonseed meal	6	70	acid	high
fish meal	5	70	acid	high
activated sludge	4	70	acid	high
steamed bone	2	70	alkaline	high
tobacco	2	70	alkaline	high
garbage tankage	2	30	alkaline	high
peat	2	20	acid	high

Source: Laurie, Alex, *Soilless Culture Simplified*, McGraw-Hill Book Company, New York, 1940, p 23.

If you're growing indoors, you have your choice of containers. A collector of ephemera (stuff that doesn't last) in England is reported to have over 120,000 different kinds of yogurt containers. In light of that, the question "In what shall I grow my marijuana?" takes on cosmic dimensions.

Just about anything will do. File cabinets. Plastic paint buckets. Toilets. Aquariums. Quintupled large grocery bags. Wooden buckets. Wash tubs. Windowboxes. Pottery. Buckets on dollies. Flowerpots. Growing beds.

Avoid galvanized buckets and tubs.

The criteria for any container for mature marijuana are simple. The container must allow for adequate drainage. It should be inert. It should hold about six quarts of soil per plant, and allow for a layer of gravel at the bottom for aeration.

Depth of the soil in any container ought to be at least 12 inches. This allows for good root penetration. If the soil is not too rich, Cannabis wants to put down a strong root system. But it is generally satisfied with a foot, though more is never bad. The container has to minimally allow for three feet trunk to trunk between mature Cannabis plants. This pretty much means individual containers, or an indoor situation such as a barn or garage with a dirt floor. In most cases, individual containers are still more convenient.

Indoor soils salt up rapidly when you're using chemical fertilizer which there is little need to do anyway except for supplementation with potassium near maturity. So don't fiddle around with any additions to the soil while the plant is growing. Enrich the soil you are going to use in advance and leave it in the ground until you are ready for it.

Use a layer of sand on top of any indoor soil to reduce its attraction as a home for bugs.

Every time you start a fresh crop of Cannabis, use fresh soil. If you can, it's a nice idea to have a compost heap and to keep your general living soil composted. Remember Cannabis does not do well later on with nitrogen, but early in life it is very good. So dig your soil from a lightly dressed area which has been well-worked and aerated for a whole winter.

One of the most beneficial agents an indoor grower can use is the worm. Indoor soils compact severely with repeated watering. Introducing a few earthworms into the prepared soil will aid immeasurably in root development and nutrition uptake of the plants, increasing the vegetation appreciably. Worms are sensitive creatures and react to the same things plants do — too much water, overdoses of chemical fertilizers, highly compact soil, etc. If worms thrive in the beds, chances are good the plants will.

It's depressing to contemplate how many good plants have been ruined by lack of attention to the indoor environment.

A critical factor in the photosynthetic process is the ability of a plant to rid itself of the poisons it manufactures in the course of the organic conversions it goes through. These processes depend upon a steady flow of water; from the soil, through the root cells, transported up the stem, passed through the leaf tissues and discharged into the air as water vapor. The escape velocity of the water vapor molecules from the stoma is very low, consequently discharged water vapor tends to hang around the leaf surfaces, preventing further discharge, until it is swept away by breezes.

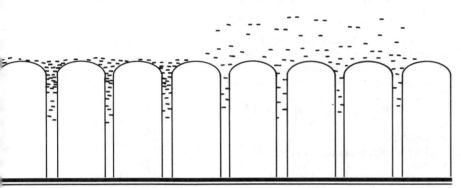

(Left) Leaf cross-section showing pores. Poison-laden water vapor cannot be discharged without adequate ventilation.

(Right) Water vapor being carried away.

These little bubbles of water vapor form a deadly shell which can suffocate Cannabis, which depends on a high volume of water passing through its tissues, very quickly. Indoor growers should take great care to provide for constant input of fresh, unsaturated air and for exhaust of saturated air.

Another common source of death and destruction among indoor Cannabis plants is tobacco smoke. If smokers are using the same air supply which the plants must breathe, you must try to filter the air somehow or take great risks with the plants' survival up until the third week, and their health beyond that. This goes for both Cannabis and tobacco smokers. If you are growing indoors, switch from smoking marijuana to eating it.

We've already reviewed the overall soil moisture characteristics which will affect Cannabis. All that remains is to look at the pattern of water uptake. These patterns are important, particularly for the indoor grower, because they give clues as to the critical growth stages where deprivation of water will have very negative effects.

Water is a critical variable in Cannabis cultivation. Too much water drowns the plant. Too little slows or stops growth and leads quickly to wilting. Wilted marijuana plants can be brought back to life by a thorough ground soaking, provided their internal fluid-carrying vessels have not collapsed. Water requirements vary radically with the growing situation, so the following guidelines are offered as general considerations.

For the first four weeks, the soil should be uniformly moist, though a little surface drying is not a problem. Water should be added slowly, ensuring complete dispersion. For indoor soils, one pint of water per gallon of soil will drench the growing environment. Outdoors, the earth should be moist an inch or two under the surface. The most common problems with early seedlings is overwatering. The soil should be drenched at planting and left alone for about a week before more water is considered.

For the fifth through fourteenth week, Cannabis requires a soil which is dry near the surface, but has deep moisture available. One thorough watering a week, or a drip irrigation system adjusted to the plants' water requirements, will do the job. If using drip irrigation, use a very slow trickle rate and if surface evaporation is a problem, use a system which you can partially bury. During the fifth to fourteenth week period the soil should be moist six inches down, but it need not show a lot of moisture in the top six inches of soil.

In maturity there are a number of water options. A great deal depends on the genetic program of your plants, on environmental conditions like wind, sun, and soil, and on your choice of a harvesting schedule. As a rule of thumb, it is OK to stress Cannabis by depriving it of water for a week at a time, once it has passed its fast growth period (when she may be growing several inches a day) and has settled into her reproduction period.

week	A AIR = 75° F. SOIL = 75° F.		B AIR = 75° F. SOIL = 60° F.		C AIR = 60° F. SOIL = 75° F.		D AIR = 60° F. SOIL = 60° F.	
	wild	comm'l	wild	comm'l	wild	comm'l	wild	comm'l
1	60	210	50	175	80	150	70	60
2	70	200	40	100	80	190	45	100
3	130	290	85	105	85	190	50	120
4	125	380	65	240	105	260	65	180
5	160	650	105	420	110	380	90	240
6	155	560	115	420	125	430	120	260
7	175	730	80	470	170	530	100	430
8	140	650	100	490	200	610	135	430
9	175	730	120	540	140	540	70	530
10	140	850	120	530	155	840	100	670
11	150	850	60	560	90	650	75	450
12	160	670	105	470	125	600	100	420
13	150	770	110	470	90	620	45	480
14	160	750	105	510	105	600	50	510

Key points to keep in mind when inspecting this chart are:

Air and soil temperatures will be equal (columns A & D) under normal indoor conditions. Bottom heating will produce the difference noted in columns B & C.

The figures given are per plant per week, indoors, under lights.

The water uptake figures are given in milliliters, which are equivalent to 1/1000 of a liter; thus 500 ml = ½ liter (or ½ quart) of water, and so forth.

The figures given for the wild strain represent the *minimum* requirements for a healthy plant. The figures for the commercial strain, grown for fiber, represent about the average under temperate conditions.

A healthy mature plant outdoors in the hot summer sun will actually transpire far more than shown, up to several gallons a day.

70   Enriched
Water for   The
Enhanced Growth   Carrotometer   The
Black
Feast

To produce enriched water which has shown extraordinary results in promoting seedling growth, take two ounces of any seed and soak overnight in a quart of distilled water. You can use any seeds you wish, marijuana or otherwise. If you are sprouting seed for food, using such nutrient storehouses as alfalfa or mung bean, then simply save the water in which you've done your preliminary soaking. The soaked seeds are then either sprouted or discarded.

Using the seed-soak water just as you would regular water, you will find a substantial improvement in the growth and health of your Cannabis seedlings. Soak water is an excellent source of high energy for seedlings to be harvested for potency at the two to three week stage. There have been no controlled experiments done yet using this approach, but casual observation of a group of seedlings raised on soak water compared to seedlings raised on distilled water shows noticeable differences in height and leaf mass.

The water in which seeds are soaked for 8-12 hours shows a rich concentration of amino acids, natural sugars and inorganic elemental minerals. Under natural conditions these growth enhancing factors would leach out of the seed and be returned to the soil when the rains and the natural soil moisture were imbibed by the swelling seed. In the soak water they are available in concentrated form to the seedling and apparently prove beneficial through the plant's whole life.

The fresh green leafy top of a carrot makes an excellent soil-moisture indicator. Slice off the top of a carrot leaving about ½ inch of carrot attached. Imbed the carrot top in the soil so that just a bit of orange is showing. As long as the leaves stay bright and healthy, your soil moisture is fine. When they begin to wilt, the soil is getting dried out. The perfect soil moisture for Cannabis is just about where the carrot begins to lose it and die, so if you can keep the carrot top on the very edge of good health, the marijuana will do just fine. It is not a bad idea to change the carrot top every two weeks or so.

A number of experiments have shown that Cannabis is highly stimulated by a concentration of carbon dioxide in the air. Plants take in carbon dioxide, strip off the carbon to use in building their structures, and breathe out the oxygen. The black ash of smoked marijuana is the carbon which the plant took from the air in its lifetime. The more carbon dioxide a plant can get (again, up to a point) the more raw material it has for growth. Carbon dioxide is for plants what protein is for humans: a body builder.

Indoor cultivators can take advantage of this responsiveness to CO_2 on the part of their plants by placing a small chunk of dry ice in a pan in the environment with the plants. More is not better in this case. One chunk the size of two ice cubes per day is enough for air space the size of an average closet. Put the ice as far from the plant as is reasonable. You don't want to chill the air, you just want to feed the plant an extra ration of carbon. A simple, effective approach is to blow the CO_2 vapors across the ceiling of the growing space, using a small fan. The CO_2 will gradually settle during the next hour if the air is undisturbed.

This technique works best when you wait until the plants are six weeks old. The plants seem to prefer to have their carbon feast in mid-morning. There is a lot of room for work with carbon dioxide feeding of marijuana plants. Needless to say, you should not be doing any deep breathing exercises in the growing area while doing CO_2 feeding.

Water is in the soil in three forms. In its hygroscopic form, it is chemically bound with the earth's materials and isn't available for the plant. Utilization and release of this hygroscopic moisture is one of the many functions served by the holy earthworm. The next form of water in the soil is gravitational. It comes from above, rain, flood, or irrigation. It is gross soil water, coursing through channels and along veins of the soil, rushing past the thirsty roots and giving relief but not nurture. The nurture comes from the third type of water, the capillary. Capillary action is water working its way toward the surface against the pull of gravity. Thus, the extent to which a soil can help hold water against gravity is a good measure of that soil's effectiveness in supporting plants. Hot and dry conditions not only increase the plant's breathing, they also increase evaportion. A soil's ability to hold water against the pull of dry space is as important as its ability to hold water against gravity. Soil is what holds water in suspension between the underworld and the air so that plants can drink and grow. The heat and winds of the upper world and the enormous unrelenting draw of the underworld strain the thin membrane of water which moistens this planet's six inch thick skin.

Even indoors, capillary action is an important quality of the best soils. But if the water isn't pure and neutral pH, your plant will be injured in even the best soil. In many places tap is acid or alkaline. You can lower pH with aspirin and raise it with calcium oxide. But rather than mess around some more with already overtreated water, use fresh distilled water if at all possible.

The pattern of your plant's water uptake is simple. The growth period, roughly the first half of life, is characterized by steady water uptake. The period of maturity is characterized by steady water uptake that is directly related to photoperiod.

To thoroughly soak soil in an indoor container will take about one pint per gallon of soil, a gallon being the absolute minimum size for mature plants. This is a flowerpot roughly eight inches diameter at the top.

Water uptake is related to growth only to a point: when the plant is prepared to flower. From then on, growth ceases. But the plant will still take up water if allowed. The plant is like any female bearing young. She will accept the most comfortable conditions afforded by the environment.

Yet, while a mild climate and all she can drink is acceptable to the female and her consort, the easy life does not bring out her best.

After the plants show their first primordia it is time to cut way down on water. It is also time to turn up the light and heat and, perhaps, shorten the day cycle a bit.

(Below) Young polyploid leaf (a plant that has double or more multiples of the normal number of chromosomes. See photograph page 143.

In Colorado once I saw the relationship between water uptake and resin production dramatically demonstrated. The plants were Afghani females, dark and rich green with a misty red halo about the whole plant. They were grown indoors in early spring in the Rockies, moved outdoors for the whole summer, and were back indoors, mature, five-month females at the time I am describing.

Some of the plants were kept on relatively dry regimens while others were allowed to drink all they wanted. The cultivators wanted to see whether a lush meadow environment or a dry plateau atmosphere would be best. A combination of heating, blowing, and watering was used to simulate each environment. Lighting was skylight plus Gro-Lux.

Each day the plants were inspected and rated by a group of us. We noted such things as how the leaves and clusters of these unfertilzed Afghani plants felt, looked, smelled and tasted. As part of our testing, we did not smoke since the experimenters' thought we might get too attached to one plant or another, thereby biasing the results. So, each day for a week, we dropped by in the afternoon and rated the plants, not knowing which were on the high- or low-water intakes.

The plants with the low water intake were consistently rated better in appearance, aroma, and moistness. These high ratings, I'm happy to say, were later reciprocated by the highs given to each of the judges by a gift package of the winners in the great Afghani Drinking Contest, Colorado, 1976.

Outdoor growing is risky business unless the cultivator is able to locate a remote and untravelled piece of ground, preferably on very private property. Backyard growing is especially risky unless steps are taken to shield the plants from the view of everyone, including neighbors, garbagemen, meter readers, postmen, police helicopters, and boy scouts who are often trained in anti-dope surveillance by their leaders!

Inverting a basket over the plant (see the Traumatic Basket section of the *International Cultivators Handbook*) works well, but people might wonder what all those baskets were doing in your backyard. High fences work unless you have higher-up neighbors.

You might fool some of the people some of the time by intercropping your marijuana with sunflowers or corn, but your unusual choice of backyard foliage would probably attract the eye of some garden buff, who might then really pay attention, and who might or might not approve of your herbal fancies.

Greenhouses are very nice and are basically operated like any other indoor growing situation, except that for marijuana they are kept hot and dry and very brightly lighted. Whether or not you can get away with greenhouse cultivation without risk depends largely on other factors — how likely is any element of your lifestyle to attract undesired attention? Do you do anything, or look like anything, which potentially marks you as a suspicious character? The more your community image is above reproach, the more your private business will be respected and the more private you can be. It's all a question of how relatively risk-free a cultivator wants to be in states where there are penalties for growing dope.

Where I live, I can no longer risk growing these beautiful plants because of my public exposure as author of this book. But if I could, crazy law being what it is, I wouldn't use my backyard, even with a greenhouse. A greenhouse on a farm, perhaps, but not in the city or near the suburbs. If you are a person already

*(Below) Opposite leaf branching pattern
which occurs in normal young plants.
See photograph page 87.*

known as a gardener, you're in good shape as long as you limit your visitors to the greenhouse with a deft ploy like "Ruins the ambient atmosphere, you know, opening or closing the door — would you like a nice cup of tea?"

But there is something terribly suspicious about a neat little greenhouse sitting in a backyard of a house with a ragged lawn and untrimmed shrubs like mine. If you are going to cultivate marijuana in an outdoor greenhouse, make your house and yard look like a gardener lives there or is on the payroll. In short, a greenhouse has to look like it belongs. If your home looks right, consider a greenhouse. For me, it would be like landing on "Go directly to jail."

If you must grow outside in the city, keep it low. When your plant reaches three feet or so, prune it back six inches. Every two weeks or so, prune back the new stems that develop below the cut — two for one in the same manner. Cannabis is like the mythical hydra. It grows two heads for every one you lop off.

But this hydra becomes a tree of life.

If planting in your backyard without a greenhouse is your only option, chances are that you're going to have to do some work before the yard will be suitable for Cannabis. Your yard will more likely be a problem if the house is new, or old with a neglected yard, than if the yard has been taken care of over a number of years. If you have a nice green carpet of grass in the yard, you may have a problem with acid soil if the previous tenants used a lot of potent chemical fertilizers, pesticides and herbicides to achieve their Utopia. In another vein, many houses have no topsoil at all, especially in the backyards, so you will be starting with a hard surface and little if any organic content below the surface. Another common problem with backyards is that there may be all kinds

of old construction equipment just under the surface — broken brick, plaster, cement, glass, insulation, conduit, nails, sheetrock. An excessive amount of such materials may have resulted in alkaline soil conditions.

The first thing to do is to remove any such junk from the plot you intend to work. Most people won't be planting a whole backyard, so choosing the most secure location, with good sun exposure and drainage will often move you away from the house and hopefully away from the area of most debris.

Your first move will be to spread straw and peat moss, three inches thick, on the surface of your plot. If there's a definite sod layer, remove it before spreading. Also remove any large plants, rotting softwood, and trash.

After a rain, when the surface of the peat moss is beginning to dry, indicating that most of the moisture is on its way down to the subsoil, rototill the straw and peat into the soil. Next, spread some well-rotted manure over the surface, adding dolomite if necessary, and rototill this into the soil as well. Then sow sweet clover over the bed. Most of this work should be done in the early fall of the year before you plant. If weather permits an early enough start, you can work your backyard this way in February for a late spring planting. You can expect some very improved soil conditions by planting time.

Fish emulsion is an extremely potent fertilizer, excellent for yards which are being worked for the first time in years, if ever. Fish emulsion is not a replacement for other organic matter worked into the soil for airiness and moisture retention, like mulch. Be sure to read the label carefully.

Of course, you can always do what both new and old world cultivators have done

(Below) Hermaphrodite plant (male and female flowers on seperate shoots). See photograph pages 38/39.

for centuries. Bury a fish 14-18 inches down in the soil, work in straw, garbage, dried grass, and manure with dirt excavated from the hole and re-fill the hole. Allow the hole to lie undisturbed for a month, then plant the seeds over the fish, six to eight seeds per mound with the intention of thinning to one plant by the third week. Creating a fertile plug like this in otherwise inhospitable soil is an attractive alternative to working a whole area in order to plant a few marijuana plants. As long as drainage is adequate, the fertile plug method works as well as any outdoor Cannabis cultivation technique.

The post-hole digger is especially well-adapted to this work and is an excellent tool to have and to share with others.

If you are composting garbage and other organic material for fill dirt in fertile plugs (or any other application), you should add one cup of lime for every five-gallon bucket of compost, mixing it into the compost pile as it is built. Compost is frequently acidic. The additions of lime are required to assure neutral pH as well as to provide a happy environment for the microbial life that is essential to good compost.

Greece is a hard land, yielding only stubbornly to cultivation, yet marijuana growing is an art which goes back centuries in this land of the original recorded enlightenment. Greek scientists are among the most creative in the study of Cannabis. Recently two top researchers announced in a United Nations report that "for the past 10 years, our laboratory has been concerned with the experimental cultivation of Cannabis for a high resin production under standard ecological conditions."

These scientists report five factors necessary for high resin production. The first four are fairly common knowledge:

potent genetic background, a good photoperiod, adequate nitrogen, phosphate, potassium, and distances of at least 60 to 80 centimeters between plants (varying with the strain of plant). The fifth factor in high resin production according to the scientists is *"Temperature of the ground at time of sowing."* The absolute minimum ground temperature at sowing is 44° F. and, if the ground is at that temperature, the crop will tend toward the low end of the resin production curve. The optimum ground temperature at sowing appears to be 62° F.

These scientists have concluded that production of THC, CBD, CBN, and other Cannabis creations "depends to a considerable extent on the ecological conditions under which the plant is grown. According to our experience, this

is the main reason for the yield of poor quality resin during the cultivation of Cannabis in nurseries and greenhouses with limited ultraviolet light."

The action of environmental factors in altering sexual expression and vegetative development in Cannabis should not be considered in isolation from some of the plant mechanisms which interact with environment to produce the changes we've been discussing.

Enzymes play an important role in sex expression. The enzymes *adrase* (male) and *gynase* (female) are produced by all Cannabis plants in the seedling stage. How much of each is produced, and how much of each is utilized by the plant seems to be determined by

environmental factors, in particular the photoperiod. While both enzymes are produced in every hemp plant, hermaphroditism is rare under normal conditions because the male enzyme has a self-inhibitory quality.

The complex interaction of environment and enzyme may be viewed as a trade-off situation. If environmental conditions are strongly in favor of production of the male-associated andrase, its self-inhibitory powers come into play so that the female-associated enzyme can influence sexual development at least to the point where the plant will be hermaphroditic. This seems to be a self-preservation and reproductivity-retention mechanism, for without it, only male plants would be produced under radical environmental conditions and the plants would not be able to propagate.

Under conditions highly conducive to the production of the female-associated gynase, a process occurs which has the same outcome from the plant's point of view — the plants retain the ability to propagate by becoming hermaphroditic.

Under normal conditions, of course, Cannabis has no need to protect itself by going through these genetic gyrations and in the ordinary course of events the cultivator will not have to worry about manipulation of sex in his plants. If, however, the cultivator is interested in producing a high ratio of females to males, deviating from the normal 1:1 relationship, then an awareness of what is happening — the plant's survival capability is being challenged — should make the cultivator more sensitive to changes in his plants. Most important, the cultivator should not try for high 9:1 or 9.5:1 female ratios unless willing to pay the price of hermaphroditic plants with potential genetic defects in future generations and highly variable drug potency.

There are a few good clues which your plants will give you if they are being starved of any of the really essential nutrients. The following discussion should be useful as a guide, but before acting upon leaf analysis, it is highly advisable to check for soil acidity, which can produce many of the below symptoms by limiting nitrification and promoting excess uptake of toxic salts. Use litmus paper to test for acidity, and simply follow the directions on the package. Litmus paper can be easily obtained at many drug stores and always at chemical supply houses and nurseries. Again, any pH reading above or below 7.0 should be corrected.

It's difficult to attempt to use natural, organic materials to redress soil deficiencies once the plant is growing or anytime near planting. If you've waited to check the soil until planting time, you'll probably want to use chemicals rather than organic materials in many cases. Keep in mind that well worked soil, to begin with, should have no nutrient deficiencies.

NITROGEN DEFICIENCY

This is the most common problem which users of natural soils will encounter. Nitrogen is absolutely essential for the production of protoplasm, for construction of photosynthetic cells, and for all basic plant tissues.

Cannabis shows a nitrogen deficiency by a yellowing of the older leaves. The young leaves will remain green, except in severe cases, because the older leaves, in the face of starvation, give up their nitrogen for the young. The plant sends whatever nitrogen it can draw from the soil to the youngest leaves first.

Use of organic fertilizers like manure or chicken dung, plus plowing in some nitrogen-fixing plants like beans, will assure that you won't have this problem. Chemical remedies include sodium nitrate, potassium nitrate, and calcium nitrate. For nitrogen excess, work in hardwood sawdust.

PHOSPHORUS DEFICIENCY

Phosphorus is another element essential for plant health. Its function appears closely linked with nitrogen. It is needed for the plant's metabolism of sugar, from which much of its energy is derived.

The mature leaves of Cannabis will show phosphorus deficiency first. They will appear a dark, dull green, curled up a bit at the edges. The undersides of the leaves, particularly close to the veins, may show a purple tint.

In acid soil, work in lime and bone meal. In alkaline soil, work in humus and bone meal. Rock phosphate is another good source.

MAGNESIUM DEFICIENCY

Magnesium is an integral part of the chlorophyll in all green plants and serves in other important ways, including the distribution of phosphorus.

Symptoms occur first on older leaves and consist of a yellowing of the tissues around the veins of a leaf. The leaves will develop a general "varicose vein" look very quickly. The yellowing then spreads over the whole leaf.

Many of the magnesium sulphur compounds available in commercial fertilizers can correct this condition. Agricultural epsom salts will be the most easily available.

CALCIUM DEFICIENCY

Calcium is absolutely necessary for the uptake of other minerals and is used by Cannabis only in minute quantities. But it is a must.

The symptoms of calcium starvation are difficult to detect. They consist of the stunting of buds which are in the process of becoming leaf clusters and a wilting of the tips of the fine lateral roots. Most cultivators of Cannabis won't have to worry if their soil is of sedimentary origin. Commercial remedies for calcium deficiencies are readily available, or you can work bone meal and chicken feathers (not in large quantities) in to soil you suspect of being calcium deficient. Calcium sulfate should be added if you are late. Calcium deficiencies are common in acid, wet soil in the East and on the Gulf coast.

MOLYBDENUM DEFICIENCY

Many soils lack the trace amount of this element which is essential for Cannabis in nitrogen fixation.

Symptoms are a yellowing of the sections of the leaves between the major veins, and this yellowing occurs first on those leaves near the middle of the plant, progressing rapidly to the younger leaves at the extremities. The younger leaves will, in addition, become severely distorted and twisted. The yellowing may not occur if you have been using ammoniated nitrogen fertilizers, but the twisted young leaves will be a giveaway sign.

Be sure to use a plant food containing a trace amount of this essential element.

CHLORINE DEFICIENCY

This disease can be confused with many others, because the symptoms are a general yellowing of the leaves, and a gradual turn in color to bronze or bronze-orange. The one sure indicator is if the tips of the lateral root system become swollen, and if they are much shorter than the normal five to seven inches radial spread just beneath the soil surface. Potassium chloride is useful.

This is a very uncommon problem, and will not occur at all if any care is taken in seeing that the major nutrients have been supplied, as the chloride ion is associated with many of the major nutrient compounds.

ZINC DEFICIENCY

This disease will begin to show along about the fifth week in Cannabis, and will result in very small leaves which are wrinkled around the edges and which are faintly yellow along the veins. The distance between nodes on the stem will also be greater than you would expect on a normal plant, in some cases only the top knot of leaves will be viable. It is a common problem with alkaline soils.

Any plant food containing zinc compounds will do the trick if the problem is caught in time.

(Right) Leaf sample grown from Thai seeds

IRON DEFICIENCY

Cannabis requires only trace amounts of this element, though it is an essential link in the photosynthetic process, as well as in respiration. Iron deficiencies are common in alkaline soil.

Deficiency symptoms look the same as magnesium deficiency symptoms, except they occur on the younger leaves first. Most plant foods contain enough of this trace element to assure no problems. Ferrous sulfate, ferric chloride, and ferric citrate are the chemicals.

POTASSIUM DEFICIENCY

Relatively large amounts of potassium are needed by Cannabis at certain growth stages. This element functions as an activator of essential metabolic activities, including assimilation of the energy of light, produced by photosynthesis.

Again, the older leaves will show deficiency signs first. There will be a slight yellowing of the leaves initially, followed rapidly by dark spots, and the edges of the leaves become bronze-gray. Potassium sulfate or potassium chloride. Seaweed mulch, granite dust or greensand can be used organically.

SULPHUR DEFICIENCY

This deficiency is uncommon except in the Pacific Northwest. Most other soils contain a sufficient amount of sulphur.

The symptoms usually occur first in the younger leaves (opposed to the normal Cannabis pattern) and amount to a slight general yellowing. This condition soon spreads to the rest of the plant. Agricultural sulphur is widely available. Sulphur is also available at local pharmacies at very reasonable prices.

BORON DEFICIENCY

This element is necessary for the development of strong stem tissues. There is usually enough in the soil to prevent problems but alkaline soils tend to be deficient.

The symptoms are a bit difficult to detect unless they are critical. This would include swelling near the base and the stem would crack open revealing the inside to be very dry and rotten looking.

Most plant foods have enough borate in them to prevent this kind of problem. In an acid soil, work in seaweed, clover, or vetch.

To one gallon of hot water, add two pounds of fresh, chopped seaweed, or a double handful of dry seaweed meal. Let the mixture soak overnight, then strain and use undiluted. Spray thoroughly over and under the leaves of deficient plants. Repeated sprayings may be necessary for stubborn cases. Dry seaweed can usually be found in health food stores, and less often in plant supply stores.

*Minerals in
Seaweed*

sulphates	4.18%
potassium	2.83%
chlorine	1.72%
calcium	1.54%
silica	1.48%
magnesium	1.01%
bromine	0.68%
aluminum	0.22%
phosphorus	0.18%
iodine	0.17%
manganese	0.016%
iron	0.010%
copper	0.002%

plus traces of arsenic, boron, cobalt, molybdenum, vanadium, zinc, gold and other elements.

Source: *Organic Gardening and Farming*, February, 1978.

*Organic sources
of major and minor
nutrients*

nutrient	source	% available
nitrogen	blood meal	12-15%
	activated sludge	5-6%
	ground animal hide	10%
	feathers and hair	15%
	bone meal	5%
	pigeon and chicken manure	5%
phosphorus	burned, ground bone	30-35%
	burned cucumber skins	11%
	dog manure	10%
	ground oyster shell	10%
	milorganite	3%
	burned potato skins	5%
potassium	burned banana stalks	48%
	burned banana skins	42%
	hardwood ashes	6-9%
	granite dust	7%
	burned corncobs	50%

micronutrients	sources
boron	vetch, sweet clover, granite dust
iron	most legumes, vetch, peachpits
copper	spinach, dandelions, hardwood sawdust
manganese	red clover, carrot tops, alfalfa
zinc	ragweed, hickory and poplar ashes, cornstalks
molybdenum	vetch, alfalfa
calcium	dolomitic limestone, ground glass

The use of chemicals instead of organic fertilizers has several advantages under specific conditions. Chemical quantities can be regulated rather closely with established plant requirements. Some of the best research done on marijuana's nutrient requirements was by Sister Mary Etienne Tibeau in 1934. Sister Mary writes of her work with her plants with the systematic vision of a fascinated researcher. Her work concentrates particularly on the nutrients required to produce the largest and thickest leaves and the greatest amounts of resin. Sister Mary is every grower's spiritual mother superior.

Commercial preparations (called salts) of all of the important agricultural chemicals are available for the cultivator who wants to make a personal formula for hydroponic or soil growing. Remember when buying these chemicals in sacks to transfer them to separate tight containers when you get them home, if you're going to store them for even a few days.

The chemicals which are generally available from nursery suppliers, agricultural chemical dealers, and elsewhere, are the following.

SALT	NUTRIENTS SUPPLIED BY SALT
ammonium sulphate	nitrogen and sulphur
boric acid powder	boron
calcium sulphate	calcium and sulphur
copper sulphate	copper and sulphur
iron sulphate	iron
magnesium sulphate	magnesium and sulphur
manganese sulphate	manganese
monocalcium phosphate	calcium and phosphorus
potassium nitrate	nitrogen and potassium
potassium sulphate	potassium and sulphur
sodium nitrate	nitrogen
superphosphate	calcium and phosphorus
zinc sulphate	zinc and sulphur

There are four basic solutions of metallic salts which occur in one form or another in many fertilizers. Such formulas were devised by Sister Tibeau in her groundbreaking experiments with Cannabis growth response to different nutrients. The formulas are very easily compounded. Simply purchase the desired chemicals, and use a large bowl to measure out the amounts required by the formula.

If a formula calls for two parts of one chemical and five parts of another, and 4½ of a third, then simply translate that into ounces or cups of material, and mix the ingredients together in a large plastic or wooden bowl. Any time a formula calls for a very small quantity to be mixed with a large quantity, be sure to grind it thoroughly before adding it to the mix. Take a pestle and grind the mixture until no crystals remain, then put it in a dry, tightly closed container. Formula strength (how much to dilute it with water) depends on the individual formula.

In addition to the formulas below, developed by Sister Mary, I would like to offer a formulation which has worked very well and is very easy to measure out, mix, and use.

calcium sulphate	6 ounces
monocalcium phosphate	4 ounces
magnesium sulphate	6 ounces
potassium nitrate	8 ounces
iron sulphate	1 gram

*Four basic supplemental
solutions of
the essential salts*

85

Mix the dry ingredients together, carefully pulverizing the iron sulphate before adding it to the mix. With this formula, use a level teaspoonful per gallon of water.

Approximately the same strengths apply to Sister Mary's formulas. Without going into the calculations, if you mix these formulas using ounces of the chemicals for the parts expressed in the formula, you will wind up with a nutrient mix one level teaspoonful of which in a gallon of water will make an excellent experimental solution.

When using any fertilizer, weak doses on a frequent schedule are better than strong doses at long intervals. Though it is tempting, with nutrients, more is not better. A good sized container, filled with good soil, will provide all the nutrients needed for the first six weeks. After that, a watering with any good soluble fertilizer every second week will be more than adequate for most Cannabis in most situations.

FORMULA 1

high potassium	ratio (parts)
KNO_3	2
KH_2PO_4	2
KCL	2.5
$MgSO_4$	1
$Ca(NO_3)_2$	4
K_2SO_4	4.5

FORMULA 2

high magnesium	ratio (parts)
KNO_3	1
KH_2PO_4	1
$Ca(NO_3)_2$	4
$MgCl_2$	3
$MgSO_4$	4

FORMULA 3

high calcium	ratio (parts)
$Ca(NO_3)_2$	15
KH_2PO_4	1
$CaCl_2$	11
$MgSO_4$	1
KNO_3	1

FORMULA 4

high nitrogen	ratio (parts)
KNO_3	1
NH_4NO_3	17
$Ca(NO_3)_2$	4
KH_2PO_4	1
$MgSO_4$	2

*Effects of the use
of supplemental solutions
of essential salts*

*(Right) Alternate branching
pattern which occurs
shortly before flowering
or after topping. See
photograph page 159.*

FORMULA 1

FOLIAGE AND RESIN

Production of very large leaves stimulated; calcium oxalate crystals are heavily concentrated; resin production is inhibited if a potassium overdose occurs after the tenth week. Sex ratio 7:3 females. Potassium is very essential in the early stages of life, but has substantial negative effects at maturity if too great a concentration is continued.

STATURE AND GROWTH

Potassium yields greatest height; stem is large and thick, very low on fiber, woody and brittle; leaves are thick, healthy, dark green; growth cycle is shortened by about a week.

FORMULA 2

FOLIAGE AND RESIN

Foliage is more sparse than with high potassium dosage; older leaves wilt readily. A magnesium shortage will inhibit or prevent resin production. Sex ratio 6:4 males. Magnesium is vital to overall health but conservative supplementation is advisable.

STATURE AND GROWTH

Magnesium concentrations give good height; stems will be fibrous and hollow, somewhat woody, not as strong as with calcium supplements; leaves will be healthy but pale-green in color and will brown or wilt around the edges and tips.

FORMULA 3

FOLIAGE AND RESIN

Healthy plants are produced with somewhat smaller leaves than with the other supplements; foliage is not very thick or abundant; high calcium salt concentration inhibits resin production. Sex ratio 7:3 males. Overdose of calcium in early life will stunt growth but an adequate supply is essential in the sixth to ninth weeks.

STATURE AND GROWTH

Very strong and fibrous stem which is desirable where heavy winds are common; plants do not grow high; color is dark green and flowers are swollen.

FORMULA 4

FOLIAGE AND RESIN

Foliage is abundant, healthy, dark green and leaves are thick; excess nitrogen promotes water loss and can cause wilting; nitrogen deficit at maturity stimulates resin production. Sex ratio as high as 9:1 females. Excess nitrogen will cause plants to grow fast in seedling stage and to appear healthy, but they will die off at the time of sex differentiation.

STATURE AND GROWTH

Plants will be short, squat and very leafy. Nitrogen should *not* be cut back until after the sixth week.

Bottom
Heating
Effects

(Left)
Alternate
branching

89

In the section covering planting frames we will talk about bottom heating, the process of raising soil temperature above that of the surrounding air; but since this is an environmental manipulation, we'll present this chart here. Before you go through the expense and effort of using this procedure on your plants, be sure to refer back to this chart and get an idea of the relative advantages and disadvantages.

A AIR = 60° F., SOIL = 60° F.	B AIR = 75° F., SOIL = 60° F.
Lowest water needs; approximately 40% less than (D).	Water needs are substantial.
Lowest rate of nutrient uptake occurs between weeks five and seven in the growth cycle.	Lowest rate of nutrient uptake occurs in the twelfth week.
Mean number of leaves on mature plants equal to (D), but female plants are more sparse.	Lowest mean number of leaves per plant for both males and females.
Leaf area is substantial; color and thickness good.	Leaf area is very low, and leaf thickness is considerably less than under all other temp./air conditions.
Use of a 16-hour exposure to light daily at this soil-air temperature level produces mainly female plants.	A 15- to 20-hour light exposure will produce a sex ratio of 6:4 females.
Height at maturity is low compared to (B) and (D).	Height of mature plants substantial.

C AIR = 60° F., SOIL = 75° F.	D AIR = 75° F., SOIL = 75° F.
Water needs are substantial.	The greatest water needs occur under these conditions.
Lowest rate of nutrient uptake occurs in the third week.	Lowest rate of nutrient uptake occurs in the fifth to seventh weeks.
Mean number of leaves per plant is the greatest, but females have fewer leaves per plant than the females in (D).	Mean number of leaves per plant is less than (C), but females have 40% more leaves per plant than (C).

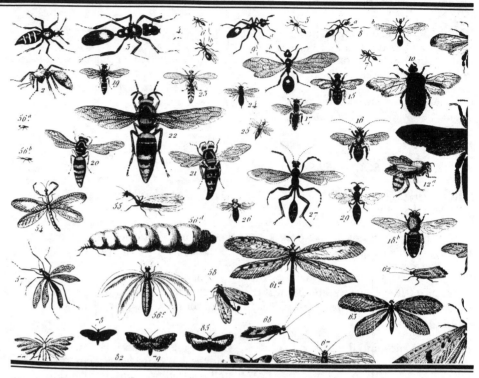

Carefully controlled recent studies (1975) support the conventional notion that a mild, unvarying temperature range in the environment of 72-80° F., day and night, is optimal for generation of potent flowering tops. The precise relationship of environmental temperature to root temperature in producing potency in marijuana has not yet been effectively studied, although the Greek studies mentioned earlier suggest the critical importance of the relationship.

When you consider the worldwide decreasing effectiveness of chemical poisons in controlling insect and animal pests, it makes sense to think in terms of natural controls. Folk traditions include remedies for almost every sort of predator — bunnies, bugs, deer, fungus. Every pest except the fleet-footed narc (*sus scrofa*) is subject to natural control through the use of herbs or natural enemies. The narc, of course, has many natural enemies but remains unaffected by herbal barriers and is, currently, a protected species.

Rabbits and deer simply love young Cannabis shoots. Many an outdoors cultivator has returned to a new garden in the woods or fields only to find bare ground, hoof and paw prints, and those little nugget calling cards. Fences aren't much help and they can be a bit conspicuous way out there in the middle of nowhere.

One method that is reportedly successful is to drink a fair amount of beer, down a quantity of B6 Vitamins, and pee copiously around the perimeter of your garden. This apparently announces that humans are about. (Or maybe it ruins little creatures' appetites.)

Another trick is to scatter a combination of ammonia crystals, mothballs, camphor, and kerosene in a minefield about five meters deep all around your garden. If little furry creatures do manage to hold their noses and penetrate this barrier, you can try planting garlic heavily all through your plot.

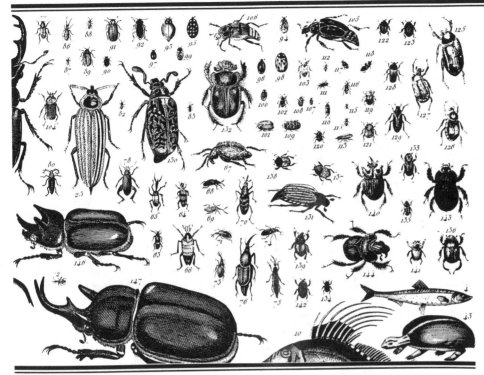

All these measures presume that Bambi or Thumper haven't tasted marijuana before. If you are in an area of the forest inhabited by experienced animal heads, forget it. Plant somewhere else.

Insects can be a problem, indoors or out, particularly if your plants are unhealthy to begin with from poor drainage, overwatering, or overfeeding — the three principal sins of cultivators.

Try natural predator controls. For instance, praying mantises and ladybugs are both wonderfully eager eaters of anything that flutters, buzzes, or hums, and they don't eat leaves or flowers. After they have cleared out an area, however, they flee through the flaw in the flue, leaving you unprotected for the next round. Frogs and lizards are also bug lovers with the additional advantage that, if introduced to your garden while still young, they rarely leave if adequate living conditions exist.

Healthy Cannabis is rarely bothered by insects. Probably Cannabis, like most plants from harsh environments, has learned to protect itself from hungry bugs chemically, by making itself inedible.

Just for insurance, however, you can brew a fine insect repellent with garlic, yarrow, chamomile, horseradish, very hot ground pepper, oregano, and sage. It's sort of like spraying liquid pizza on your plants but it doesn't hurt them and it drives away most bugs. Take eight ounces of garlic and ½ ounce of each of the other herbs plus ¼ of a small bar of ivory soap. Steep them for 30 minutes in a gallon of boiling water. The cooled brew, strained, is mixed in a 1:2 ratio with water. Re-apply the spray after each rain. Some people don't like the taste of plants receiving the pizza treatment and I must admit I've tasted better. So try your alchemical hand on one or two plants before treating your entire crop.

There are many interplantings that have been recommended at one time or another to reduce garden infestations. A preliminary step is to keep all weeds and other unwanted plants out of your garden, since any plant can supply food or cover for insects. Planting of marigolds is reputed to ward off many beetles, but may attract spider mites. Zinnias and geraniums are frequently used to disgust little buggers. Basil is planted with tomatoes to ward off several voracious worm species. Radishes and nasturniums are used to repel beetles. Catnip repels various fleas. Thyme is used to control leaf-eating worms. Chives are planted to eliminate nematodes and rust flies. Horseradish is supposed to be effective in controlling aphids and an array of small flying bugs.

There are mechanical approaches to predator control that are available to any Cannabis gardener. A very effective device is to remove the bottom of a small paper cup and slip it over a young plant, wide end up, burying the bottom in the soil about ¼ inch. This acts as a barrier to climbing insects. Use cheesecloth to protect beds and frames from egg-laying insects. Newspapers, rolled loosely, moistened and placed on the ground around the garden, will soon become home to vast numbers of bugs. The papers can then be picked up and burned. Aluminum foil placed on the ground around the base of young plants will often discourage small crawlers. And finally, there is the traditional can filled with beer and buried with its lips flush with the soil level. This traps slugs and other carbohydrate-loving insects.

Soil-less marijuana cultivation has many advantages and the techniques are quite simple. The problems which arise with this method are subtle. Soil-less cultivation requires an interest and attention on the part of the cultivator which is not needed when one plants outdoors, walks off, and comes back once a week to check.

Laboratories have been raising Cannabis in soil-less mediums for years. A major center of such research is France, where the hemp industry has long supported efforts to find out what makes a Cannabis plant bigger, healthier, and stronger. Of course, the aim of French research is not to produce smokable plants, but to produce plants for the fiber industry. Still, in the course of their investigations, French scientists have come up with some very nice ideas, adaptable to the more refined aspects of hemp culture.

Ordinary laboratory procedure in French Cannabis experiments is to germinate the seeds in vermiculite flats and, at a height of one inch, transplant the seedlings to the soil-less medium. This is usually a mixture of sphagnum moss and washed sand, in equal parts. The containers are most often 12″ x 15″ clay or plastic pots.

In formulating, the French are particular to use only absolutely sterile water. This is fine for experiments but, in the field or in your room, the use of such pure water is optional. Besides, the use of well water and even some city tap water can provide important trace elements. Polluted or over-treated water is, of course, never very good for your plants.

Using the following low-nitrogen formula, a team of French researchers recently reported their most impressive growth in female plants, measured in terms of height and foliage mass:

$MgSO_4$ — 2 milligrams per litre
$CaNO_3$ — 3 milligrams per litre
KPO_4 — 1 milligram per litre

Plus a solution of trace elements — iron, boron, zinc, manganese, and copper were used — just a dash, 10 cc per 50 litre batch of formula.

Using very high Phillips (The GE of Europe) lamps, 400 watt mercury fluorescents, one bulb per row supplemented by one 150 watt incandescent bulb per fixture, centered and above the plants, the plants were given 16 hours of light daily by timer and were demand-watered by a wick system.

The French experimenters found that plants which were kept on the low-nitrogen diet had a much higher ratio of females, stood taller, weighed more, had fewer sexual abnormalities, and responded more readily to lights than plants raised on several formulas richer in nitrogen.

Cannabis is not a luxury lover. Over and over we get that message. Plants, begun under harsh conditions, thrive under what would be deprivation for another plant. They seem to do their best when there has been a struggle. Where the light is rich, the soil moist but not wet, and the diet lean but not sparse, this noble plant does well.

Now let's touch on a few ideas for the hydroponic growing of Cannabis which most growers can use in common situations.

In the first place, hydroponic cultivation of marijuana is both simple and inexpensive. There is no need for fancy equipment or kits and, even for more elaborate setups, everything except the pumps and timers can be built yourself.

The Basic Bucket is probably the easiest hydroponic growing device for marijuana cultivation. Take an old, sturdy table and drill a one inch hole in the center. Insert a three inch long piece of one inch plastic tubing through the hole. Shim it with paper if it doesn't fit tightly into the hole. Allow about ½ inch of the tube to protrude above the table surface.

Now take the plastic tub or pail and, in the center of the bottom, cut a one inch hole. Set the bucket over the tube, reach under the table and pull the tube down flush with the bottom of the bucket. Put some broken tile or pottery shards in the bottom two inches of the bucket. Try to assure that the drain hole is not plugged. Then fill the container with aggregate — preferably hadite, an aggregate used in lightweight concrete.

Depending on the dryness of your growing medium, you may have to pour nutrient solution through the aggregate twice a day, or perhaps just every other day. The trick is to keep the medium moist but not wet. Do not be fooled by the surface. Check the moisture below.

Under the table you have the collection bucket and a piepan. The piepan is to catch nutrient which will run through before you can get your bucket poured out and back under the drain.

The nutrient solution should be made fresh every week. The bucket should be flushed through every week with several gallons of fresh room temperature water. This is a very effective planter, provided adequate nutrient is used and the lighting is good. Its only drawback is the need for frequent attention. But if you have the time, this approach will work well.

This simple, inexpensive alternative to straight hydroponic gardening is easily adapted for the cultivation of superior marijuana. The growing container is made of wood and is a bottomless box. To build the box, use 1 x 12 inch boards, or the equivalent. Make a box, square or of any length, from 18 x 18 inches up to six feet by any feasible length.

have been needing and not getting from your nutrient solution. A very successful utilization of the Mittleider Box is to layer the soil beneath the box with nutrients in the order that they will be needed by the plant. The top six inches of the soil directly under the box should be rich in phosphorus for mid-life growth, using bone meal or ash well worked into the soil months before. Under that, you

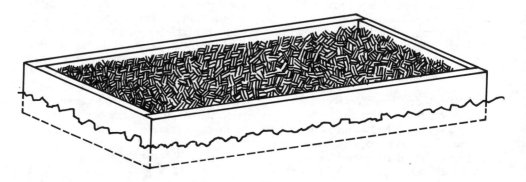

Set the box in the ground so that four inches are below ground level. Then fill the box with a mixture of sand and vermiculite, and about 10 to 15% peat moss. Fill to within one inch of the top. This means you will have seven inches of growing medium. Either germinate directly in the box if you are far enough south to grow outdoors by late April, or germinate the seeds in peat pots, setting them out when the weather turns, after hardening in a cold frame if necessary. Use a good hydroponic solution, and adopt a feeding schedule of about once a week, watering with pure water as often as needed.

Since the plant receives practically no nutrients from the growing medium, nutrients will have to be provided as in normal hydroponics. The difference is that after the plant is established and puts its roots down seven inches, it hits soil! At this point, the plant begins eagerly sucking up everything it may

should have a two to four inch thick stratum of soil rich in potassium. Potassium is what marijuana needs in the prime of life and what stimulates it to high resin production. This potassium rich layer can be achieved by working in burned or fresh banana skins at least three months prior to the time you will be digging the soil for use in the layer.

So, for the first two months of her life, Cannabis will be drinking in the high energy of nitrogen, phosphorus, and potassium from a basic hydroponic formula. Then, sometime in the second or third month, the roots will strike the rich layer of phosphorus. The plant's branches will start spreading and the foliage will increase. Then, after a time, the roots will reach down into the banana potassium and the flowering spikes will vibrate with energy. Your plant will shine with a rich, dark green.

Plants get off to a roaring start with this
method, as they do with most soil-less
cultures. It is in midlife and maturity
that most hydroponically grown plants
get in trouble. The problem is that the
plant feeds from the soil in different ways
at different times. People don't want the
same diet when they are old that they
had when they were young. Neither does
Cannabis. It is difficult for cultivators to
keep up with a plant's total needs in
hydroponic situations, which is why the
soil remains Mother Earth and Man
remains — well, man.

For the initial solution in the Mittleider
Box, any good hydroponic fertilizer will
do. Watering and feeding will be less
frequent than usual in the hydroponic
setup, because the soil beneath the box
will hold moisture. It is important that
there be good drainage beneath the box.
Don't set your box over hardpan or the
plants will die in a few weeks.

If you're going to try to stay away from
pumps, you'll be considering the gravity
feed approach. In this system, the
nutrient solution is poured into a tank
above the growing bed. The nutrient is
then released to the tank by a
controlled-flow valve. It runs through the
medium or, in more elaborate setups, is
piped through the medium and
ultimately emerges from a drain at the
bottom of the growing bed into the
collection bucket.

The amount and frequency of use of a
nutrient solution will depend on many
factors including the individual setup.
Nutrient solution shouldn't be used more
than four to five times because it picks
up waste each time it is flushed through
the growing beds. Broken tile or one to
two inch diameter, clean, inert, jagged
stones should be spread four inches deep
on the bottom of the tank. The tank
should be 16 inches deep allowing at least
12 inches of growing medium such as
gravel or hadite.

96

(Below and Right)
Seedling germination
sequence

The
Good
Seed

Working With Young Marijuana Plants

When you consider the amount of time and energy that goes into preparing for cultivation, whether you plan on a large-scale operation or just a couple of plants grown in some little nook, it doesn't make a lot of sense to take a cavalier approach to seed selection. This is particularly true when it is so simple to assure yourself that the seed you're using is of good quality. Seed genetics are *the* single most critical factor in the potency of your harvest.

External appearance will give you a good set of clues to the seed's state of health. Viable seed will be well fleshed out and not be all crinkled up. It will be bright gray, gray-green, or gray-brown and will appear glossy if rubbed between the palms of your hands.

To test further for seed quality, several methods are suggested. It's a good idea to carry testing beyond a glance at the seed's appearance, because a number of internal conditions affect their germinating ability and these are not always detectable by appearance and the water test.

Crack open several seeds selected at random from the batch which will be used. If they have a musty, oily taste, they are pretty old and may well have gone bad. Another test is simply to germinate a group of ten seeds and count

up those which fail to sprout. This will give you a rough estimate, by percentage, of what you can expect overall. Anything above 50% is pretty good for a bunch of seeds acquired at random on the streets of North America these days. Considering the traumas which most marijuana goes through before it reaches the domestic market, it's a wonder that any seeds remain viable.

If you have cracked open a few seeds and note that the insides are black, then fermentation has set in and there is no chance that they will germinate. Conversely, if they are pale and dusty on the inside, they are overage and will produce feeble plants at best.

Another test is to drop a few seeds onto a red-hot iron. If they burst with a noticeable crack, they were good seeds. In Thrace, seeds were thrown upon red-hot stones, and "their perfumed vapor, so obtained, used for a fume bath which elicited cries of exultation from those enjoying it." A great idea for your backyard sauna, if you are a profligate sort of soul.

Incidentally, Cannabis seeds are considered excellent bird food because they are fattening and stimulate egg production, so I'd be very careful with those brownie recipes if I were you, population freaks.

Seeds can provide an important clue for those who are breaking the law by purchasing lids. Since the optimum time for harvesting marijuana for drug potency is at, or shortly after, female flowering, the greater proportion of seeds in such a plant will be immature. Conversely, if all the seeds in the lid appear to be ripe; that is, bright gray or brown the chances are good that not only was the plant overage when she was harvested, but she had also probably been pollinated, which will have lowered her effectiveness as a drug.

Seeds can amount to almost half the weight of a lid purchased on the street. Most tropical strains of marijuana will have over 1,000 seeds per lid. When buying marijuana there are two basic prohibitions: (1) Don't buy cleaned marijuana where you cannot see the intact flower buds and tops. (2) When buying buds and tops, look for a minimum of seeds, which are unusable weight, and try for Sinsemilla or lightly seeded varieties. Look out for immature marijuana, as mentioned. Just hold out for a lid of good tops with a minimum of seeds.

Once you are fairly sure of the vitality of your seeds, you should soak them overnight in a starting bath of distilled water. Actually, any pure water will do, but if you are city-bound, you would do well to invest in a bottle of store-bought water to avoid the chemicals and crap which might damage the swelling embryo beyond saving.

There are a couple of general points covering the use of additives with particular significance for Cannabis, if you decide you want to experiment a little.

Most growth regulators and stimulants in the pre-germination and germination stages require that temperature and moisture levels be held constant, usually between 65° and 75° F., and 30-50% relative humidity.

Commercial preparations are manufactured to cover a wide range of plant response levels, and therefore aren't necessarily good for one specific plant. It seems more sensible to design your own growth stimulator, even if it is simply adding a little soluble nitrogen, than to waste money on commercial products.

Most plants seem to benefit from application of growth stimulants at later stages in their growth cycle. Cannabis *sativa* is no exception. Limiting stimulation to a carefully controlled environment and perhaps some nutrients seems to be the best policy at the pre-germination stage.

If you think that your seeds have had a rough time in transit, you should be particularly careful in using stimulants at the early stages of life. Let the plants try to make it on their own, rather than forcing them to exceed capacity in a weakened state.

Particularly after applying stimulants through the starting solution (but this precaution applies generally), one should exercise care in handling the seeds because they are going to be swollen and tender. Sterilized tweezers are the best instruments for handling the seeds in transfer from the starting solution to the germination beds. The seeds should be picked up with the lightest possible touch, and should be picked up by the sides of the seed rather than the ends. To put pressure on the ends might damage the embryo root permanently.

level at this critical growth stage. Second, the plant has to exert a great deal of force, after the tap root is extended, in lifting its head, enclosed by the two halves of the seed pod, above the soil and in forcing the pod off its back so that it can spread out its two embryo leaves to begin the photosynthetic process. Carelessness on your part can exhaust any but the most hearty seedling at this stage, resulting in a feeble plant in later life.

The seed should be placed about ¼ inch to ½ inch under the soil surface. As it develops, it should not have to expend large amounts of energy pushing through the soil because it will need the energy later on to stand erect and throw off the seed coat.

The germinating Cannabis seeds go through several distinct stages, and it may prove worthwhile to pull one or two sprouts each day to check on development according to the following time table. If the seeds do not develop approximately in the sequence and at the time indicated, something is wrong. You

Seed improperly positioned—the pointed end is down. Tap root makes natural bend out of the seed, but then has to reverse itself. Vital seed energy is lost.

The seed should be placed in the earth with the pointed end up because as the primary tap root emerges from the pointed end, its natural tendency is to make a turn and grow downward. If it has to twist and turn in order to seek its proper direction, two negative effects will result.

First, a great deal of energy stored in the seed which should be going for root extension will be expended in root positioning, resulting in a lowered energy

may save yourself weeks of work, a substantial electric bill, and some disappointment by checking on these growth stages.

Upon germination, the primary root emerges from the stylar end of the seed (the pointed end). The seed is split in half, but the halves remain together protecting the emergent leaves. This primary tap root undergoes rapid growth.

After approximately 48 hours from germination, the tap root should be around 1½ inches long. Root growth normally slows at this point.

After from 72 to 96 hours, a fine lateral root system should begin developing just below the soil surface. At this point, the seedling will begin to force itself above the soil surface and to exert pressure to throw off the seed coat.

The seedling stem begins to stand erect during the fifth day, and the seed coat falls away or remains at the soil surface. The embryo leaves are slightly oval in shape and are not serrated. They should be yellow-green at this point, and have a moist, waxy appearance.

The stem of the seedling below the embryo leaves lengthens steadily from the fifth to about the tenth day. The first leaf node where the embryo leaves are attached should be 1-1½ inches above the soil surface. During this period the first pair of foliage leaves will appear. This first pair will be simple leaves, slightly oval, and will show serrations. They only last a short time, and the second and third pairs should appear by the twelfth day.

The embryo leaves, which have functioned as photosynthetic and food storage organs for the first few weeks, yellow and fall away during the early part of the third week.

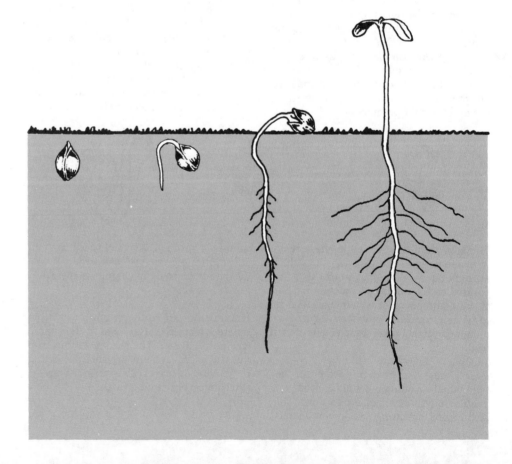

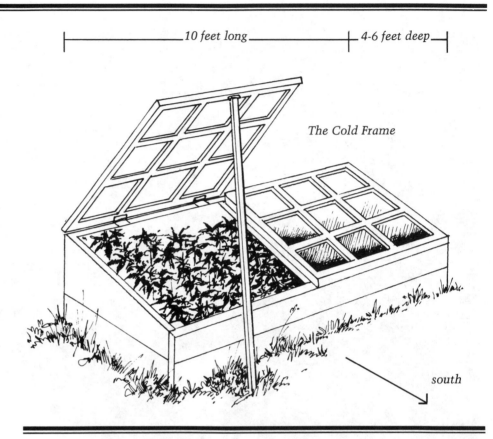

10 feet long   _4-6 feet deep_

The Cold Frame

south

To assure maximum survival of Cannabis seedlings during and after germination, care should be exercised in choosing the medium and the environment. For outdoors starting, the cold frame and hot frame offer superior environments.

There are advantages to both the cold frame and the warm frame. Warm soil provides for optimum nutrient uptake by young plants. The cold frame, however, hardens the young plants, and makes their transfer into an outdoor growing situation much easier for their delicate systems. A lot depends on what you are going to do with the plants later in their growth cycle.

To make a basic frame, which can be either heated or cold, choose a location with a southern exposure. Most people locate their frames alongside the house, facing south. Be sure it is not in a place where water from the eaves will drip onto it during rains.

The frame is a wooden box-like structure painted black, and should be no deeper than six feet, so that you can reach in and work the back plants easily, and no longer than ten feet, so that you have good temperature control. The soil in the frame is usually slanted, back to front, and the frame itself is 24 inches high at the back, 18 inches high at the front. For a lid for the frame, many people use old windows, hinged to the back of the frame.

To make a heated frame, you will need to buy heat tapes (wires, actually) which can usually be located through nurseries or through your local electric utility. Another option, if you're good at plumbing, is to use hot water pipes running under the bed of the frame. If you are using heating wires, do not let them touch or cross, but lay them out in successive loops on the bottom of the bed. In an outdoor bed, use the following procedure:

After you have constructed your wooden frame, excavate the soil inside the frame down about a foot, and lay in the heating wires (or hot water pipes). On top of the heating element, lay about six inches of composted material, or well-rotted manure. On top of this layer, place your soil, building it up to within six to eight inches of the top of the frame, front and back. The soil should, as we've pointed out, be a sandy loam with good humus content. Now you are ready to plant, germinate and start your little seedlings in a wonderful, warm environment. Cannabis prefers a root temperature of at least 60° F., and even a little warmer is OK. A soil thermometer is a worthwhile investment if you are using heat over which you have some control. Use cheese cloth to cover both cold and hot beds. Also frames to prevent egg-laying insects.

You make a cold frame the same way you do a heated frame, excavating inside the frame and layering as described above, but of course you omit sources of heat and rely on the sun, and the biological processes in the bottom layer to provide what heat may be needed, so you will excavate deeper, and use fresher manure in a thicker layer.

Air temperature in the frames is controlled by propping up the lid and allowing air to circulate. At night, the lid of the frame is always closed to conserve heat and to keep out the night moisture. You should not allow the temperature in the frame to exceed 85° F., day or night.

Moisture content in germinating soil is a critical factor. The surface of the germinating soil should be almost dry, and the subsurface soil not so moist that it adheres to the finger. Testing for good moisture is much like testing gingerbread to see if it is done — as long as any soil sticks to a pencil thrust to the bottom, it is too moist. Care should be taken, however, to see that the germination beds are kept within a range of moisture, neither too wet nor too dry. If too wet, the seeds are likely to rot and ferment; and if too dry, they are apt to sprout weakly, if at all.

Several authors state that germination can be accomplished in many mediums — even wet paper towels — but there is substantial evidence that subjecting seedlings to transplant shock twice in their early growth stages is as harmful as would the case be if germination takes place in a non-nutritive and impermanent medium.

Almost any container the imagination can devise will do for a germinating box as long as it meets certain size and depth requirements. Coffee cans, plastic basins, window boxes, jars, bathtubs, etc., all have been used for indoor germination.

A few tricks to remember which might make indoor germination a good deal more simple and reliable:

If the seedlings are to be transplanted at any point, it will be helpful to germinate them in containers. This makes transfer to the planting soil easy and non-traumatic. Germinating the seeds in ice cube trays or similar devices allows for easy transfer.

While almost any container will do for your sprouting medium, a shallow wooden or plastic tray is ideal. Mix your sphagnum moss and washed sand in a ratio of 2:1. Don't provide too rich an environment for the young plants because this increases the possibility of trauma at transplanting time. Line the bottom of the tray with clean gravel about one inch deep. On top of this add the sphagnum and sand mixture.

There are several kinds of germination cubes on the market in most places. With these cubes, you will have no container problems.

Jiffy-7's are the most common. They come square and round and are little pieces of compressed peat wrapped in a very thin plastic net. When the cube is watered, it expands to approximately two inches high and 1½ inches in diameter. Place one or two seeds just below the surface of the peat. Water and set in a warm well-lighted environment. When you are ready to plant or place the seeds in a hydroponic unit, remove the netting.

Jiffy-9's are in every way similar to the Jiffy-7's except that they don't have the plastic net. This means that they are a little more prone to crumbling than the 7's but are easily handled and do a fine job.

Sudbury makes a cube, treated with liquid seaweed extract having special growth-promoting elements, that does a great job for seedlings. The cubes are Sea-gro. They are competitive with the Jiffy cubes in price, but are otherwise better.

Fertlcubes are also little blocks of peat but with perlite, vermiculite, and nutrients mixed in to form an ideal environment for Cannabis seeds. They also expand with watering and are crumbly, but are probably the best of these three methods for sprouting Cannabis. Any of these cubes may be placed directly in either the soil or a hydroponic unit. There is no need to remove the seedling from the cube to transplant.

Paper cups are good germinating containers, too, because you can cut them away and leave a well-shaped ball of soil. But be sure to use one big enough to not cramp the roots of the germinating seedling — at least a 12 ounce cup.

A substantial exposure to risk comes during transplanting for the Cannabis seedlings, but there are a series of steps which can be taken to minimize the danger and promote healthy adaptation.

A primary consideration is the receiving soil. It should be as similar to that used in germination and sprouting as possible. It must be fertile, neutral or slightly alkaline, loose and friable, moisture-retentive at the sub-surface levels, well-drained, spaded to a depth of at least 12 inches, and reasonably clean of weeds and mold. A few earthworms introduced into the transplant soil would be very beneficial if they are available.

It is at this point that a number of critical differentiations occur in the plant's environment which determine in large part whether its ultimate usefulness will be for its fiber or for its resin.

One of the most important determinants is the crowding which young plants experience. A general rule may be stated; for fiber, the closer together the better, and for resin the further apart the better. Plants which are crowded closely will produce, other things being equal, rather good fiber and rather sparse leaves. Cultivators after the leaves, rather than the fiber, have to work largely by inference on spacing, but several sources indicate that plants should be spaced at least two feet away from any other if leaves are desired, with a three foot spacing even better, for those who have the room.

Another factor bearing upon the ultimate use to which the plants are to be put is the lighting which they receive as seedlings. The sprouts should be exposed to at the very least eight hours of sunlight or its equivalent before and after transplanting. While the specific lighting requirements of Cannabis are discussed in a later chapter, it is most important at this early stage that lighting be consistent. Reducing the amount of lighting the sprouts receive immediately after transplanting seems to speed development of the mature plant by about one week. This reduced period of lighting, the lower limit of which is seven hours per day, should be discontinued after the fourth to sixth day of seedling growth and the plants put on the light regimen which you have decided to follow through their lifetime.

When the time comes for transplantation, you should have all your equipment at hand, and have the germination beds close to the transplant beds so that there will be minimum exposure.

It is really a good idea to perform the transplant under green light of low intensity. If no green light is available, a green filter will do. The green light is the cultivator's equivalent of the photographer's darkroom red. It allows him to see well without danger to the plants, because green light is the least active part of the spectrum for photosynthetic processes in plants, and tends to shut down the major metabolic processes which, if active during transplant, will put a great strain on the seedling.

In a more general sense, any time you perform any operations which entail exposure of the delicate tissues of your plants to light, use green light and you cut your radiation damage risks to almost zero. This is particularly important if you leave the seeds in the starting bath too long and the embryo root has begun to emerge. Seeds in this condition should be gently, but swiftly, placed in earth in the proper heads-up position described earlier.

One of the most traumatic experiences which seedlings can undergo is to be transplanted. This is true of Cannabis even though it is a hearty plant in later life. In cases where the cultivator takes the outdoor hit-or-miss route there will be no worry about transplantation. Indoor cultivators, careful outdoor cultivators, and experimenters will all want to germinate their plants under a controlled set of conditions and upon successful arrival of the plants at the seedling stage, transplantation will be necessary.

Several steps can be taken to assure maximum survival:

The soil which is to receive the seedlings should be completely ready; that is, there should be no need to disturb it for a week after the seedlings are planted. It should be fertile, friable and thoroughly spaded. Earthworms should have been introduced at least two days prior to transplant, or their introduction should be delayed several days after transplant if they are to be used.

Transplanting should take place in the evening if the climate's kind; if not, then in the morning. The plant's respiration

naturally heads downwards as it prepares to go into nighttime hibernation. Water loss is kept to a minimum in the newly transplanted seedling, so dehydration shock is not piled upon transplant shock. But coping with transplant shock during respiration is nothing compared with transplant shock and chill.

Transfer indoors should take place under a pale green light, and the place should not be subject to drafts or temperature variation.

All instruments should have been sterilized, and sterile cotton gloves should be worn, if possible. If not, washing your hands with soap which removes surface oils on the skin should help prevent damage to the seedlings.

Where at all possible, the receptor soil should closely approximate the donor soil.

Overuse of fertilizers at this stage is not recommended, but several commercial preparations for stimulating transplant setting are readily available and work well when directions are followed.

If possible, the seedling should be lifted with a ball of the original soil surrounding the roots, and this placed in a hole in the prepared growing bed. When lifting the seedling, it is best if the ball of soil can be lifted without the necessity for touching the plant in any way. If the plant must be handled, it is best to grasp it lightly right near the soil level, supporting the plant's weight from above and that of the soil from below. Exposed roots and the upper stem and embryo leaves of the seedlings should not be handled.

Seedlings should be placed in an upright position in the receptor beds with their leaves oriented to the principal light source. Phototropic (light-seeking) movement in newly transplanted

seedlings can be detrimental to good secure rooting. The hole should be deep enough to allow the young root to extend to full length, as it probably will be somewhat cramped from the germinating beds. The root should not be mashed down into a shallow hole, or the plant will not be able to summon energy enough to establish itself. The soil should be gently built up around the seedling to a level equivalent to that of the germinating bed. Piling dirt too high up the stem can be harmful, leading to stem rot within hours.

The soil in the transplant beds should be dry enough so that when you add water after the transplant is finished, it will be absorbed rather than pooling around the roots. Adding water helps the transplanted seedling by, in effect, bonding the ball of original soil to the new soil, and makes root penetration of the new soil much easier. A teaspoon of water at room temperature will be enough for a transplanted seedling on the first day, provided the soil is fertile and contains enough moist humus to begin with.

Care should be taken during transfer that the seedling is not jolted or bent, and that the stem is not strained by being forced to support any weight. During the transfer roots should be exposed only to green light.

Don't cramp
the roots.

Less than
one-half cup
of water

109

If any form of treatment is undertaken
before transplanting is completed — such
as Colchicine treatment described
elsewhere — special care should be taken
to protect the roots either with moist
cotton or filter paper, or with a plastic
film wrapped gently around the ball of
soil to preserve moisture and
compactness.

All plants undergo transplant shock;
some seem to die and eventually recover
and some die; but the majority of plants
transplanted correctly will survive and

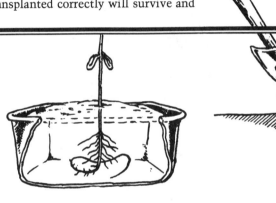

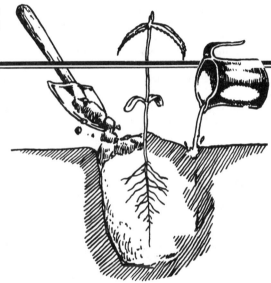

thrive with no apparent bad effects. If
some of the transplanted seedlings
yellow, droop, and even appear to die,
leaving them alone is the best policy,
after checking to see that the bending
over has not exposed the delicate white
flesh of the root.

With proper precautions and adequate
soil, moisture and lighting conditions,
the cultivator indoors should expect at
least a 75% survival rate for transplants
while outdoor transplants will have a
lower survival rate in a less controlled
environment.

Immediately after the transplant is in
place, it should be watered with a
solution of transplant shock stimulant.
These special conditioners are available
in nurseries under names like

110

Planting
on the
Planetary Diagonal

Planting
in
Peat Pots

Transplantone. They are the equivalent of megadoses of vitamins for humans under severe stress.

If you're transplanting in rows, be sure that they run Southeast-Northwest or Southwest-Northeast, rather than North-South or East-West. Planting on the planetary diagonal staggers the plants in relation to the sun, whereas planting them oriented toward either pair of cardinal points means that the southern most plants are blocking some of the sun which otherwise would reach the northermost plants. This consideration is minor for cultivators in the south, where the sun is more nearly overhead, but in the north where the sun's rays fall slantingly upon the earth, it can mean a significant reduction in vigor, and therefore in yield at harvest, for much of the crop.

Transplanting is a time-honored practice of cultivators in the cooler zones of the earth. It is often desirable to start your plants before the weather permits outdoor growing. The marijuana plant is especially sensitive to frosts. The plants with tropical ancestry, and therefore greatest genetic potency, will require a long growing season to reach peak maturity.

For cultivators who prefer to work with the soil, who love the feel of the earth, seed beds are the best approach to germination and transplanting. It is satisfying to dig up the plant with its ball of soil and midwife it as it adjusts to its new outdoor home. But other cultivators are not so involved with the Earth Mother aspects of gardening. They simply want to grow marijuana outdoors as efficiently and practically as possible. For these cultivators, peat pots may be the answer for an early start.

Peat pots are small pots formed from pure peat moss. They are great for

germination. When the time comes to transplant, just stick them in the outdoor soil and the plant grows right through as the pot dissolves. There are plenty of good brands.

Fill the peat pots with the outdoor soil in which the plants eventually will be transplanted. Before putting the seeds in the pot, moisten the soil thoroughly in the morning and allow it to drain until evening. Then, take seeds which have been pre-soaked and poke two or three of them into a ¼ inch hole in the soil. Smooth the soil over the hole to cover, but don't pack down. Do not water. Put each pot inside a plastic baggie, but don't close the baggie. The plant needs circulation. Put it in a warm spot, not exceeding 90° F. The baggie acts like a little greenhouse, so adequate ventilation is needed.

After several days, some or all of the seedlings will have sprouted. Remove the baggie. After a week, the healthiest seedling in each pot will be obvious. The others must be removed. This is done by slicing them off at soil level with a sharp blade. A single edge razor is best. Don't pull these seedlings because their roots may be intertwined with the roots of the ones you want to keep.

112

Hardening
Young
Plants

Protecting
Seedling
from Heat

Pruning
for Mass
Potency

Use a very light hand watering the young seedlings in their peat pots. The outside walls of the pot should always feel dry. When the time comes for transplanting, dig a small hole in the outdoor soil, make several deep scratches on each outside face of the pot, and bury the plant with the top of the peat pot just a fraction of an inch below the soil surface. The newly transplanted seedling is then given a good soaking. This single watering should be sufficient for the first week unless drying conditions are severe and soil moisture is quite low. This set of conditions is unlikely in the climates calling for transplanting.

Cultivators living in the northern U.S., Canada, and Northern Europe, will probably want to harden their plants against the cold nights of the early growing season. This is done by gradually exposing the seedlings in their trays of pots to the outdoor conditions, if you are not using a cold frame. Begin with 30 minutes a day exposure, starting at around 10 A.M. and increase exposure by 30 minutes a day up to the time of transplanting. The farther north you are, the cooler the nights in the early season, and the more valuable the practice of hardening. You might also want to de-bug the outdoor spot used to harden the seedlings. Cold bugs are hungry bugs when the sun finally comes up.

In warmer regions of the world, inventive marijuana farmers have reported success with protecting newly transplanted Cannabis from the excessive heat of the day or chill of night. They turn paper bags upside down over the plants. (Peg the bags down with popsicle sticks or something similar.) Holes are always cut in the sides of the bags to allow ventilation. White bags are preferred over brown because white reflects the wilting sun more effectively. A plant should never be bagged just because the day is somewhat hot and dry. Cannabis has an inborn love of such

conditions. It is when the temperature in April goes unexpectedly to 98° F. two days after transplanting and a dry wind rushes in from the desert. Then you need to be alert and put some protection over your plants.

The most common form of pruning is to force side growth, and entails removing the top of a young plant by cutting off the head between the fifth and sixth sets of branches. By the time a plant has reached 18 inches, it will have developed at least six nodes if its growth is normal; and if it's not an exotic strain such as Afghani or Moroccan, which behave very differently. A node, please recall, is a point at which branches diverge from the main stem. Removal of the top of this young plant will cause multiple shoots to develop, one on each side of each node, into vigorous, growing, principal stems. Once these stems are well established, and have themselves developed a minimum of four nodes, each of the tops is removed. On each of the stems a number of new shoots will emerge at each of the remaining nodes which will in turn grow vigorously into the equivalent of a principal stem (the strongest from the upper nodes, the weakest from the lower), unless strong side lighting is provided — a practice highly recommended in *all* pruning operations. If, then, once these stems are all well established, some training over of the tops is performed, the cultivator will have a squat, compact, very dense marijuana bush that will, if all else is right in the environment, develop an almost solid mass of flowering tops at maturity, yet will take up a little room and will be easily shielded from prying eyes.

Another form of pruning involves the pinching-off of the growing tip of a young, vigorous plant of at least four weeks age — better to wait till the sixth week to begin.

At the very top of the young plant, observe a small, bright green bud form, and begin to swell. This bud is the genesis of the next set of leaves which the plant is going to make in its climb toward the sun. Just as a rock climber sets pitons in the sheer face of a cliff, securing the progress made so far before climbing further, so the plant at each increment of growth sends out new sets of leaves to anchor itself in the growing space by securing sun-energy to support the next surge upwards.

If this surge is prevented by the removal of the growing tip, the plant's energy will seek expression at established levels, and strong new shoots will bud forth at the nodes. If, as these new shoots grow strong and develop a minimum of four nodes themselves, you remove the bud at the growing tip of each, they will in turn bud forth at the nodes, and you will then have the makings of an extremely bushy plant.

There are limits to the clipping you can put your plants through. Not only will excessive clipping eventually sap the plant's vigor, but it will also create a top heavy structure, and radically increase competition for available light, CO_2 and nutrients among the multiple heads. For the more delicate, slender varieties of marijuana, such as Mexican, a plant with five to eight good shoots is about at the limits of effective growth. For the sturdier varieties, eight to 12 heads represents a good compromise between enthusiasm and realities.

Pruning operations should cease after the plant has passed the 3½ month mark, to permit full recovery before it leaves the rapid growth period and enters maturity. The exception to this general rule is that at harvest time, many growers practice a form of radical pruning which will, given healthy plants and proper care, result in a second harvest of flowers and small leaves. This operation works both indoors and outdoors, but is generally more effective indoors under lights.

Cut your plants back to three feet, and treat the harvested tops in your preferred way. Also remove about 75% of the leaf clusters which remain on the lower three feet of the plant. Don't clip off any branches, just remove the leaf clusters by pinching them off. Leave only healthy leaf clusters — remove any that are deformed, withered, or otherwise imperfect.

114

Heavy
Head
Production

Inhibiting
Vertical
Growth

Maintaining the 12 to 13 hour dark cycle used to bring on flowering, bring your lights down as close to the tops of the plants as possible, and use strong side lighting as well. Water the plants well after harvesting, and feed them with a complete fertilizer. If the soil is dry and resists soaking, add six drops of Ivory liquid detergent to a gallon of water, and water with this instead of regular water. The detergent acts as a wetting agent, and the water will penetrate even the driest soil quite easily.

Within two weeks, the new crop of flower buds will be in evidence all over the plants, and in six to eight weeks a complete flowering will occur. This second harvest will weigh between ⅓-⅔ of the weight of the original harvest, and will be Sinsemilla as well, provided there are no late-blooming males around. It is often possible, with vigorous plants under lights, to repeat this radical pruning operation.

Maturing females can be encouraged to develop large numbers of flowering heads by several methods. One of the easiest, and least traumatic to the plant, is performed on plants which have begun to develop substantial flower clusters at the top of the principle stem. Such plants will normally be at least four feet tall. Locate an internode space about ⅔ of the way up the stem, and attach a length of soft cotton twine, or whatever string you have available. Drive a stake into the ground about three to four feet out from the base of the plant, angling it away from the plant. Now take the string and pull the plant over as far as it will go without apparent strain — about 1½ feet away from the vertical at first — and tie it down to the stake. This pulls the plant over in a gentle curve, not too extreme. Give the plant two to three days to adjust to this new position, and then shorten the string by another six to 12 inches, pulling the plant over more nearly horizontal.

Repeat the operation every two to three days until the top ⅓ of the plant is in fact horizontal.

Even before you get the plant trained horizontally, the side branches in the top half of the plant will begin to raise themselves toward the vertical, and within a week or so they will begin to develop horizontal branches of their own, and will show beginning development of extensive flower clusters. Depending on the inherent growth energy of the plant, this treatment can result in the development of a dozen or more solid masses of flowering heads where, on the same plant left untreated, you might have harvested only a few small clusters.

Yield of this horizontal female can, of course, be increased by careful clipping of the heavy clusters, so long as the plant has not passed from the stage of vigorous growth into the relative passivity of maturity.

It's unlikely that you will need to support plants which you have trained to the horizontal, but if you have a particularly hearty plant which develops many heavy clusters, you might need to support the main stem with a stake. A simple stake cut from a tree branch, with a Y-crotch at the top for the Cannabis plant to lay her heavy head in, is the simplest sort of support.

If your plants can't grow up, they will grow out. What this means for you is that both leaf mass and the highly potent flowering tops of your plants can be increased significantly — as much as 100% — by limiting the upward potential of your plants.

There are several ways to do this effectively. Pruning has been discussed as has the effect of keeping your lights right on top of the plants, and side-lighting them.

Another simple way to inhibit vertical growth is to take the flexible top six inches of the plant and bend it over so that it is pointing almost downwards. Plants should be at least two months old to benefit from this procedure. Some plants will be more flexible than others, but all will allow you to bend this top at least to the horizontal without breaking it. When you've determined how far you can bend the top over, then secure it in that position using a paper-covered twist-tie of the sort that come with plastic garbage bags. Wrap one end of the twist tie around the upright stem of the plant, and make a hook in the other end to secure the bent-over top in position.

If you have bent the tip radically downward, keep it bent over in this position for only two to three days at a time — keeping it longer can cause structural damage as the plant strains to right itself. However, the operation can be repeated after three to 10 days, and within a short time you will have a plant with noticeably increased leaf mass, and vigorous top growth.

With a less radical bend to begin with, no harm comes from leaving the twist-ties in position until the plant has conformed to her new growth pattern, at which point the tie can be removed. Obviously, on plants with more than one stem, you will want to bend over the tip of each stem. Cultivators report that plants can be trained into dense, compact masses using this simple approach. It is absolutely essential that strong light be provided when training your plants, so these operations are best done indoors, unless you live in an area with strong, dependable sunshine. Additionally, wind movement during each training can be harmful, and thus the indoor environment takes on even greater desirability.

Once the best plants have been trained into a horizontal profile, they are in an excellent position to have a technique called layering implemented. With this process, genetic duplicates of the best plants may be made without going through the lengthy process of growing from seed.

To begin, one should choose a vigorous branch on a healthy plant. Tie a soft but strong cotton string around the branch, about halfway between the stem and the tip, and attach the string to a stake in the ground, or to some similar anchor. Use this approach for training a vertical plant over to the horizontal, and gradually shorten the string each day until the branch is trained down to ground level.

Once the branch is trained down, fill a large container with a good soil mixture, assuring that there is good drainage in the container, that the soil is nutrient-rich, etc. Next, remove the string from the branch, and slip the container underneath so that the branch is lying on top of the soil in the pot. If the branch is trained down properly, it will actually press into the soil a little, with no tendency to spring away.

Next, choose a point where the main stem of the branch is in contact with the soil, and make a shallow cut on the underside of the branch using a sharp, clean blade. Scoop out about 2" of soil at the point of contact, and allow the cut point on the branch to come to rest in this shallow depression.

Take a 10–12" piece of coat hanger wire, bend it into a U-shape, and stake the branch down. Don't stake directly over the cut portion of the branch. Fill in the hole with dirt and pack it down lightly, then water.

An environment has been created in which the branch of the marijuana plant will begin putting out tiny root fibers at the point of the cut. It is important that this environment is kept moist, but not wet, for the next couple of weeks. It is a good idea to water with a rooting compound — any of the commercial brands available at nurseries will work just fine. In addition, the layered branch should be mulched over, preferably with a fine cut straw or some similar natural material. Peat or any other acidic material should not be used for a mulch over a layered site.

Within three weeks, roots strong enough to support the branch as a whole new plant will have developed at the layering site. The next step is to separate the clone from the parent. To do this, simply cut the branch where it enters the soil on the side toward the main stem, and seal the cut with grafting wax. This is now a fully rooted independent plant, which will grow to maturity and produce flowering tops with all the desirable characteristics of the original.

This technique is an excellent way to take the best plant of an outdoor crop and reproduce it for indoor growing during the off season. Layered cuttings are more vigorous and disease and insect resistant than seedling plants of similar height, and will make rapid progress through the vegetative stage into flowering. Layering is an excellent way to share the best plants with friends, and to multiply yield of the very best, most vigorous plants without having to wait until the next growing season.

There is no problem at all in layering several branches of a single plant at the same time. Just be sure that healthy, lower branches are chosen, and that they are trained to stay down to the level of the containers being used prior to beginning.

For many years folks have wondered how the growers in Colombia produce those beautiful characteristic golden buds. Now that Colombian marijuana is not only becoming relatively scarce, but what comes through is also increasingly contaminated with pesticides used during cultivation, many growers would like to be able to reproduce this Colombian growing technique at home.

The process is very simple, and is adapted from a standard horticultural technique known as "girdling" a plant. To girdle a plant, wait until it is in flower, but before it has started to produce the red hairs characteristic of full maturity. Girdling works much better with Sativa plants than with Indica, because the blooming pattern of Sativa is continuous, whereas Indica tends to bloom in successive flushes.

Using a very sharp, clean blade such as a single edge razor, simply cut in a full ring around the plant's main stem, about 12" above ground level. Make this cut a shallow one, severing just the outer 1/8" or so of the plant's stem. Make a second cut fully around the stem just below the first, and remove the plant tissue between the two cuts. This cuts the layer in which the principal fluid and nutrient transport from the root zone to the leaves takes place. By completely severing this layer, you interrupt these processes vital to continued growth are interrupt without actually killing the plant outright, which would result in radically lowered potency.

Over the next few weeks, the plant will gradually turn the golden brown color characteristic of fine Colombian in its heyday. This method is an excellent way to conceal a bright green marijuana plant in the fall, when all the foliage around it is turning yellow and brown, as well.

It's pretty obvious why it is a felony in most places to grow marijuana, while it is only a misdemeanor charge for possession. The marijuana bought keeps the system going, the system which employs tens of thousands of police, lawyers, judges, drug rehabilitation workers, and politicians. The marijuana which is homegrown means that one is taking oneself out of the loop, and that means the freeloaders who depend on the continuing illegal status of drugs for their jobs get nervous facing the possibility that their paycheck could be affected. Hence, a person is really trashed for growing his or her own, and is treated as lightly as possible for possession — certainly not harshly enough to deter a person from stepping right out and buying some more smoke.

The war on outdoor growers is being carried on by every sort of means available — infrared satellites, light aircraft, Boy Scouts turned into police informers, cancer-causing herbicides, and much more. Plus, every outdoor grower faces the most dangerous threat to marijuana known — his or her friends. There's something about a nice little crop of marijuana that turns one's closest brother into a thief in the night. More marijuana is ripped off every year by friends of the growers than by all of the policework in the country combined.

The dangerous atmosphere for home growers means that many folks have moved their growing operations indoors — which has its own kind of exposure problems. Here I want to offer a couple of countermeasures which have proven effective for a number of grower friends of mine over the years. These tricks may not work for everybody, but they might. Even if they do, I suggest that cultivation is done very carefully — without telling even the closest of friends what is going on! It may be satisfying to tell others about how well the plants are doing, but it is even more satisfying, and much less dangerous, to lay a few wonderful buds on each of them as a total surprise at harvest time.

TREETOP MARIJUANA

The main trouble with finding places to grow marijuana outdoors is that it is such a distinctive plant that it's easy to spot almost anywhere on the ground. Although a single plant is relatively hard to spot from the air, and impossible to detect from outer space, any pothead walking within a hundred yards will be able to spot a mature female no matter how well hidden. That's why the Treetop Marijuana trick works so well — people walking on the ground rarely look up, and people in the air can't effectively spot a single plant, especially this kind.

The technique is simply described. Take a lightweight container, like a good quality plastic trash can, and fill it with a lightweight growing media, such as a 50/50 topsoil and pumice mixture, and hang it in a tree, far enough up that nobody on the ground will spot it unless they know where to look. The container should be of an appropriate color, like dark green. To prepare the container for hanging, simply bolt two pieces of wood together, one on the outside of the container, the other on the inside. Put the bolts right through the sidewall of the container, and tighten the nuts down hard. This rigid reinforcement can then be used to hang the container in the selected tree, using an eye hook or similar piece of hardware.

The best type of tree is one with extensive branching on the lower levels, and a good, green canopy. Choose a tree on a south-facing hillside with good exposure. Also, choose a tree which will not start turning gold and red with the first frost, because your plants will pop right out of such foliage with their vigorous bright green leaves. After starting the plants indoors or outdoors, and being assured that they are healthy and growing vigorously, one should climb into the tree and position the container in such a way that it receives maximum solar exposure with minimal obviousness from ground level. Make the climb with each container just prior to watering, so that it will be at its lightest. If the plan is to water the treetop plants from a hose, be sure to attach them no higher than can be reached with normal water pressure. If a backpack pump, or some similar pumping device, will be used, also check its maximum reach. It is not a good idea to run water lines up into the tree, because any such setup is bound to attract someone's eye. Also, watering should be done at night, because anyone spotting someone watering the top of a tree is bound to wonder what's going on.

A technique which is far more effective than watering with a hose or pump is to install a section of the Leaky Pipe described later (pages 158–164) in the lightweight plant container, and to anchor a water reservoir above the plant in the same tree. Simply attach the empty water tank in a secure spot, and fill it in whatever way you can — hose, pump or (gasp) by making multiple climbs with a bucket. A marijuana plant will transpire between 1/2 and 2 gallons of water per day, depending on several factors such as its state of maturity, how hot the environment is, how much direct sun the plant gets, and how strong the wind is blowing. Even at the maximum rate of 2 gallons/day, a 50 gallon tank of water anchored above the plant in the tree will feed it for almost a month without refilling. This makes treetop growing not only convenient, but also pretty secure.

In short, while there is no universal formula for growing treetop marijuana, if a people take sensible precautions, and *can keep from bragging to anyone*

about how clever they are — they should be able to grow an excellent crop unmolested.

ROOFTOP MARIJUANA

Rooftops offer great solar exposure, and in many cases offer pretty good security from casual peeping. Of course, there are many situations in which rooftop growing is impractical — a ten-storey apartment building next door, a neighbor with second floor bedrooms overlooking the rooftop, etc. Another serious drawback to raising plants on the roof is that an 8' mature female on a roof is pretty easily spotted, even from ground level, and it certainly stands out from the air.

However, if one is planning to do a little rooftop growing, in many areas of the country it is relatively easy to find the proper rooftop growing situation, and if one is a renter, it's usually pretty easy to find the right sort of location. Which is, ideally, a flat or slightly sloped roof which is not in the direct sight of neighbors, with one or more trees growing along the north side of the structure, close to the roof and even overhanging it a little. If a person has, or can find such a situation, he or she has the ideal beginnings of a clandestine rooftop garden.

As I mentioned, even if there are no neighbors looking directly down on the rooftop, an 8' female standing proud at maturity is pretty easy to spot, so rooftop growing isn't just a matter of putting a couple of containers overhead and growing away. What must be done is to start the plants in adequate-size containers, and set them on the roof as close to the overhanging trees as possible. Under the containers, place a long board, with a number of eye hooks along the board. As the plant grows, progressively tie it down so that instead of growing vertically, it will grow horizontally. It is an easy matter to train marijuana to grow along the ground, or along the roof in this situation. Simply begin with a young plant no more than 24" tall and, by tying a soft strong cotton twine around the midpoint of the stalk and attaching the other end to an eyehook, gradually shorten the string over the course of several days until the plant is bent horizontal.

It will keep trying to grow vertically at the tip, so every week or so another loop of string will have to be attached around what is now the upper part of the main stem, and drawn down horizontally. As the plant grows along the rooftop, it will send up side branches which turn into multiple main stems, each with its own crop of side branches. If these get too tall, they will either have to be pruned back or tied down also.

This type of growing setup is very difficult to spot from the air, especially if there are the overhanging north-side tress mentioned earlier. If there are not these trees, one should consider not doing the project, because they are essential to prevention of overhead detection. A bright green roof garden automatically attracts the eye of police in spotter aircraft, who increasingly make the rounds of cities in the late summer and early fall, looking for just such a setup.

With rooftop marijuana, a person would also have to be careful when and how to come and go from tending the plants. It is an easy matter in most cases to thread a watering hose up the downspout and along the gutters, so that watering is simply a matter of turning on the water, and nobody is likely to spot such a system, whereas even a dullard would wonder at seeing someone climbing a ladder with a garden hose dragging behind.

I recommend consideration for using a length of Leaky Pipe installed in each of the containers on the rooftop (see pages 158–164).

Another excellent technique for concealing horticultural activities from prying eyes and light-fingered night visitors is known as production of "Vine Indica." The Indica plant is extremely responsive to training by various forms of pruning but none so radical or interesting.

I first saw Vine Indica in California, growing alongside the house of a friend who also raised a wide variety of grapes in an arbor setting. This person had planted an Indica plant in the ground at the base of the arbor, in among the grapevines which climbed all over the structure. As soon as the Indica was about 24" tall, the grower began systematically pruning away the sun leaves and fan leaves, leaving only a topknot of leaves intact. As the plant kept growing, the cultivator kept pruning each new set of leaves as they appeared on the stem. He tied the growing Indica plant to the arbor, training it vertically alongside the grapevines. Over time, the pruned stem of the Indica grew to resemble its neighboring grapevines, and the topknot of sun and fan leaves mushroomed into a huge halo. Within four months, the top of the Indica was at the top of the arbor, where the cultivator trained it over and secured it.

Maintaining his pruning all along the stem, and leaving only the topknot intact, the cultivator waited patiently until the Indica went into flower, with its massive buds fully concealed among the grape leaves and grape clusters at the top of the arbor. To anyone walking along below, the woody Indica stem was indistinguishable from the other vines, and except for the distinctive skunk odor there was no readily detectable sign of the presence of the massive twenty-ounce head of buds growing above. This technique isn't limited to grape country either — the vinelike character of radically pruned Indica offers some very interesting possibilities in many different environments.

*(Right) Intersexual flower
(pistil formed on male
flower) initiated by
short daylength*

Marijuana and the Light

There are many important differences between types of light used in cultivating plants.

Sunlight, as it comes from the sun's surface, is a continuous radiation spectrum. Sunlight appears white for the same reasons that metals glow white with a blue tinge at high temperatures, and only red-yellow at lower temperatures (the higher an object's temperature, the further its light emission moves toward the short wavelength, very high energy end of the spectrum).

We often think of light and color together. Color actually is any light with one part or another of the spectrum missing. A 100% reflective surface would appear to be pure dazzling white. Surfaces which absorb certain parts of the spectrum and reflect other parts, appear to be the color they reflect. Color is not a property of the world — in fact, there is no color in the world. It's all in the human mind.

The plant is not green. It is just that the light we call green bounces off the leaves while all the other colors sink in. When a leaf "yellows" it is because chemical changes in the leaf cause the surface to reflect yellow. Color is a clue to the world, not a fact of it.

The sunlight which falls upon the earth's surface has already been filtered through several layers of atmosphere, each stripping away different wavelengths, mostly in the far ultraviolet range. Very little ultraviolet light reaches the earth's surface, which is fortunate, because ultraviolet is ultra-high energy and blows living cells to pieces on impact, cutting through many layers of tissue.

Of the light reaching our surface, about half is infrared and half visible. The infrared is not a continuous band because certain wavelengths are absorbed by water vapor and carbon dioxide.

The processes of photosynthesis require a certain energy level to start them and keep them going. The molecules involved in photosynthesis must absorb enough energy to excite them and loosen them up so that they can enter into reactions with other molecules. This process is the same one which takes place in our eyes, and explains why we have a visible range of light. Too high-energy light (ultraviolet) freaks out the molecules in the eye, gets them so excited that they can't go through their reactions in an orderly fashion; and too low-energy light (infrared) isn't heavy enough in energy to get the molecules up for interaction. Photosynthesis in plants requires that the plants have energy levels which they can "see" — what is light to our eyes is life to a plant. This is the reason that infrared light produces such odd changes in plants — they aren't getting enough energy to go through with their normal processes, so they have to come up with some abnormal processes, and thus some abnormal growth patterns, in order to draw enough energy from the environment to survive. The phenomenon seems analogous to an organism such as man, who, when deprived of life-giving or life-sustaining substances such as air and heat, stretches out toward life in an agony of death, distending the normal limits of his

122

Daylength
and
Growth

Growing
Where
You Are

physical being, his muscles and internal organs all reacting violently to the low energy input.

People had long suspected that daylength played a role in the flowering of all plants. But it was not until 1912 when Jean Tournois demonstrated conclusively in Paris that Cannabis responds to varying daylengths that the affair was opened up for serious investigation.

It is completely appropriate that the marijuana plant was the first plant to prove the relationship between daylength and flowering. There are a great many varieties of Cannabis with a wide variation in response to daylength. Plants with temperate zone ancestry are relatively more responsive than tropical strains. But all strains of Cannabis are very responsive to the sun.

All strains show short-day response, meaning that the onset of flowering is moved up by shortening the days. In a number of experiments with two tropical strains, one from India and one from Panama, it was found that lowering the daylength to nine hours of light daily brought on flowering within six weeks of germination.

There are, of course, trade-offs in doing this, not the least of which is that these early bloomers are quite small. The normal span of flowering for tropical varieties is from six to nine months under light in excess of 16 hours per day.

The number of hours of light received daily affects the marijuana plant in terms of (1) numbering of weeks to first flowering, (2) proportion of females in the population, (3) the leaf mass of the mature plant, (4) the vitality and health of the plant, (5) the height achieved and (6) the amount of resin produced by the plant.

The relationships between these factors are fascinating and complex. We'll deal with them as we go through this chapter. A general principle to keep in mind for marijuana plants of tropical strains is that the longer the daylength, the longer the time to maturity; but also, the better the growth, and, all things being equal, the better the resin production.

Daylength varies with location on the planet and is an important consideration for the northern outdoor cultivator. Under natural conditions, an average marijuana plant will need about six months to mature, and will also require short days to bring on flowering, and the development of those much loved clusters. In the north, it's hard to squeeze in enough growing time between the last frosts of spring and the first frosts of fall to bring a plant to full-term maturity, and to give it the short-day treatment it needs to bloom, without resorting to indoor starting in the spring, and the use of special techniques for the induction of flowering. For cultivators who live north of about 35° North Latitude, such measures are best taken in mid-August, with flowering proceeding to full bloom by mid-September, in plenty of time for harvesting at full potency before first frost.

If you are cultivating outdoors in the north, and your plants are from a long-life equatorial strain, you'll have problems with unwanted attention after all the rest of the plants start turning brown and dying. Big, bushy, green marijuana plants become increasingly obvious as the surrounding foliage drops to the ground.

The most obvious solution to the problem is to cultivate early-maturing varieties — those which don't come from the equatorial regions. Most Mexican varieties are early maturing, for instance.

If you prefer equatorial strains, and they are growing in movable containers, you can bring them indoors, into a darkened room, for all but six to seven hours of direct sun once they have reached an acceptable height and just before they are about to become obvious due to their greenery. The sudden shift will bring on the flowering response, usually within two weeks, often in as little as a week.

If your plants are not movable, you will have to cover them with a light shield for all but the six to seven hours needed for basic health. Many growers use heavy-duty plastic bags, tying them over the entire plant before sunrise and removing them around noon, before the heat of the day, so the plant can breathe.

Effects of short daylight on flowering has been looked at in research and in popular books on marijuana from a number of points of view. Without doubt, decreasing daylength progressively after the plant is a month old brings most plants to flowering sooner than ordinary. There are problems with doing this, which we'll get into shortly.

But it is helpful to know where your seeds are from. Strains which have thrived for generations in the equatorial sun are going to have a different reaction to short days than plants whose ancestors have bathed in the sun of the temperate zones.

The plants from temperate zones will be used to a light cycle which begins with 12 hours of natural light in the spring, rises to a peak of 16 hours in the summer, and falls off rapidly as the first chill winds of the fall blow in. These plants will have the rhythms of their ancestors fixed into their own growth programs. They will read short daylight as a signal to hurry up and flower.

Other strains are going to be from the tropics and are going to flower with or without a short-day period. Their ancestors never experienced any short days, so they have no short-day response pattern. The reason these plants flower earlier than usual under short-day induction probably has more to do with traumatic energy loss than with the onset of a natural program.

The best genetic material in marijuana comes from equatorial plants, generations of which have matured under very long steady days and predictable, nurturing nights. The strains from farther north have a short-day expectation build into their system. They hoard their juices. If you are raising plants which come from Colombian or Jamaican marijuana, you will want to give them strong, close, steady light and just barely varying nights to fulfill their seasonal pattern. All annual plants have this pattern, even equatorial strains. The juices of these tropical strains flow freely in the light and disseminate through the tissues at night.

When a plant is raised on a light program which is different from its implanted code, it experiences stress. Continuous stress exposes otherwise concealed genetic characteristics. Plants grown under stress can give up on trying to flower, or they may flower early at low potency.

It is legitimate, in a sense, to fool the tropical zone strains into earlier flowering by raising them on short days. It is unfair to force them into blooming as a kind of gag reflex, choking on a lack of radiant energy.

What are these plants anyway? Should we treat them the way we treat our animals? Is their spirit some convenient little motor, making them go while they grow? We need to ask ourselves if we respect what we are consuming. I'm a hypocrite, too. A lot of this book is about manipulating the marijuana plant. But I do feel respect for the great herb, our intimate friend. This plant is the bearer of a high order soul. Let us praise this being who has followed us all over the earth, keeping us company, clothing us, opening our eyes and other senses to ourselves and the world, bringing us back some of the joy of our childhood. I have no doubt that we will one day owe our integrity as a species to some of the clear-seeing of self and life that the marijuana plant has afforded us. It is only fair that the herb be given its drink of life to the fullest, and harvested at its natural peak.

Of course, it is fun to experiment. Cultivators love to inquire, manipulate environments, learn, and generally play with this responsive being. There is no harm done in a spirit of friendly inquiry. This plant is not afraid of us. The evidence of human-marijuana association exhibits something very much like love. In its own way, this plant loves humanity.

Many of us smoke the marijuana plant. Relatively few of us grow the plants we smoke. We allow them to be grown for us by exploited laborers in remote valleys. We support whole kingdoms in the mountains, legions of narcotics police and the military. We support the empires. We support the armies. We support all the games that are sowing fear in place of flowers and violent death in place of peace. This is our circus. We pay for its performance because we buy marijuana instead of growing it.

How badly do we want the world to change, to be the way we say it should be? How much responsibility for these changes are we willing to take?

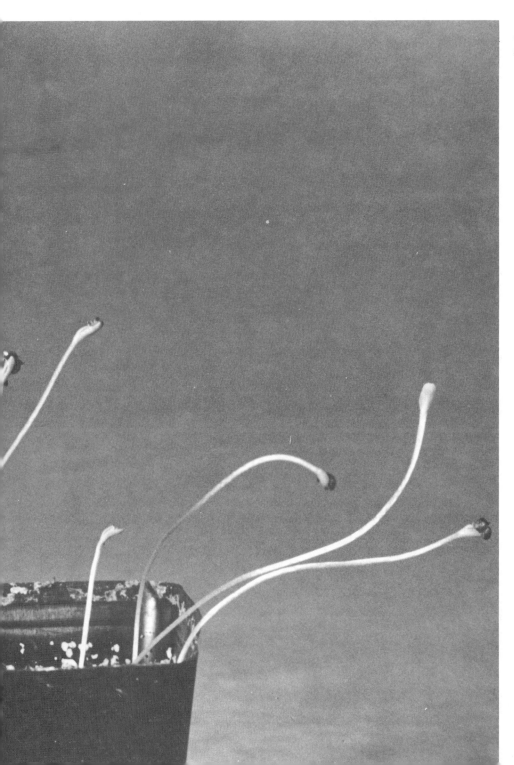

*(Left) Etiolated seedlings
caused by
insufficient light*

126

Spread
a Little
Light

(Right) Normal seedling
with cotyledons
and first true leaves

Cannabis reacts to the visible spectrum
of light and certain parts of the spectrum
are more active than others. To get the
concept of spectrum clear, because we'll
be dealing with it a lot, the following
diagram may be helpful.

It's clear that the plants need richer
concentrations of red and blue than they
do of the green center of the wavelength
spectrum.

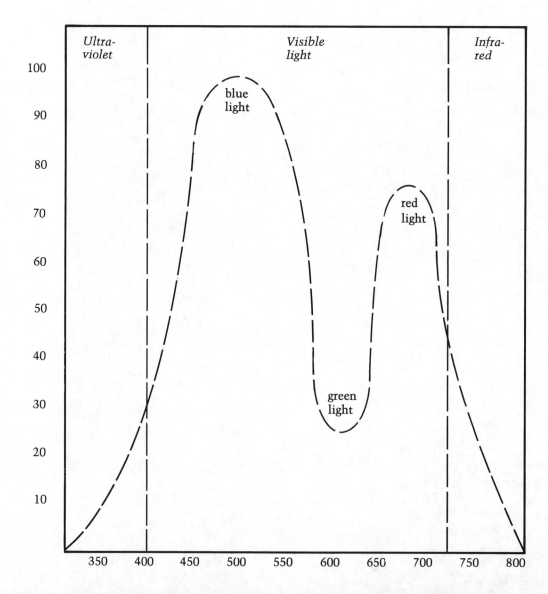

Relative amount
of usable energy

Ultra-violet   Visible light   Infra-red

blue light

red light

green light

100
90
80
70
60
50
40
30
20
10

Nanometers   350   400   450   500   550   600   650   700   750   800

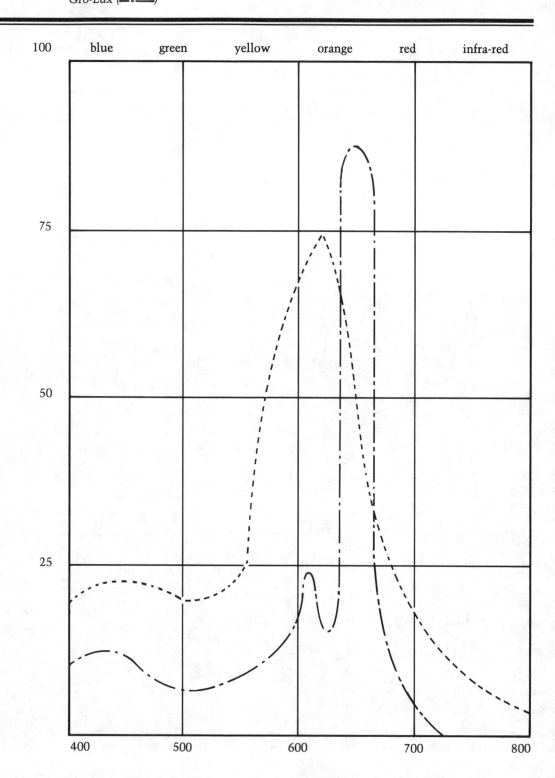

*Comparison of
Wide Spectrum (------)
and standard
Gro-Lux (—·—)*

100   blue   green   yellow   orange   red   infra-red

75

50

25

Nanometers   400   500   600   700   800

There isn't a light in the world that's yet brought the sun indoors, though a lot of brand names make the claim. Fire has been brought to the hearth, yes, but the sun stays in the sky.

Gro-Lux standard bulbs put out a spectrum which nicely mimics the sun's own. I have no doubt that a supercharger light market is about to develop and that before long photon accelerators will be used to grow astounding marijuana. But for the moment, consider the humble, limited, Gro-Lux Standard Spectrum.

Just about right. A nice rising flood of radiation through the violet and blue wavelengths, a falling off through the green and yellow, a sharp high peak bursting with reds, and a rapid, precipitous falling away with no infrared at all.

Supplemental lighting is the answer to the problem of no infrared. When you look at the profile of a Gro-Lux Wide Spectrum or even that of an ordinary 100 watt incandescent bulb, you'll see how nicely they complement the other growth-lights.

If you want to keep your plants from flowering, keep them under continuous light. Or, if you want to delay flowering, interrupt their night times with as little as five minutes of full strength illumination, sometime between 10 P.M. and 3 A.M., a couple of times a week from the second month onwards. If you want to bring on flowering, give your plants 12 to 14 hours of darkness each 24 hour period. Young plants take longer to respond with flowering to long nights and short days than do physiologically mature plants. Young plants may need as much as 28 to 34 days of long nights to bring on flowering, whereas mature plants can often be brought to flowering in less than a week. Many cultivators utilize a long-day, short-night illumination schedule to prolong growth, and prevent flowering, until maximum size and weight have been reached, and then switch to a short-day, long-night schedule to bring on flowering at the plant's ripest moment. Once flowering has begun, attempting to reverse the process is bound to decrease vigor, yield, and potency. Flowering is, for the plant, very much like orgasm for us — it's fine to prolong it, up to a point, but once release has begun, it's debilitating to experience anything but a freely-flowing rush of energy.

It may be very helpful to keep these spectrum energy charts and general observations about light in mind throughout the rest of the book. The normal light-bulb which is used to provide indoor illumination emits much light in the red to infrared range. Thus, such light is very low energy with well over half of the emissions being in the invisible infrared part of the spectrum. Many plants have been ruined by people who in good faith have believed that putting a blue filter in front of incandescent bulbs produces blue light, which they have been told is beneficial to plants. Blue light is high energy light and plants do need a certain amount of this to go through their photosynthetic process efficiently. But what you get when you put a blue filter in front of a source which is emitting primarily red light is not blue light — the filter does not generate light, it only passes the remnants of what is being generated. So what you have here is a very small amount of predominantly *green* light being passed, and green light is the least active part of the spectrum in supporting photosynthesis.

An additional caution: overexposure to infrared light at the earliest stages of seedling life will prevent the plant from standing erect. In order to raise itself and spread its embryo leaves, the plant must absorb red light at about 660 on the spectrum. This promotes the growth of longer cells on the inside of the curved

130

*Growing areas lighted
by tubular
fluorescent lamps*

Fluorescent
Lights

length of lamp	number of lamps	lamp wattage	growing area in sq. ft.	size of growing area
24"	1	20	1	24" × 6"
24"	2	20 end to end	2	48" × 6"
24"	2	20 side by side	2	24" × 12"
48"	1	40	2	48" × 6"
48"	2	40 end to end	4	96" × 6"
48"	2	40 side by side	4	48" × 12"
48"	3	40 end to end	6	144" × 6"
48"	3	40 side by side	6	48" × 18"
48"	4	40 end to end	8	192" × 6"
48"	4	40 side by side	8	48" × 24"
96"	1	72	4	96" × 6"
96"	2	72 end to end	8	192" × 6"
96"	2	72 side by side	8	96" × 12"
96"	3	72 side by side	12	96" × 18"
96"	4	72 side by side	16	96" × 24"

Source: Cherry, E., *Fluorescent Light Gardening*, D. Van Nostrand & Co., Princeton, N.J., 1965, p 37.

portion than on the outside, pushing the plant erect as though there were extensor muscles at work. Exposure to far-red and infrared light, however, cancels this effect and the seedling will remain bent over. So keep supplemental incandescent or wide-spectrum light away from seedlings until after the first week.

anufacturers of growing lights include Westinghouse, Sylvania, Duro-lite, General Electric, and Verilux. In Europe and parts of Canada, Phillips is a dominant grow-light manufacturer. Most of these manufacturers put out a full line of sizes, from 8 inches to 96 inches. The bulbs come in four kinds: special incandescent, standard, wide spectrum, and Very High Output (VHO). Wattages run from 20 watts to 1,000 watts per bulb. New shapes are being introduced to the market with the claim that these shapes increase the light energy. Fixtures are available in a wide variety, from simple strap suspension units to self-contained units on trolleys, some with built-in humidifiers and air-flow controls.

All fluorescent bulbs have certain things in common. They all produce light by creating an electrical arc in a glass chamber filled with very low pressure metallic vapor. The electrical arc causes the vapor to give off heavy ultraviolet radiation which strikes the phosphor crystals coating the inside of the chamber wall. These crystals glow with excitement when bombarded with radiation from the super-heated metallic vapor, and produce a remarkably sun-like fluorescent light.

Since the electric arc is most intense at its center, the phosphor in the center 12 inches of any fluorescent tube will emit the light of greatest intensity. Plants should be rotated under the centers if more than one plant is using a fixture, or you can rotate the lights. Either way, it is a good idea to even out the light energy received by your crop. Typical fluorescent bulbs put out from 50-80 lumens per watt and a lot of these lumens are accounted for by the center 12 inches. Over a five month growing period, an unrotated plant could run a significant deficit of light energy. Rotating will also create more females in your crop.

Fluorescent bulbs start losing energy from the very first, though new bulbs give about 10% more light energy than their rating for the first 100 hours. Regardless of the rating, even some of the 12,000 hour bulbs lose so much of their energy-producing capabilities by the 5-6,000 hour point that it's not wise to burn these bulbs past 6,000 hours or 50% of their rated life. This is because, just as your plants' light energy needs are going up, the energy input from your fluorescents is going down. This is the

equivalent of putting your plants on a short-day program, which tells them to hurry up and flower, and to hell with the leaves and the resin. Significant energy loss does not begin to occur until about two full growing seasons of 16-18 hour days for five months each season. So, figure on changing your 12,000 hour bulbs every two growing seasons. For other life-ratings, figure on using only half of the bulb's lifespan for cultivation.

Another reality with Cannabis is that fluorescent lighting will need supplementation by incandescent lighting. Since you have to use incandescent lighting for supplementation anyway, why not use an incandescent grow-light. There are several on the market.

Fluorescent lighting can be conspicuous for its intensity but if your lights' glare can be seen, just set the timers so that the hours roughly coincide with the habits of your neighbors. Nobody ever thinks anybody who is like them is suspicious.

When working with fluorescents, use flat white surfaces and spread white sand beneath the plants to reflect lost light back to the plants. The walls of the room should be glaring white if possible. One of those great train station tile restrooms where flesh colors just wash out would be perfect. On a less grand scale, showers are often just right if you have someplace else to bathe. Talk to your plants, but never shower with them. That's not intimate, that's pushy.

Lights are usually hung from swag hooks or simple hardware in the ceiling with the line tied off wherever in the room is most convenient. The distance of a light source from the plant varies with the bulb type, wattage and age of the bulb. As close as you can get without wilting the growing tip of the plant is best: and that's a matter of experience. If the seed

*Illumination from two or
four 40 watt standard
Cool-White fluorescent lamps**

distance from lamps (inches)	two lamps used† (footcandles)	four lamps used† (footcandles)	new (footcandles)
1	1,100	1,600	1,800
2	860	1,400	1,600
3	680	1,300	1,400
4	570	1,100	1,300
5	500	940	1,150
6	420	820	1,000
7	360	720	900
8	330	660	830
9	300	600	780
10	280	560	720
11	260	510	660
12	240	480	600
18	130	320	420
24	100	190	260

*Lamps mounted approximately two inches from a white-painted reflecting surface. Center to center distance between lamps was two inches. Source: USDA (in) Cherry, E., *Fluorescent Light Gardening*, D. Van Nostrand & Co., Princeton, N.J., 1965, p 77.
†These lamps had been used for approximately 200 hours.

genetics carry a low-profile, bushy model for growth and the environmental conditions are appropriate, then this little squat tropical female would welcome even the strongest light slung down to within two inches of the top leaves. This plant is not going up so much as out. If, on the other hand, your seed bears a program with the design of a tall, slender female with delicate but powerful flowers — perhaps a Colombian mountain lady — then keep your high lights up and side-light her.

Another factor is the speed at which your crop is growing. How often do you want to move the lights?

High Intensity Discharge Metal Halide lamps combined with Lumalux are reported in use by professional, experienced cultivators with excellent results. There is much more vigorous growth than can be achieved with even VHO fluorescent lamps; improved production of flowering heads; and one grower in Boston swears that the flavor is vastly improved under HID Metalarc lamps. She likes 1,000 watt Lumalux made by Sylvania and grows her crop in a loft. HID lamps are offered in a range of wattage, from 100 watts to 1,500 watts. Each wattage comes in a variety of lighting options. *Clear* produces the best spectrum of all levels. The life of HID bulbs is very good but depends on a number of factors, principally operating temperature and number of starts. The 400 watt lamp puts out the most usable energy for the money.

HID lamps must be operated from a fixed position with respect to the horizontal. Since they generate a lot of heat, provision must be made for heat dispersal, such as the use of a growth chamber or very high ceilings with ventilation. A 400 watt HID bulb will generate about 1,500 BTU's per hour of operation. At a rate of one 400 watt bulb per 16 square feet of floor space, a growing room with 10 lamps would generate 15,000 BTU's per hour. In greenhouse operations, much of this heat is recoverable and reusable. Thus the heat output of HID lamps is converted to an asset.

Self-ballasted HID lamp units are available but they have a significantly shorter life than the modular-ballasted units. Both G.E. and Sylvania will provide detailed application information on request and will respond to a request on letterhead from professional plant growers who ask for help in designing HID systems.

No one who is beginning cultivation needs to get into HID Metal Halide lighting right away, unless high technology is a must. To gain initial experience with the marijuana plant, a nice little fluorescent setup is more than adequate and allows the cultivator to get used to the plant's habits under normal growth conditions.

With seedlings, six to eight inches of space between the new leaves and the bulb's surface will give any seedling all it can handle, especially if there are good nutrients and good ventilation. Watch growth with seedlings and keep an eye open for any signs of wilting due to excessive heat. The temperature at ground level should not exceed the low 80's. If you've got hot burning lights and can't get them close enough to fully feed the plants, back off the fluorescents and side-light from 18 to 24 inches with an incandescent on either side. With cool fluorescents, come down to two inches if you like. The plant will like it.

Heat from light sources is not only a problem for the plants, it's a problem for the light bulbs. Most modern fluorescents operate best when the bulb temperature is 100° F., but in unventilated situations they burn a good deal hotter.

The solution, which allows you to bring your lights down close to the plants as well as giving your maximum bulb life and output, is to build an "isolation barrier."

Plant experimentors have been designing and building such barriers for years. The basic idea is simple. Your fixtures are placed inside a lightweight box with a plastic or glass bottom or a material which has a high, continuous transmission of light in the visible and infrared parts of the spectrum. This plastic is semi-opaque and makes an excellent window covering for those who wish to grow plants indoors by light from windows but are concerned about visibility to those outside.

hours burned per day on first start	average service life in hours	80% of average service life (replacement time)
10	11,200	8,960 hrs. (2.5 yrs.)
12	12,000	9,600 hrs. (2.2 yrs.)
14	12,500	10,000 hrs. (2 yrs.)
16	13,000	10,400 hrs. (1.8 yrs.)
18	13,500	10,800 hrs. (1.7 yrs.)

Source: Cherry, E., *Fluorescent Light Gardening*, D. Van Nostrand & Co., Princeton, N.J., 1965, p 49.

Nurseries often have supplies of such material. This chamber is then ventilated with fresh air, cooled if possible, drawn in at one end, over the surfaces of the lamps (drawing away their heat), and exhausted at the other end. The exhausted hot air is piped well away from the plants which are right beneath the plastic or glass. Since 42% of the heat generated by the bulb comes from the surface of the bulb and since this is just the area cooled by the isolation barrier chamber, you will have cut your lighting system's total heat output by almost half. The barrier cuts the total light energy available to the plants by only 10%. This is more than made up for by the increased possible closeness and the increased efficiency of the lighting system which will pay off in higher light output and longer bulb life.

When you are working with water and electricity, it is essential to ground the electrical apparatus. If you have a grounded, three-prong socket system, plug into that. (You may have to rewire your fixture. A two-prong plug into a three-prong socket does *not* ground your equipment.) If you don't have a grounded electrical system (two-prong sockets are not normally grounded) you will have to ground your lamps to a water pipe or radiator or pipe in the ground outside.

Attach a bare end of insulated wire to the fixture and run the other end to your ground (the pipe, etc.) and attach it there with bare metal contact. Use a little electrician's tape to secure the contact and protect it from contamination. For any sort of complex wiring, be sure you know what you're doing. Get help if you need it. Fires attract a lot of attention and the heat is bad for your plants.

Before spending a sum of money on new fixtures, check wrecking yards, salvage companies, etc. Tell folks that you are looking for old fixtures for your workshop in the garage. If you don't walk in with your "Marijuana Forever" T-shirt on, you probably won't inspire any darkening of the junkyard proprietor's beetled brow. In many places, you are going to have to do some real looking around to find second-hand fixtures. Sometimes demand outstrips the limited supply.

There is some experimental evidence that the use of incandescent sunlights, high in ultraviolet radiation, significantly enhance resin production during the second half of a plant's life. The role of uv in resin production isn't understood, but just as our skin produces melanin to tan and protect us from the sun's uv, resin must in some way protect the plant.

If you are going to use a sunlamp as a source of uv, get it at least five feet away from the plants, six feet if you can. It's not just the heat. It's the flood of ultraviolet that comes pouring out of a sunlamp which, even at an increased distance, is hard for a plant to take.

Position the sunlamp so that its energy falls on the upper shoulders of the plant (if you can't have it vertical). It should not be left on long at first. For best sunlamp results, begin with 15 minutes exposure an hour after midday when the sun would naturally be at its highest and the natural uv would be most intense. Using a timer, burn the light off once a day, moving up to 30 minutes for the second week, 45 minutes for the third. The upper limit for sunlamp use depends on how far away from the plants you have the lamp(s), what the wattage and heat situation is, etc. It may be that a rheostat rigged with an inexpensive self-cycling timer, or controlled by a personal microcomputer such as the TRS-80 or the Apple II, could quite effectively operate an entire lighting system, and perhaps a fertilizing and watering system as well. The whole area of fine control of light and other variables in Cannabis cultivation is open to interested growers. *The Journal of Marijuana Cultivation* will feature results obtained from well-done experiments. We will most certainly be publishing our own results in the near future. As with a good vineyard, the successful cultivation of marijuana seems to take man seasons to establish. Both indoor and outdoor cultivation of marijuana seems certain to become defined by region and cultivator, much like the fine wine regions of the world. It only remains to see which regions begin soon, and which wait, and sulk.

Both fixtures and tubes should be cleaned every three to four weeks. Just as dirty windows cut down on available sunlight, dirty fluorescent bulbs prevent full-energy, full spectrum light from reaching your plants.

After cleaning your tubes, wipe them with a silicone-impregnated cloth or pad available in the household cleaners section of any big supermarket under many brand names. The manufacturers of fluorescent bulbs put a silicone finish on them at the factory, but it is wiped off by cleaning. Without the silicone, the glass loses some of its insulating properties, and on high humidity days this can mean considerable energy loss through leakage into the atmosphere. Loss of insulating properties can also mean difficult starting, particularly on fast-start systems, and this in turn can materially shorten the life of the tubes.

There are a number of darkening problems associated with fluorescents. Any time the operating tube comes in contact with an object such as the top of a plant, a cool spot can develop causing the metallic vapor inside the tube to condense at that point. The resulting dark spot rarely goes away, and can significantly reduce light output.

Darkening of the entire tube is normal at the end of service, but darkening should not begin to be obvious until around 1,200-1,500 hours of operation. If the ends of the tube begin turning black in the first half of its rated life, there is a problem with the starter, the ballast, the wiring, the voltage, or with the tube itself. If, however, the blackening at the ends of the tube disappears after a few minutes of operation, you have no problem.

If your tube begins flickering, it is a sign that the end of life is near. If the lamps are new, you have cause for suspicion. You may have a defective starter, ballast, wiring setup or just a bad tube. In a new tube, the light will sometimes wiggle and squirm around for a few minutes and then settle down. This snaking of the

136

Calculating
Wattage
Level

A
Subatomic
Excursion

light in a new tube is normal, though it doesn't always happen.

With respect to the fixture, keeping it clean to enhance reflectivity is the major maintenance task. Many fixtures have nice, shiny, baked-on white enamel paint that looks like it does a great job of reflecting light, but which actually is *less* reflective than a flat white enamel finish. Manufacturers know that glossy white looks more reflective, and that they can sell more fixtures by painting them glossy white rather than flat white, but if you can't find a flat finish fixture, buy a can of flat white enamel spray paint and do it yourself when you get home. Be sure to cover the sockets while spraying, and remember you only need to do the inside.

To find out the wattage level that the wiring in your house or apartment will bear, locate the fuse which serves the room in which you plan to grow your plants. Multiply the amperes on the fuse by the voltage of your system — probably 110 or 120, although laundry rooms, basements, and kitchens, especially in newer houses, may have 220 volt wiring.

Voltage times amperes equals wattage capacity of the circuit. Thus, if you have a 30 amp fuse and your house is 110, you have a circuit that can carry a maximum of 3300 watts. Leave a 25% safety margin, particularly if your lighting is ballasted. The initial power draw of your ballasts may exceed their rated limits, especially if either the lights or the fixtures are older. A system which exceeds the circuit's capacity will, at the least, blow a fuse, but the consequences could be much worse.

The wattage drawn by your lights can be roughly calculated as follows:

Standard fluorescent tubes draw 10 watts per foot of length;
High output fluorescent tubes draw approximately 16 watts per foot;
Very high output tubes draw 25-30 watts per foot (depending on type);
HID lamps draw varying power, depending on their ratings.

Let's take a little side trip into the whole relationship between wavelength and photosynthesis which may be helpful in understanding what the plants, all green plants, but particularly Cannabis, are doing with the energy they draw from the sun.

The controlling processes in photosynthesis begin at the atomic level, with the nucleus of the atom and its electron ring. Each orbit around the nucleus of an atom has a variety of potential energy levels at which electrons can move and still remain in orbit. If the electrons exceed the energy limits of their orbits they are forced to leave — to move into an orbit further from the nucleus and therefore an orbit which requires more energy to complete. This movement is the famous quantum leap which we have been using for years to describe an exponential increase in energy required to move from one plane to another. Knowledge, among other things, seems to operate according to this principle — you can acquire vast amounts of knowledge and still remain on the same plane, but there comes a point where the cumulative knowledge in your head — the cumulative creative energy you're trying to deal with — requires a leap into another plane. Once you've made that first leap, you realize that, while knowledge is a cumulative process, it is not a progressive phenomenon. You do not move from plane to plane in a smooth, harmonious progression merely by storing up knowledge. You move from level to level, but always within the same orbit or plane, until you reach a point where you can no longer contain the creative energy you have been accumulating and remain within the same plane. So you make the quantum leap. And find yourself starting all over again, gathering energy on another level, always with successive levels above you, levels which are accessible only through the accumulation of vast amounts of knowledge, until once again the leap is within your ability.

The life process of photosynthesis in plants proceeds in this way, by quantum leaps of the atomic particles into a higher, more energetic plane. Following this leap, the electrons lose energy, their orbits decay, and the quantum leap occurs in reverse, liberating energy as the fall from the outer orbits to the inner orbits occurs. It is this energy, made possible by decay in the orbits of the excited electrons back to their original plane, which drives the engines of life. This is the conversion process which is essential to all life on earth. Without the ability to perform this leap, and the subsequent energy-liberating decay of electron orbits, all life would disappear and the earth would be stone and sand.

So you are very close to some very essential things when you are manipulating the light your plants receive, and there is no replacement for knowledge and understanding in dealing with these processes. You are moving close to life itself, to the process if not the meaning.

We'll use, as a reference point, a line drawn between Washington, D.C., Louisville, Kansas City, Colorado Springs and San Francisco. Along this line the hours of sunlight available throughout the year break down approximately as shown on the chart on page 141.

This breakdown is deliberately very loose, and does not take cloud cover into account. Therefore, the amount of effective sunlight will vary considerably. Nevertheless, some generalizations are possible which help greatly in determining the optimum planting times for Cannabis along this line, and if you are located either far north or far south of this line you will be able to adjust to fit your own seasonal picture.

The number of hours of sun available is balanced with other considerations such as how early a plant may be set out, what the cloud cover is, and other factors. By the time you are ready to plant, there will be plenty of sun in most places.

In northern New England and upstate New York, and all of southeastern Canada, seed can be sown by mid-May. Seedlings can be set out by late May, by which time they will be getting more than sufficient hours of light for best growth.

The best time for planting in the deep South is late winter in most places, since there is plenty of sun available even in February and the late summer can see killer conditions of heat and humidity.

In most of the Southwest, there's plenty of sun available, as soon as the weather permits planting. June marks the beginning of the dry season in most places, so it's a race in the spring to get Cannabis in the ground early enough so that she will achieve substantial height by late June. The southwestern summer in many places duplicates the environment of Cannabis' native central China, and it thrives.

In the Rockies and intermountain basins, seedlings should be started indoors in April with a mid-May transplant date. They should be in vigorous health by then, especially if they have been started

*Normal April daily
minimum temperature
(Degrees Fahrenheit)*

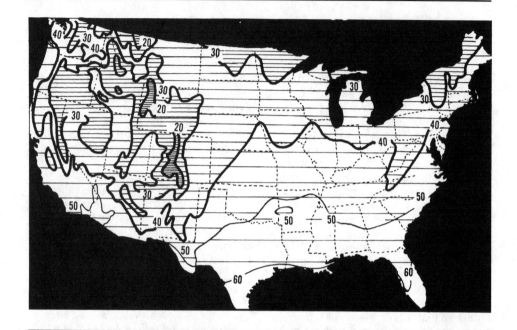

in a frame, and gradually hardened to the ultraviolet sun, the dry air, and the temperature extremes. By June, the spring cloudiness will be over and the high mountain sun will shine down 12 to 13 hours a day.

In the Northwest, watch out for June. In the normal growth cycle of Cannabis, June in the Northwest is the middle of growth month #3. And June can be awfully cloudy in the Northwest, permanently stunting your crops growth, and dramatically lowering resin yield.

Midwestern planting cycles extend all throughout the central belt of the country, east to the Atlantic. In many places you can start indoors or in a frame by April 1. Planting outside from May 1-15 assures Cannabis of immunity from frosts and of increasingly long days.

Of southern California, Arizona, New Mexico, and sunshine, little need be said.

Experimentors have always loved playing with Cannabis and photoperiod. This is one of the most light-responsive plants. Cannabis reacts definitely to varying daylength, intensity, and spectrum shifts; to breaks of light in the dark cycle and plunges into darkness during the daylight cycle; to varying photoperiod/hormonal stimulus; and to various combinations of light sources.

There is no doubt of Cannabis' response to light. The findings of many experiments may be summed up in a few general guidelines:

For daylight extension to plants receiving eight or more hours of sunlight per day, incandescent light is adequate, though a grow-light is better. If you are using a cold or hot frame, for instance, and are starting in April, you may want to put the seedlings on a full summer daylength for your area to begin with, so that later on, transplanted to a field where they will get full-day sunlight, they will not miss stride. Decide on a light cycle from the beginning and stick with it. Don't vary the light until you are ready to bring the plant to flower.

Cultivation with incandescent bulbs alone is a bust. Don't try it. It isn't worth it.

Incandescent bulbs for supplemental lighting should be five inches away from the leaves for a 100 watt bulb. Farther for higher wattage.

If sunlight through windows forms any part of your indoor lighting program, keep the windows clean. Dirty windows, even those not obviously filthy, cut available energy significantly.

Use only fluorescent bulbs designed for plant growth. Supplement the fluorescent lighting with about 50% incandescent lighting. The ratio is about two fluorescent watts to one incandescent watt. Thus, if in a fixture, you have two 40 watt fluorescent bulbs, you would need one 40 watt bulb on each side of the plant to get a 50% incandescent/50% fluorescent mix. This setup applies *per plant* in a row or, if the incandescent bulb is between rows, each bulb will do for one side of two plants.

Dollar for dollar, a longer tube gives more light energy than two smaller ones equal to a larger one in total length.

Fluorescents can be as close as heat buildup will allow. Try six to eight inches for beginning distances and see how the plants do. There's a great deal of variation in the heat output of different lamps and fixtures, so it becomes a very individual thing. Seriously consider using an isolation barrier and ventilating. Drill a few holes in the reflector shield. You lose little light, and get good heat dispersal.

Arrange reflective panels, white walls, white sand on the floor and soil surface, etc., to return escaping light to your plant. These measures increase available light 20-25%. Or, paint the floor flat white, and walk around with clean feet.

Plants with a short-day program go toward flowering if put on a progressive short-day cycle at any time in their lives. Equatorial strains go toward flowering, too, but for a different reason, which we discussed earlier. Keeping lighting at full intensity for the full growth term produces the superior plants. Plants speeded up with short-day experiments have to struggle to amount to much.

Very long days, 16 to 18 hours, are effective in promoting leaf mass and longevity of tropical strains. Beyond 18 hours a day, growth is slowed and finally even retarded a bit. Other abnormalities creep in. A daylength of 18 hours is genetically ideal in 95% of Cannabis strains.

Interruption of the plant's dark period prolongs that part of the growth cycle where the plant gains height and leaf mass — the vegetative stage of growth. A brief period of illumination in the middle of the night is all it takes to move flowering back a month or two. Thus, an early-maturing strain can have its life span prolonged and size markedly increased by merely turning on the lights for a few minutes every night from the sixth week until you want the plants to flower.

Pruned plants should be side-lighted, preferably using fluorescents. Incandescent will do, even at nice low wattage, like 60 watts.

Combinations of long days with plant hormones produce rampant sexual abnormalities. The headspace volatiles produced by such a plant could be terribly bitter. Better not push Cannabis too hard with both light *and* hormones.

*Normal daily number
of hours of
sunshine in summer*

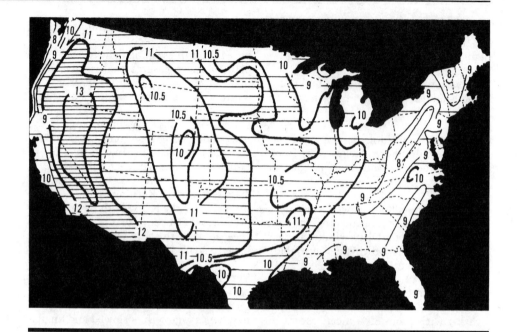

To extract more light from fluorescent tubes, overballast them. Put 30 watt tubes into a rapid-start, 40 watt ballast. Light intensity will increase over 35%, while the life of the tube goes down about 10%. A tube should be discarded after ⅔ lifetime use, at the most.

One early experimentor (McPhee) was interested in the relative effects of daylength on growth rate in Cannabis. He set up his experiment so that he could control for the variables of temperature, soil quality, growing space per plant, soil moisture, light intensity and action spectrum. By controlling for all of these factors, he came up with a pretty close to ideal experimental situation, one where he could attribute difference in growth rate to duration of light alone, with pretty good confidence levels.

The chart on page 142 is based on the principal relationship which McPhee discovered, one which has been confirmed by many people since then.

We can derive a couple of interesting principles from this chart.

First, it is clear that after you pass the seven-hour daily exposure period, you begin to see a substantial increase in the growth and development of Cannabis for every unit of light increase provided. This relationship holds up to, and including, the 16-hour day, when the point of diminishing returns is reached. Most of your attention will probably be focused in that area of the chart labelled "A" and the decision as to how much daylight you are going to give your plants will have a lot to do with the kind of results you're willing to accept. The part of the chart marked "B" presents an interesting example of energy starvation — the plants aren't getting enough energy, but they are growing at a fairly good rate anyway. This doesn't last, and is not a sign of vigor; rather, it is a sign of impending disaster just as is the elongation that occurs under infrared light.

Accompanying the growth chart under increasing amount of light are significant changes in the amount and quality of leaves produced by Cannabis. One of the best ways of judging the overall quality of your growing plant is to calculate the leaf index. The higher the leaf index in Cannabis, the greater will be the leaf mass at maturity. This calculation is a good device for a number of purposes. First, it allows you to decide in about the fifth week which plants are going to have the greatest leaf mass at maturity. (This will be important if you anticipate thinning out your crop, particularly if you want to pull most of the males, leaving only the best.) Second, it gives you a check as to the uniformity of the growing conditions the plants are experiencing. It also gives you a good device for deciding which females you want to let go to full maturity as seed producers, and which you want to harvest before they bear fertilized seed.

Add up the total wattage of your lighting system. For instance, 15 40-watt bulbs will burn 600 watts per hour or 6/10 of a kilowatt per hour. A kilowatt is 1,000 watts. Power companies charge by the kilowatt hour. You can get your rate from your company. Let's say the rate is 8¢ per kilowatt hour.

Multiply the total wattage of your system in kilowatts by the rate per kilowatt hour in your system times the number of hours a day you burn your lights. Let's say you have a total of 600 watts times 8¢ KWH times 16 hours a day. You will get the figure 768. Divide by a thousand and you have a cost of 77¢ per day to run your light system.

At any rate, some of the interesting effects of providing increasing light energy for the plants include greater leaf weight, higher leaf index, increased number of flowers, changes in rate of growth and shortening or lengthening of the time required to reach maturity, and the occurrence of branches opposite each other on the stem versus the occurrence of branches on alternating sides of the stem, which means more branches per unit of light. So don't skimp on the light. It doesn't cost that much, and it yields big returns.

Most of these variations can be adequately represented in tabular form. It is important to keep in mind that while this chart may appear to give you the ability to control certain factors in your plants, and you will in fact be able to manipulate these factors, the key to understanding does not lie in an ability to control. To reach a level of understanding which will put you into a harmonious relationship with the natural order requires that you analyze your plants with an appreciation of the ecological relationship which exists between the plant, with its hereditary potential on the one hand, and the environment, internal and external, on the other hand. What you will gain by manipulating environment will be a function of the interaction of the plant with the environment, not a simple, passive response. You cannot expect, therefore, that each plant will respond equally to specified changes you make in the environment; neither can you expect to be able to predict exactly how each change you make will affect all plants. You will be dealing with a range of potential responses, and must be prepared for variation.

Sunrise 4:30-5:00 a.m. Sunset 7:00-7:30 p.m. Hours of sunlight = approx. 14	June
Sunrise 6:00-6:30 a.m. Sunset 5:45-6:15 p.m. Hours of sunlight = approx. 12	September
Sunrise 7:00-7:30 a.m. Sunset 4:30-5:00 p.m. Hours of sunlight = approx. 9	December
Sunrise 5:45-6:15 a.m. Sunset 5:45-6:15 p.m. Hours of sunlight = approx. 12	March

daylength	effects
2-3 hours Little more than seven inches in height at maturity.	Very poor chances for survival; radically stunted growth; very little vegetation; weakness; seeds are worthless even if produced; death can be expected with a few weeks.
4-5 hours Eleven to twelve inches height at maturity.	Rapid initial growth for some plants; growth tapers off after a few weeks; large portion of seeds sterile; very little vegetation; mature height is stunted; plants are weak and pale; resin production is low; sexual character confused; leaf index low; leaf mass light; branches opposite and alternating low female survival rate.
6-10 hours From one and one-half to three feet at maturity.	Growth period lengthened, especially in artificial light; good vegetative development of most plants, sex ratios exceed 1:1 female, with 15-100% more females than males; sexual expression less confused, but flowering somewhat inhibited; seeds are viable; stem elongates and thickens; internodes spaced out; branches predominantly opposite; resin production increases.
11-15 hours Up to three and one-half to five feet at maturity.	Height at maturity increases; flowering is delayed considerably; seeds are viable; resin production is high; stem is strong; sex ratio dips a bit; sex expression is clear; growth period may be shorter than 6-10 hours in some strains; branches usually alternate; leaf index increases.
16+ hours From five and one-half to six feet at maturity.	Height not increased further; excellent flower and leaf mass; strong strong production of resin; female survivorship lowered a bit, and sex ratio appears at 1.5:1 female; seeds have slightly lowered vitality; nodes occur between 7-10 inches along stem; leaf index high.

b
energy
starvation
zone

a
point of
diminishing
returns

The
Harvest
Setting

(Below) Polyploid leaves. *
See photograph page 71.

143

Harvesting, Drying and Curing Marijuana

The best time to harvest your plants is in the heat of the day. The marijuana plant's resin output is highest during the hour immediately preceding the peak temperature of the afternoon. Try not to harvest if the day is damp and never when it is cool and overcast. Such conditions temporarily suppress resin production. The heavy dews accompanying this kind of weather radically decrease resin concentrations around the all-important flower clusters.

To harvest the marijuana plant, cut through the stalk just below the lower branches. The key to a successful harvest is a sharp blade with a handle that will let you apply your strength to the cutting and respect for the plant you are sacrificing. A short meditation before each plant's harvest is important for your own healthy outlook, as well as proper and respectful to this great being.

That fine book, *The Secret Life of Plants,* shows that plants understand what is going on around them. They know when they are about to die. Tell your plants that the time of their life is at an end. Tell them that you love them for what they mean to you. Let them know you appreciate their existence and recognize their spirit.

144

Hanging
and
Drying

Multiple
Harvests

Whatever form your harvest celebration takes, don't include any guilt feelings over killing your plants. Fear of death is a human cultural phenomenon. Your plants don't fear death. They fear brutal intent. Experiments show this clearly. Approach your work with a peaceful mind, a sharp blade and a strong arm. Your plants will end their lives with a sigh of joy instead of a scream of fear. That is as it should be.

If you are going to air-dry your plants in the dark, which I recommend, hang them rather than lay them on the ground. Hanging them increases air flow and reduces the possibility of rot and mold. However, it is a myth that hanging promotes resin flow to the leaves and flowering tops.

The source of this myth is probably reports from scientists that cannabinoids and other forms of potentially psychoactive molecules and their precursors are found throughout the plant, particularly in the root. It is true that cannabinoids, cannabinols, etc. are manufactured in the root of the plant. But it is only when they reach the leaves that they are processed into psychoactive forms. This occurs in minute glands. Nothing psychoactive is in the stem and nothing runs down to the leaves. Fluids do not flow through plants that day.

Whether you are drying your plants by hanging them or turning them on mats, remove as much of the main stem as possible. The stem contains a lot of water which will escape through the leaves. In the process, it will slightly diminish the potency of the resin. The only problem is hanging leaves and tops which have been stripped from the stem. This can be partially overcome by cutting out the stem between the nodes of the plant. This leaves a series of alternate branches held together by just a bit of stem. These pieces are easily draped over a line to dry and do not have excess stem water to process through the leaves.

The top's the thing in the play, and cultivators in Nepal and Afghanistan have long practiced a harvesting technique which gives up to 300% more weight in flowering tops per plant. The technique is simple and has begun to be used here in the U.S. with great success.

It is easier to practice this technique with a few plants than with a whole field because, in order to do a complete job, you must pay attention to each plant. As the female approaches maturity, she will, as we know, begin to develop flowering spikes or tops. As soon as each of the tops develops to a point just prior to the extension of the stigmas, or as soon as the first little white stigmas start to stick out, that flowering top is removed from the plant. One simply cuts the stem supporting the flower cluster where it joins the secondary or main stem.

If the cultivator is careful about not letting the female flowering tops reach the point where even one of them sets seed, then each time a flowering top is removed, a new one will appear in its place within several weeks. The plant will keep trying to produce young. If even one flower cluster gets pollinated, however, the plant will shift gears radically. It will be under a whole new set of chemical direction and will not usually produce any more flowering spikes for those lopped off.

Sooner or later, the female is going to get tired of all this trimming and she'll start wishing she was a creature with teeth so she could bite you. So when you've cropped her two or three times, why not call it enough and let her go ahead and develop a full flowering?

And then, of course, on with the harvest.

If you've given normal care to your crop of Cannabis, by the time harvest comes you will have put a lot of thought and energy into the plants, and they will be ready to give back what has been invested.

A little care in drying your plants will assure that they will retain the potency and vigor which is present at the moment that they are severed from their roots.

It almost seems too elementary to point this out, but the object of drying is to remove enough moisture from the leaves so that molds can't survive, enzymes can't go to work, and the processes of organic decay, which thrive on water, cannot set in as far as the resin is concerned.

Moisture being removed from the plant tissues must be converted to water vapor and then pass from the interior cells of the leaf on through the skin and the stomata and out into the air. The air which is to take up this water vapor should be circulating freely so that it doesn't get saturated and thus resist further uptake. If this happens, the leaves will not dry evenly and thoroughly. A second thing to watch for is that the temperature isn't too high.

If it is, the water vapor near the surface will boil off quickly, creating a dry gap between the surface of the leaf and the moist interior, causing the skin tissues to shrivel up and resist any further water passage. The water will then be trapped permanently in the interior of.the leaf, and the resin content will deteriorate far more rapidly than if it were not exposed to moisture.

Like all living plant material, marijuana leaves and flowering tops are mostly water. In addition, when harvested live, they contain a delightful complex of volatile and aromatic oils and many other components such as chlorophyll. These begin to break down immediately upon the death of the plant.

In the process of drying Cannabis, the object is to drive off water without disturbing the psychoactive molecules and their aromatic cousins, which constitute only about one tenth of one percent of the plant weight. The volatile oils of Cannabis are the substances which give flavor and aroma to the smoke, and are a large part of the enjoyment of smoking. All of the essential oils and psychoactive compounds of Cannabis are very sensitive to light, water, air, and heat. The drying of your marijuana is central to its ultimate quality.

The process is not complex. The key to successful drying is control of the environment, and time. A slow air-drying with minimal exposure to light, plenty of air circulation, a consistent 80-90° F. temperature, low humidity and careful handling will produce superior aroma and taste.

A well-ventilated drying environment doesn't mean one with breezes. The hanging flowers and leaves should not bob and sway, nor should dust devils dance in the fine shake on the floor.

While light should be kept to a minimum, when you do turn on a light to check for mold, you will want a good strong light. Also, when you are hanging the herb in the first place, be sure to leave room for yourself. Be able to inspect each piece without brushing against others.

If you discover mold on your marijuana, the mold you see will only be a forerunner of things to come. A few specks of mold anywhere in a closed environment usually means numerous colonies in a day or so. The discovery of mold on drying marijuana signals the need for a new drying approach immediately. By the use of shielded floor heaters (or whatever device is appropriate for you), the air temperature in the drying room should be raised to 110-120° F. Increase airflow around the plants and to the exhaust vents a bit. Use exhaust fans at the vents. Do not blow directly on the marijuana. Place sacks around any of the marijuana showing signs of mold but otherwise do not disturb it. Cut a few, small, narrow slits in the sacks to allow moisture to be driven off while containing any mold which might want to spore. Continue to dry at the high temperature until the marijuana is ready. If there is room, put an ultraviolet lamp or two in the room. This will prevent further colonies from forming while the heat is being raised. After the heat reaches 110-120° F., no new colonies will form. After the marijuana is dry to your satisfaction, remove it from the drying room and either put it in direct high sun for a few hours or put it under a sunlamp. Turn each piece gently to get maximum exposure to ultraviolet, just in case any hardy spores survived. Then store the marijuana in bundles as small as practical, just in case re-infestation occurs.

An alternative to the heat treatment for marijuana threatened by mold is to simply take the entire batch out into strong sunlight laying it out on white sheets or some other reflective surface (not concrete! Too hot, will destroy potency!). Sun-drying of moldy marijuana is an improvement over the fast indoor-dry because there will not be a lot of marijuana-smelling exhaust to deal with. On the other hand, a yard full of pot on sheets is hardly inconspicuous.

In any case if you have to heat-dry or sun-dry your crop, be ready to accept a harsher smoke with less flavor and perhaps lowered potency if exposure to the sun lasts more than a day.

One variation on sun-drying that is used effectively with tobacco (whose aromatic oils present similar problems) is to dry the plants in the sun, shaded by a cheesecloth awning. The same poles which support the awning support the lines on which the herb is hung. Shade-drying of marijuana with a mold problem is not effective, since the ultraviolet of direct sunlight is needed, but under warm, dry conditions, outdoor shade-drying of marijuana is every bit as good as indoor slow-drying as regards flavor, potency, and texture, and mold rarely forms in the first place.

The U.S. government has studied many aspects of marijuana, including the optimum drying conditions in an artificial environment.

Some friends and I built our first dryer on a farm outside Eugene, Oregon, and prevailed upon a good-hearted dope grower to let us dry several pounds of his fine crop as a trial run. Well, we didn't burn up his dope and it smoked pretty well.

Now, it is nice to have scientific confirmation of our blind flying.

The marijuana used in the state experiment was eight-week-old plants from Afghan seed. (The government has no problem getting good stock.) The plants were stripped of their leaves and air-dried at room temperature for one day. They were then ground through a 60 mesh sieve. (Not a good idea for smoking, but for this experiment the objective was measurement, not pleasure.)

The marijuana was oven-dried at various temperatures for varying lengths of time.

Weight loss of the THC was kept at a minimum by drying for 16 hours at 65° Centigrade.

In another part of the experiment, weight loss of the leaves themselves was measured. It was confirmed that 65° C. was the most effective temperature for

(Below)
Construction of
drying boxes

Curing
Marijuana

147

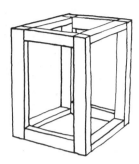

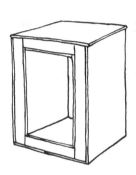

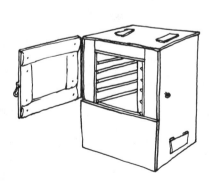

driving off excess moisture in the leaves without shrivelling them and destroying other constituents.

There is no indication in any of these experiments what the effects are of drying time and temperature upon plants of varying resin content. Nor is there a comparison of the drying characteristics of flowering tops and leaves. But it seems fair to assume that destruction of the THC would proceed at the same rate whatever the resin content, tops or the whole plant. Also, a 65° C. temperature is excessive when one takes all desirability factors into account. As mentioned before, a drying air temperature from 80-90° F. is very good. Different marijuana strains will vary, and the individual cultivator will want to play around with heat control a little.

Your plants should be dried to the point where the leaves crease readily when bent and break but not so dry that they crumble to the touch or the stems snap with one twist. When your plants have reached the proper stage of dryness, they are ready for curing. Curing is not a necessary operation in many cases — but when a plant, even after proper drying, still gives a heavy body effect, curing can be valuable in helping the clean high come through.

A number of books recommend flash-curing of freshly harvested marijuana, but I do not believe it is such a hot idea. It is too easy to end up with a pile of pre-smoked marijuana on the cookie sheet. Still, for folks in a rush for a rush, who simply must flash their stash, it's easy enough to do. Take the leaves (never flash tops) and spread them out on a cookie sheet so each leaf cluster is equally exposed. Turn the oven to broil and put them in, six inches under the broiler element. Do not let your attention wander, even for a minute. Don't answer the phone, don't get thirsty, don't get horny, nothing. Watch those leaves! As soon as they curl and you see the first wisp of smoke, get them out. Keep a hot pad on hand. If you have to look for one, it will be too late by the time you find it. When they go, they go up fast.

One of the main reasons I don't like flash-curing is that it really isn't curing. It's just fast drying. Curing is a biochemical process in which the chemical constituents of the resin and the plant material expand in several directions and mellow out. In short, well-cured dope may not be more potent than flash-cured, but it is far more pleasant to smoke.

The only time flashing your marijuana makes any sense is if you are going to eat it instead of smoking it. Since the smoke of marijuana is every bit as dirty and carcinogenic as that of tobacco, more and more people are eating rather than smoking. Most recipes call for an hour or so at a moderately high temperature, around 350° F. This is because raw marijuana requires heat to convert and release its psychoactive components. You can't just eat it raw and get off. If you are too rushed to cook, flashing your marijuana brings it to readiness quickly. It will require about five minutes. Spread it on a cookie sheet and place it six inches below the broiler element just as before. Watch it carefully for smoke. Remove it quickly when you sight the first wisp. Give it 10 seconds to cool and pop it back in. After five minutes of this treatment, it is ready to eat. How you go about making dried marijuana palatable is up to you. Mixing it with honey is the best I've come up with. It is best to eat marijuana on an empty stomach. You should eat about twice what you smoke for a comparable high. The high lasts far longer when eaten than when smoked, so you get back in time what you give up having to use more. The high is different, too — largely because your body does not have to contend with all that garbage in the smoke. Onset of the high takes about 30-45 minutes and it creeps up on you. You eat it, go about your business and all of a sudden you realize — ping!

In *The International Cultivators Handbook* I discussed the ancient Himalayan practice of curing flowering tops with goat dung. The flowers are buried in alternate layers with the dung in a pit with smoldering coals on the bottom. The pit is covered with a layer of dirt and the whole mess stews in its warm juices for several days. Well, the key to curing marijuana *is* heat and an enclosed space. However, it can be done very nicely without the goat dung, Thank Shiva!

The first step is to sort the plants. Be sure they are well-manicured, with all stems, branches, and as many of the seeds as possible removed. Separate the males if you have saved any.

Take a large green or black plastic bag and lay it out flat. Place the marijuana in the bag in layers with newspapers (not the color comic strips) or paper towels between the layers.

Spread out the material inside the bag evenly. Tape the open end of the bag shut and roll the bag lengthwise into as tight a roll as possible, the way you'd roll a sleeping bag. When you get a tight roll, tape it, and use an icepick to poke several dozen holes randomly through the entire roll.

The rolls of marijuana will need to be stashed in a warm but not hot place. Attics are good spots, so are backyard sheds, garages, etc. It is best to store the rolls high up in such places in order to derive maximum benefit from the dry heat. Air temperatures should not exceed 130° F. nor the marijuana more than 140° F. in the curing process. Poke a thermometer through one of the holes into the center, and check it occasionally.

During the curing, the plant material will change from bright green to mellow brown. The flavor will be much improved as will the odor of the smoke. Curing is not a necessary step. It is a refinement. Avoid sprinkling coca-cola or other sweet concoctions over the plants before curing. It doesn't help and the burning sugar when you smoke tastes terrible. This whole practice began with unscrupulous commercial growers who added sugar to their marijuana primarily to add weight and, secondarily to make compression easier. There are no advantages to the smoker at all.

After the fifth day, or sooner if they are getting too hot, the rolls should be undone, stirred around a lot, and re-rolled. This should be done for the next three or four days in a row. If the contents look or smell moldy, a day in the hot sun should take care of the problem. A sunlamp or strong sunlight will also do the job since it is the ultraviolet light that kills the mold. Don't re-roll such marijuana.

Most marijuana is ready after seven to 10 days of curing. The readiness of a particular batch will be a matter of judgment. Don't cure longer than 10 days. The decomposition of the plant material can proceed quickly to where you have an unsmokable, composted mess.

After unrolling the marijuana at the end of the curing process, spread it on clean sheets or mats in the shade or under indirect heat indoors, until it reaches your favorite smoking texture. Watch it carefully during this final stage of curing, turning the piles often. Get it in its storage containers as soon as it is ready.

All cultivators relish heavy, aromatic flowering spikes, but even the most top-heavy Cannabis plant needs her lower leaves, which are major energy-conversion organs for the manufacture of biological fuel. These broad lower leaves, however, remain low in potency throughout life, and are frequently treated as discards by people seeking the high-impact flowering tops alone.

In addition to the lower leaves of high-potency plants, cultivators are often faced with the question of what to do with culls from their crop — the low-potency males pulled to produce Sinsemilla females, perhaps some of the younger plants pulled to thin a field. Also, people who do not cultivate Cannabis can find themselves stuck with a purchase of low-potency marijuana which has to be smoked in nauseous quantities before even a slight buzz becomes apparent. Then, of course, there's that low-potency wild weed which grows profusely in so much of our Midwest and border state territory. For years people have been looking for a way to use wild weed effectively.

In the mid-70's, several teams of researchers began following up on rumors that street people in parts of the Northeast were boiling their marijuana in order to increase potency, and what they turned up was a process that works very effectively. There are a number of variations of the process, but the basics are quite simple.

Take a non-metallic container, such as a Pyrex bowl, and cover the cleaned marijuana with just enough distilled water so that no leaves are exposed. Bring the water to a boil, then reduce the heat to a simmer, and maintain the heat for several hours, adding hot water periodically to keep the leaf mass immersed. The whole process is better carried out in a darkened room, since light degrades THC quickly in the presence of heat and moisture. Three hours of low boiling will be enough. The leaves should be stirred frequently to assure even heating.

During the boiling period, a number of things happen. A great deal (30%) of the weight of the fresh or dried leaves of marijuana consist of sugars, pigment proteins and other water-soluble substances, and these are dissolved. This in itself increases the concentration of THC in the leaves once they are dried, since the leaves will weigh less after these substances are dissolved, but the THC which was in the leaves beforehand will not dissolve during boiling, and so will be concentrated. But the boiling does more than simply concentrate the existing THC. The marijuana leaves contain a great deal of THC-Acid, which isn't psychoactive; however, the heat of boiling converts this THC-Acid into psychoactive THC. Actually, boiling isn't absolutely necessary, since THC-Acid converts smoothly to THC at a temperature of 103-105° F. Boiling does help to dissolve the soluble, non-psychoactive substances in the leaves more so than soaking in 103° water, and in no way harms the psychoactive elements of the resin, so it is more desirable than it may seem at first. In fact, competent studies show that the boiling treatment increases the amount of available psychoactive THC in marijuana by up to 1.4 times the original content.

During boiling, some of the THC-Acid is liberated from the leaves and rises to the surface of the water, where it stays. It doesn't evaporate, but the heat does convert some of it to psychoactive form, and thus the marijuana tea produced by boiling is also psychoactive. An additional benefit derived from the boiling treatment is that the smoke obtained from the treated leaves is much cleaner than the smoke from fresh or dried leaves, since so much of the sugar and other substances are removed.

The boiled leaves will look shrivelled and brown-black after drying. Many people simply pour the contents of the boiling pot through some cheesecloth, retaining the liquid that is poured off and squeezing the leaves in the cheesecloth to remove the maximum amount of water, and then either spreading the leaves out on trays in a dark room to air-dry, or putting them in a nylon stocking and drying them with a hair-dryer. Whatever the drying method used, the leaves should be evenly dried, and if air-drying is used they should be turned frequently to prevent mold.

After the marijuana tea has cooled, it should be stored in the refrigerator to prevent mold. If this tea is taken on an empty stomach, about one cup, just before smoking a joint, the effects of the high will be increased and prolonged. For the more exotically inclined, an enema with the tea is a different kind of experience — quite effective.

Drinking or otherwise using marijuana tea makes sense only if you are sure that your herb has not been treated with poisons. If you are at all suspicious that your marijuana may have been chemically treated, the tea should be thrown away, as it can have concentrations of herbicide, especially if you have boiled down a good deal of water in the process of treating the marijuana.

The dried marijuana, even though it is shrivelled and dark, is used just like untreated marijuana for smoking, only it will be from 30-50% stronger because the original THC is more concentrated and because some of the THC-Acid has been converted to psychoactive form. Since scientific studies establish that none of the psychoactive resin elements in Cannabis are adversely affected by even prolonged boiling, this treatment will prove useful in any situation where low-quality marijuana is all that is available. This treatment doesn't produce tasty marijuana, but it is an effective way to use otherwise unusable marijuana.

The only serious harm done to our bodies by marijuana is caused by the gases in the smoke we inhale. Carbon monoxide is the principal harmful smoke element and it is a serious health threat. Carbon monoxide binds the hemoglobin in the blood, so that the red cells cannot carry the oxygen to the brain, organs, muscles, and other body systems. As the blood's hemoglobin becomes bound, its oxygen-carrying capacity is often drastically reduced, and the entire body's principal energy source is correspondingly diminished.

If smoking is chronic, the energy level in the body can be permanently depressed. All smoking, not just marijuana, does this.

People have used a combination of care and ingenuity in coping with the oxygen deprivation that accompanies smoking. The Oracle at Delphi in ancient Greece offered two fundamentals for living. The first was: Know thyself. The second was: Nothing in excess. Though this second maxim, no doubt, also includes moderation, the "middle road" is an excellent idea most of the time, if not always. Moderation in smoking speaks for and recommends itself. Ingenuity in reducing the side-effects of smoking has generally been limited to a vast array of pipes and devices designed to cool, mellow, and smooth the smoke inhaled by the pleasure/consciousness seeker. These instruments are generally effective at limiting the particulate matter reaching the lungs and mouth, but have very little impact on the carbon monoxide concentrations in the gases.

The key to dealing effectively with lowered energy levels due to carbon monoxide poisoning is to work to raise the oxygen-carrying capacity of that portion of the blood which does not have the hemoglobin bound by the insidious gas.

The first approach, which seems to come naturally to most people after a certain amount of marijuana experience, is the adaption of a natural balanced diet. The role of diet in building strong blood is complex and more involved than simply expansion of the oxygen-carrying capacities. Still, adequate nutrition is an important factor in maintaining body energy. Adoption of a natural diet, with chronic excess and highly refined foods eliminated, is part of the change experienced by many people on the path of marijuana experience.

A second approach to relieving oxygen deprivation is to have a body that is in good condition. With regular work, care and attention, any body is better able to absorb temporary toxicity and energy deficits. Body work seems to generate a sense of well-being, conducive to the creative use of high states without serious negative body consequences.

One of the nice things about body conditioning, whether Yoga, running, dancing or any holistic means, is that a person with a body in good condition just naturally feels better about life and, therefore, breathes more deeply. Remember those magic mornings when the light is radiant, the mind clear and calm, the air good, sweet, and fresh? Remember breathing deeply, gratefully, joyfully, happy for the one eternal moment. The center of our life is breath. All systems of body knowledge observe this elemental fact. Strength and depth of breath is directly linked to body condition. When breath is used to bring smoke into the body as well as oxygen, body condition takes on increased importance.

Another approach to enhancing the oxygen-carrying capacity of the blood is rarely used by smokers, but deserves more attention than it usually gets. Since carbon monoxide binds only part of the blood and ruins its oxygen capacity, it

152

makes sense that the remaining portion of the blood will take up oxygen in proportion to its availability in the breathing environment. A simple way to enrich the air which you give your body after smoking is to keep a small tank of oxygen around. After smoking, being sure all butts and embers are out, crack the valve and take a dozen deep breaths of an oxygen-air mixture. Hold the breaths deep and long. Open up your lungs to the life-giving oxygen just as you just opened them to the consciousness-altering smoke.

There are two advantages to this approach. In the first place, the body impact of the CO and other gases and particulate matter is significantly reduced. Body processes are greatly improved. The second advantage of taking oxygen is that the high of marijuana is, in many cases, augmented. The high seems cleaner, brighter, and more creatively manageable. But don't overdo oxygen — you can get in organ trouble remaining too long with oxygen-rich air in your lungs.

A less expensive and only slightly less effective oxygen practice is to take up a breathing discipline. Most of these disciplines, however, require that a person abstain from smoking anything and, therefore, are unavailable at certain levels to those who smoke marijuana. If one chooses to eat marijuana rather than smoke it, breathing disciplines will still be effective (especially since one's CO intake will be limited to the usual car-truck-bus-industrial exhaust in the air).

While on this subject of marijuana and our bodies, it seems time to give some attention to the phenomenon all marijuana fans know and love/hate: the Munchies. The Blind Munchies. That irresistable urge to eat ravenously which strikes about a half hour after smoking,

perhaps 90 minutes after eating, marijuana.

The midnight ice cream run, usually for Jamoca Almond Fudge or Triple Chocolate Swirl. Giant pepperoni pizzas inhaled in 15 minutes and then, donuts for dessert. Who has not gobbled more candy in an hour than was ever dreamt of by a child? Who has not, after the Munchies, been sick for days?

The Blind Munchies. What they are in the language of science and medicine is a hypoglycemic reaction, ranging from mild to severe depending on body state, amount of marijuana and the biochemistry of the particular stash.

Once the Munchies are tagged as induced hypoglycemic reaction, the approach to their moderation and control is known. Simply, when your body goes into a low blood-sugar state, what it needs is a bit of very accessible protein to take up and convert to blood sugars needed to get back in balance. When most of us get the Blind Munchies our little voices inside scream for sweets, not protein. This is because, by the time hypoglycemic shock has set in, the body wants sugars and wants them right away. Sweet wine merchandizers know this, and exploit us this way, as do so-called soft-drink companies, and many others. So the messages of the body combine with the deep and often suppressed craving for sweets most of us have. The mind interprets the body's need and promptly consumes large amounts of refined sweets, far more than the system can handle. The person gets whipsawed between the two states of low blood sugar and excessive blood sugar, which is toxic.

The accessible protein can easily be provided by taking in 20-30 grams of easily assimilated protein just before marijuana use. This is most simply done using protein wafers or tablets, though a banana, an egg, some tuna, or many other foods would do. But these foods may not be as readily drawn upon as pure protein in powder or liquid form. The cheapest, and best source is yeast blended in a drink. With the precautionary step of having some protein in the stomach, much of the impact of the Munchies can be avoided, and the gorging and weight gain so many people find to be an undesirable side-effect of getting stoned can be reduced or eliminated.

Dealing with the psychological need to be satiated, often with sweets, may be more involved than just building up to drinking an ounce of yeast, or popping a few protein tabs. In close analysis, much of this behavior is an affair of the soul.

A final sensible precaution that smokers of The Herb may want to know about entails the use of vitamin C. Most of us know that vitamin C is essential if we smoke and many of us take large amounts. That's the problem. Our bodies can't store vitamin C and will excrete any of the vitamin that cannot be used within about an hour of ingestion. In the process, crystals may accumulate in the kidneys, unless copious amounts of water are taken in. So, while the body may need several grams a day, if all the vitamin C is taken at one time, the body may take only 300-400 milligrams and pass the rest into the urine. For the rest of the day there would be no vitamin C available, though the stress and toxicity would continue throughout the day.

Once again, the solution is simple. Use time-released vitamin C, and drink lots of liquids. This insures that all of the vitamin remains available over the period that the body's need exists. The vitamin will not be excreted wholescale into the urine and be wasted. Level of intake of vitamin C is a subject of controversy, but one gram time-release in the morning and one at night should not be excessive, especially for a smoker.

There have been a number of scientific experiments in recent years which point decisively to the best ways of storing marijuana for long periods of time. While the studies themselves are technical and are oriented toward laboratory procedures, cultivators can benefit from the discoveries.

The first principle developed by the researchers is that the handling of the marijuana is very important. The glands which contain the resin are very effective containers and protect the components from oxidation, moisture, and light. But these glands will burst under only slight pressure and it is inevitable that many of them will be broken open during harvesting and drying. But if you want your marijuana to last, take care to treat it gently as possible in all stages of handling.

Of course, many methods of preparation, particularly traditional Eastern styles, involve trampling and compressing the fresh marijuana to release the resin. This is done because of the commercial value of aroma and texture and not because long-term storage is desired. In fact, most commercial Ganja will deteriorate within a year to the point where it is not smokable.

The most important negative factor in the storage environment of marijuana is light. This is true whether the Cannabis is stored in herbal form, extract, or solution. In the case where Cannabis is stored in extract and solution form, the effect of exposure to ordinary indirect sunlight is dramatic. In a number of experiments, the THC content of resin solutions went from a healthy 5-10% to practically zero in as little as a week of exposure to the level of light found in an ordinary northern exposure room. Experiments with Cannabis in herbal form showed far less dramatic drops in THC but did demonstrate that over a period of 6 to 12 months, light is the most significant factor in degeneration of THC content. Cultivators will do well to store their marijuana in a dark place or in a container reasonably impervious to light.

Another important environmental factor in the storage of Cannabis is the temperature in the storage area. There is no particular advantage to keeping your stash in the fridge. In fact, the best storage conditions seem to be right at ordinary room temperature, about 65° F. It is important to avoid high temperatures for even short-term storage. Temperatures of over 100° F. will cause significant degeneration of the psychoactive principles if they persist for more than a few weeks. The exception to this rule is the high temperatures found in the curing process. Under the special enclosed conditions desirable for curing, high temperatures have a most useful effect in converting cannabinols to THC. But for long-term storage of marijuana, high temperatures are out.

While we're talking about storage temperature, let me mention a problem more or less widespread. A few years ago a popular book on marijuana recommended that people who wanted to make superdope should put their dope in a closed container with some dry ice for a while. This was supposed to vastly increase the potency of the stuff. What really happens when you do this is that a lot of carbon dioxide crystals form in the cells of the plant material. When the dope is smoked the carbon dioxide is released as carbon monoxide, a toxic and deadly gas, present in the combustion of all organic materials but present in huge amounts in grass which has received the dry ice treatment. Also, there is no increase in potency. Clearly, this is not a good idea.

The last important factor in the storage of marijuana is oxidation by air. Many experiments show this is a primary cause of degeneration of the active compounds in marijuana. To counteract this problem requires that the cultivator be sure that the container he uses for storage is as airtight as possible. Even ordinary containers can be made reasonably airtight by using a piece of wax paper under the lid as a gasket. Also it is easy and cheap enough to buy almost perfectly airtight containers from canning supply sources.

To summarize: airtight storage of gently handled marijuana in a dark place at room temperature is ideal for keeping THC content of your marijuana at a peak for the longest possible time. The same applies for preserving seed vitality.

Science marches on! Italian researchers looking into what happens to the Δ^9-THC in marijuana when a joint is smoked, discovered some very interesting things which conform to what most heads have known for a long time.

In this experiment, joints weighing 300 mg. were machine smoked at varying inhalation strengths.

Depending upon the strength of the inhalation, from 50% to 80% of the Δ^9-THC was burned up in the fiery tip of the joint as it ate its way into the marijuana. This confirms the general knowledge that it is best to smoke a joint with a minimum of drag, keeping the fire at the tip as cool as possible. Not only does this technique lessen the amount of Δ^9-THC destroyed by fire but it also means that a minimum of harmful combustion by-products are drawn into the lungs of the smoker. In addition, the temperature of the smoke passing over the front teeth of the smoker is kept low. High-temperature smoke has been firmly identified as a contributing factor in poor dental health in smokers of all kinds.

The second interesting discovery of the Italians is that only 6% of the Δ^9-THC is lost in the smoke that floats away from the end of the joint. Six percent loss is not an amount to be concerned about and one must wonder about the real value of the many smoking toys on the market whose primary function is to prevent the escape of smoke from the joint. Still, 6% is 6%. There's no need to throw away that power-hitter just yet.

Then, there is the roach. I must confess right here that for years I thought roach eating was little more than a nasty habit ranking high on my personal nausea scale. Well, I was wrong. I mean, my aesthetic reaction still feels valid but these same dauntless Italians have determined that a full 21% of the Δ^9-THC in a joint is trapped and stabilized in the roach. It looks like that nasty habit makes sense. I'm not saying I'm going to start chewing the gummy little numbers but I can go along, less nauseously, with anyone who does.

Down to the moment of truth. Fifty percent of the Δ^9-THC is incinerated, 6% floats away and jimmies the depth perception of spiders on the ceiling, and 21% is trapped in the roach. That leaves 23% of the Δ^9-THC to do what smoking a joint is all about. Twenty-three percent of the active ingredient in marijuana makes it into the lungs of the smoker.

So that's the story of the joint, and what happens to the Δ^9-THC in marijuana as it is smoked in this fashion. I've tried to find research on other methods of ingestion to try to determine the relative efficiency of the joint, but so far there seems to be no hard data.

My guess is that pipes of all kinds offer a trade-off — hotter fire for less filtration. In other words, the joint which is drawn on gently does not burn at as high a temperature as a pipe put under equal draw. Also, the fire applied to a pipe goes directly onto the marijuana, and has to be applied many times throughout the

(Below)
Relative THC content

smoking of a given quantity, while in ordinary circumstances a joint only needs to be lit one time. This implies that more Δ^9-THC is lost in combustion in pipes of all forms than is lost to combustion in a joint.

On the other hand, the smoke from the combusted material goes directly to the lungs of the smoker, unimpeded except with dirty pipes or water pipes, and thus much of the 21% which is trapped in the roach must go directly to the smoker who is using the pipe. In a water pipe, or one using any sort of filter, some of the Δ^9-THC would be trapped. In addition, any pipe designed to cool the smoke in any way is going to cause some Δ^9-THC loss through condensation and deposition on the interior walls of the pipe.

smoke 6%

ash 50%

roach 21%

inhaled 23%

It is unclear which smoking method would prove superior in matched tests. My guess is that it would be the joint.

I have several reasons for this opinion.

First, most people prefer joints, as far as I can tell. This implies a mass subjective judgment. Since the goal of most smokers is to get high, chances are a joint does it better.

Second, it has always seemed to me that a given amount of marijuana burns faster and hotter in a pipe than a joint.

The third reason I have for preferring the joint is esoteric. I think the shape is important to people. From Moses to Glinda the Good Witch, people have been drawn to the archetypal figure of the wand or rod.

A large diversity of human experience centers around this shape. All manner of rod-shaped objects and rod-expressed functions are intimately involved with our lives. From time before history, people have gone into the world, their power increased and their fears eased by the wands cradled in their hands, and by the images of wands the human mind conceived or the eye discovered in the natural world. Through the wand, the individual's power is inspired, and expressed. The wand is one of the most versatile of objects (spear, pen, totem, crutch, Louisville slugger). Each acts as a channel for particular levels and configurations of human energy.

Energy flow in many people is chaotic. The use of wands focuses and smooths the flow.

As we have become increasingly civilized, we have become progressively deprived of the satisfaction of the wand. We once hunted with wands, planted with wands, played with wands. Now we wear suits and dresses, work in cities, and have no real wands to fill our hands.

Wands come in all sizes but they share basic functions. They are used to touch, to connect, to register one's intent upon the physical world. Wands enable us to transform the world into the terms of our will, to work upon the world's inertia and momentum, to touch its otherness. Wands allow projection and penetration into the physical world. They invoke the reality of our presence.

The popular mind conceives of wands as the instruments of fairies, a twinkling stick that goes ping, used to transform mice into horses and pumpkins into carriages. But if all consciousness could be focused through the wand upon the point described by the end of the wand — great power could be called forth. Magic is possible still.

Today great business empires are devoted to providing decadent modern man with wands made small, elegant and inconspicuous. The cigarette cult depends upon the profound nature of the need for wands to keep its tenacious grip upon people having deprived them of true, herbal tobacco. Through the various ingenious instruments designed to facilitate consumption of the chemical-vegetable blend called tobacco, the wand-need of people is met, seduced, and quieted. The combination of toxic and narcotic properties and wand-qualities of smoking, whether cigarette, pipe, or cigar, is a powerful satisfaction of the need to express energy.

The expression of energy is not in itself a positive act. Witness the gross destruction of life by the cigarette cult. But the expression of energy itself is a positive impulse. Its channeling may well take negative turns but the original need is organic and positive. In the instance of the cigarette cult, where many of its members understand the destruction they bring upon themselves, vast sums are spent on propaganda to make cult members substitute enjoyable fantasies for disturbing inner realizations.

The gun is a specialized wand as are all such instruments of killing. While it is true the gun throws a spherical object, objects as projectiles take on rod-like qualities.

Young children discover the joys of the wand very early and use the power of this shape to discover much about themselves and the world. Gun play, stick play, jabbing, prying, reaching, connecting, hitting, and other activities children get into with such satisfaction involve the wand.

One of the initial uses of the wand was for doodling in the prehistoric dirt. The discovery that lines made in the dirt made sense to others must have been startling. From this to painting on cave walls and scratching on clay tablets must have been a short leap for the developing mentality of early peoples. Art and writing probably descend from the inherent power of the wand to awaken and channel human energy. A stick in the hand may have been the initial stimulus to the development of the human mentality and was probably the key to the elaboration of ego, which is necessary before effective communication and great art can take place. One wonders if the enlightenment of these early doodlers in the dirt might have been partly because they had just come from the fire where they had breathed the smoke of the strong plant together.

So, other than its efficiency as a dry-distillation instrument, the joint is also a powerful, magical shape. Like all magic the joint has a dark, and a light aspect. The act of preparing Cannabis for smoking in a joint connects us, whether we know it or not, with an ancient human lineage. One wishing to do magic through the act of smoking will want to be aware of the significance of the act.

Small scale marijuana production can be vastly simplified and enhanced by installation of a grid of buriable soaker pipe. This is not the same thing as regular soaker pipe, designed only to be used on top of the ground. This new low technology is simple, but truly revolutionary. It will radically alter marijuana cultivation, just as it is doing with everything from vegetable farming to ornamental hedges, from cotton production to aquaculture.

Buriable soaker pipe is of different construction, and varies in quality, durability, and price. There are several brand names on the market, including "Aquapore" and "Leaky Pipe." For strength and proven durability in a wide variety of agricultural situations, one should take a look at the "Leaky Pipe" brand of soaker pipe. Leaky Pipe is manufactured by Entek Corporation in Grapevine, Texas, and in Iceland and Belgium. It is made from recycled automobile tires and a special polymer resin, and it has dozens of remarkable applications. It is cheap and easily installed, and resists clogging effectively. It seems to last almost forever as long as it's buried. Which makes sense, considering that buried tires will probably outlast mankind. Buried soaker pipe conserves water and delivers it directly to the plant root zone, where the easy availability of just the right amount of water radically improves total plant mass yield. The low moisture soil conditions discourage plant predators and disease, and encourage aeration and positive soil activities such as earthworms. With buried soaker pipe, water, nutrients, warm air, and carbon dioxide can be delivered through the same system. It can be used in multi-level environments, and will leak evenly along a great length of pipe under very little head, or water pressure.

With this buried soaker pipe, plant growth in both indoor and outdoor locations will be vividly enhanced. The plants will be highly insect resistant, and will flower with more vigor than ever before. The flowering plants will regenerate more vigorously after their first cutting, and the plant's season will be radically extended. (This characteristic, by the way, is not all good — pay attention that the marijuana plants aren't next to plantings that will be dying off in September/October, leaving an emerald green spot sticking out for any passing satellite to see.)

Before anything else, calculate the technical factors for the particular installation. Since everybody will have a somewhat different set of requirements, I will present several examples, along with the necessary calculations, and encourage those interested to work from there into their unique situation.

Example #1: The 2–6 Plant Backyard
Let's say that there is a backyard with a good layout — fences or walls in the right places, trees which overhang without blocking sun, and a good growing environment. With Leaky Pipe, one is totally free to site individual plants in the most advantageous locations, and to plant them however desired.

Assume that in this yard there are several great locations with privacy and excellent solar exposure, but these locations have very poor ground conditions. One of them is a concrete driveway, the other a rocky part of the yard, and the third an area where nothing has ever grown. In these areas, plants will probably grow best in a container. But there are several other great growing areas where there is excellent soil, right alongside the garden, so growing in the ground is appropriate in this location.

When one is potting the container plants, simply place a loop of Leaky Pipe into the container before adding the soil mixture. Leave both ends of the pipe protruding just above the edge of the container.

To hook up the system, connect the individual containers with lengths of regular, non-soaker hose. At the water source chosen — probably an outside faucet — attach a Y-connector with independent valves. Valve #1 will be used to put water through the containerized plant system. Valve #2 will be used to put water into the system of ground sites. To connect the container system, run regular hose from one branch of the Y-connector to the first container. When all the containers are attached together, using regular pipe in between and Leaky Pipe in the containers, finish the system off by attaching a 12" length of regular pipe to the outlet side of the last container. Now just tie the system off by crimping and tying this last little length of hose. Turn on the water source at low pressure, then open the Y-valve to the container system.

The garden area or ground growing sites should be served by a different system from the one watering the container plants, because ground sites like fertile plugs and garden beds will have different water draw requirements, different soil/growing media mechanics, and a different nutrient cycle from the container plants. Installation of buriable soaker pipe in a ground site is simply a matter of burying the pipe so that it doesn't crimp, and attaching regular hose lengths where the water must run on the surface. Soaker pipe can be installed easily in a garden by burying lengths of it about 8" deep, on 30–36" centers in soil with good percolation qualities, 18–24" centers in soil compacted and poorly aerated.

When all of your soaker pipe has been buried, connecting it to the water source is a matter of the system's layout. If there are two parallel lengths buried in a garden bed, a simple Y- or T-connector is all that is needed to attach the regular hose running from the faucet to the garden. If there are three or more buried parallel lengths of buried pipe, a T-connector will need to be attached to the end of each, with sections of either regular hose as a header run across the top of the garden.

At the far end of the growing bed, if the system stops there, crimp and tie off the ends of the buried pipes, and bury the ends themselves. Mark the spots where the ends are buried, for future reference. If one is putting water through the garden site, and on to one or more other ground sites, one should simply continue with sections of regular hose alternating with buried soaker pipe at the sites.

Be sure that all installation is done so that water flows from the high end of the system to the low end. The highest end of buried soaker pipe should be the entry point for water under pressure; the lowest end of the lowest buried soaker pipe installation should be the tie-off point.

Now the basic delivery rate for the system must be determined, which means determining what water pressure, for how long a watering period, will produce the best water delivery for the plants. The containerized plants will not need anywhere as much water as the ground plantings, but their water needs are more critical. Watering is a major source of stress for containerized marijuana, and stress of the wrong kind is a principle reason for poor quality. The main source of stress comes from loving, careful, but erratic cultivators who water by inspiration, or who engage in other forms of erratic, guesswork watering. When the plant's watering is erratic, the deprivation/drowning cycle is a withering

kind of stress. Under these circumstances, the moisture level rises rapidly to
a peak, and then gradually declines until
the next unpredictable time water is
added. The plant is in a situation of
continually declining soil moisture
reserves, with varying amounts of water
pouring in at unpredictable intervals. It
can never get its respiration/transpiration
cycles in phase with its uptake of
moisture, nutrients, and soil gasses. This
situation is a source of high grade stress,
resulting in an exhausted plant without
strong reserves, and without much
flowering energy. The randomness of the
watering cycle is a major contributor to
low plant energy in indoor marijuana
cultivation.

Emitter-drip systems do a better job of
delivering a steady supply of water, but
don't work well when buried, and
therefore tend to either overwater or
underwater the container soil. In addition,
drip irrigation in indoor situations tends
to promote salting up of the container
soil. In outdoor situations drip is easy to
spot, erratic in performance, and
unforgiving of crimps; it tends to clog, it
fares poorly in multilevel applications,
and it is expensive.

Until Leaky Pipe and other buriable
soaker pipe systems came along, there
was no way to achieve perfect moisture in
indoor growing soil. The ideal level of soil
moisture is just enough to supply the
plant's drawing requirements, and
enough reserve to promote healthy soil
functions, and not one drop more. This
balance can be maintained by varying
moisture input to the system as
environmental conditions change.

When the plant in nature needs
moisture, it exerts increased hydrostatic
pressure on available moisture in the soil,
and draws this moisture toward its root
system. With Leaky Pipe buried in the

plant's root moisture zone, sweating
moisture under low pressure, each plant
will exert a draw on soil moisture in its
container in a steady, two-cycle daily
pattern. The plant's draw on soil moisture
will begin to rise in the early morning, and
will continue to rise until after midday,
when it will start to decline. By evening
the draw will have fallen to 50% of its high
point near midday, and by midnight the
draw on soil moisture will be at a low
point. From there, the level of activity in
the slumbering plant begins to rise, as a
new day approaches.

With a buried soaker pipe system, one
can determine the rate of delivery of
water directly to the plant root zone by
varying the water pressure in the system.
This means that one is able to keep
moisture coming to the plants in any
situation, by figuring out their water-draw
cycle, and by using a simple timer to
begin the flow of water when their draw is
rising, and to shut the flow off after the
peak of the day's water use is past — say
6–8 in the evening.

There are almost infinite variations
possible on the basic system design just
discussed. With such a system, a
personal crop of homegrown marijuana is
within almost everyone's reach.

Example #2: The 6–10 Plant Basement or Attic

Leaky Pipe is a breakthrough for indoor
cultivators, because it takes the hassle out
of watering the plants — a major problem
with indoor growing. With a system of this
type, one is free to leave the plants for
weeks at a time, as long as the lights are
on a timer and the pressure feed set
properly for the water system. It doesn't
matter if one is using containers or beds,
soil or hydroponic media, the root
environment for your plants can be
significantly improved with use of
buriable soaker pipe for water and

nutrient delivery, soil aeration and carbon dioxide delivery, and other simple but very productive crop management activities.

For purposes of illustration, let's say that a person is going to set up a growing area in the basement. Since most basements have a water faucet, installing the system is a simple matter of positioning the containers and lighting, putting the Leaky Pipe segments into the containers before filling them, and hooking up the system as in Example #1. If plants are growing in a bed rather than in containers, simply lay the Leaky Pipe into the bed before filling with the soil or artificial growing medium.

If plants are growing indoors in a multi-level setup, at varying heights, one would have to plan the system so that the water is delivered first to the highest plants, flowing downhill to the lowest. *This assures good pressure throughout the system, and is a very important detail.*

If plants are growing indoors in a location where there is no water faucet, one can feed a Leaky Pipe system from a water tank simply by elevating it above the system. The greater the length of the system, the more elevation is needed on the tank to get pressure. For a small system of a dozen plants or fewer, one should need no more than 24" of elevation above the highest point in the system. With one system of 15–20 plants in containers, at least 36" elevation is needed. Check out the elevation needed in any situation simply by installing the system, but leaving the dirt out of the last container. When everything is in place, open the valve on the water tank and give the system a few hours to adjust. If the last length of Leaky Pipe in the last container is sweating away at a good rate, there is good pressure. If, after a few hours, the last segment is still dry, one would need to elevate the water supply

tank a bit more. Repeat this adjustment as often as required to get a good sweat at the end of the system, then fill in the last container, and it is set up to plant or transplant.

Example #3: The Guerilla Garden
Assuming there is an ideal outdoor growing site in all other respects, the use of Leaky Pipe can add that extra measure of security most guerilla gardens lack. Whenever there is television coverage of marijuana patches which have been busted, they almost invariably are nice orderly clumps of bright green marijuana standing out from the surrounding foliage, easily spotted from the air. Guerilla marijuana is usually planted this way because the plants are easier to water and care for when they are growing all together; however, it sure makes detection easy.

With a combination of Leaky Pipe and ordinary pipe, a guerilla farmer can take full advantage of natural cover, and can seek out the ideal growing spots in an environment. The principles are exactly the same as in example #1 — for the long runs between plants, use ordinary hose, and at each planting site, simply cut the desired length of Leaky Pipe and install it either in the ground or in the container. The water source, which will probably be a tank in a guerilla situation, should be installed above the most elevated site, and the water in the system should feed from high to low. That's all there is to having the most versatile, dependable water supply ever available for guerilla farming. A major advantage of this system over all others is that it is extremely water conservative. This means fewer trips to refill the water tank, which is a major security consideration.

When choosing a guerilla growing location, one is clearly going to be seeking a poorly traveled spot, which may mean that conventional growing options are very limited. Leaky Pipe is the most versatile, low tech tool I have ever seen. With a 100' length of this pipe, a few hose connectors and several hundred feet of conventional water hose, a person could lay out several dozen sites over an area of a hundred square yards. Once the sites are chosen, the lengths of regular connector hoses with the pieces of cut Leaky Pipe at each site can be assembled. When this system is completely assembled and laid out on the ground, the water source should be elevated to where it will give good pressure throughout the system, and the feeder hose for the system should be connected.

The system should be given a few hours to reach equilibrium, and then checked to compare the amount of oozing high up in the system with the amount near the low end. With proper elevation, there is a problem-free system.

This isn't to say that wild animals won't chew through the hose, or tip over the tank, or eat the buds. It certainly isn't to say that wild-eyed dope fiends won't find the patch, and declare harvest time has arrived, nor that drug-fighting commandos won't descend from the skies to blast the patch, and the surrounding countryside and watershed, with designer chemicals.

Example #4: The 1/10 Acre Plot
Let's say that I intend to make the big move — to grow a sizeable amount of marijuana outdoors. I intend to use a level, well-hidden .10 acre piece of ground near my barns and residence to produce a crop. I have chosen this ground because it is next to a 50 gpm well which I use for my residential and family gardening needs, but not for general farm irrigation.

I live in a very hot region, and plants around here transpire relatively large quantities of water at the height of the season, so I will need a system which delivers the optimum amount of water to my crop. This means that I will want to lay my pipe on closely-spaced centers, and use a large diameter pipe. A simple calculation for the footage of pipe required is: Square footage to be irrigated (.10 acre = 4,356 square feet) divided by distance between centers. For .10 acre to be irrigated on 4' centers, about 1,100' of pipe will be needed, 3' centers will require about 1,500' of pipe, and 2' centers will take roughly 2,200'.

The best way to choose the proper distance between centers for a system is to perform a simple little experiment. Simply take a 10–20' section of soaker pipe, plug the far end and install a hose coupling at the near end, then bury the hose at an even depth in the center of the ground which is going to be planted. Then turn on the water at low pressure, and wait for a few days. After the pipe and soil have had a week to stabilize, simply use a shovel to determine how far to either side the moisture zone has moved. If there is good moisture at low pressure 18" on either side of the pipe, one can feel confident in planning maximum 3' centers. If the moisture zone is only 12" either side of the pipe, one will need to lay the laterals on 2' centers. Lay the pipe far enough apart to avoid extensive overlapping of the moisture zones, which would create potential wet spots, but not so far apart that there are gaps between the moisture zones, which would create dead spots.

To calculate the amount of water which can be delivered, begin with the fact that 17,000 gallons per acre equals 1" of rainfall on that acre, or: 17,000 gallons per acre equals 1 acre per inch, or 1,700 gallons per .10 acres equals 1 acre per inch. Assuming constant irrigation, you divide 1,700 gallons by 168 hours per week, and find that it will take approximately 10 gallons per hour to produce the required 1 acre per inch per week. Since I have a 50 gpm well, it will take less than 1 minute per hour of the well's output to water my acreage with 1 inch per week. One's own water requirements could be calculated in the same way.

The next step is to estimate the amount of water which the field will need on a weekly basis. Clearly, as the season progresses, the sun gets hotter, the days get longer, and the plant mass growing on my acreage will increase — all factors which will increase the water requirements of my crop throughout the growing season. Most of the studies I have seen conclude that marijuana under conditions of intense sun and a semi-arid environment consumes and transpires between 1 and 3 acres per inches per week, on a per-acre basis. Under highly ensolated, semi-arid conditions such as we encounter in the southwest, I have estimated that my plants will require at least 3 acres per inches per acre per week in mid-summer, which means that I will have to devote about 2 minutes per hour of pumping capacity in order to maintain my 4,300 square feet (.10 acre) plot during the hottest times of the year. How much water an individual crop will consume is a factor of so many variables that it isn't practical to offer a simple formula. However, it should be clear that even a low capacity well can provide enough water for effective irrigation of marijuana acreage when using the Leaky Pipe system.
So, now that I have decided that I need 2,200' of pipe, and have had it delivered, my next step is to install the system. Entek Corporation sells a very effective Leaky Pipe planter for $1,000, or will furnish plans for those who want to build their own. All that is required is elementary welding to be able to build your own installer for less than $150. On the other hand .10 acre is not all that big a plot of

ground, and installing my Leaky Pipe by hand-digging the trenches is not out of the question either.

But let's assume that I have built my own installer, and with a reel mounted on the back of my 16 horse-powered tractor, I now lay in the Leaky Pipe laterals at a depth of 8" on 2' centers. With my laterals laid, I now install my plugs at the far end of the grid, my Tees and connectors at the near end, and my PVC Header main pipe, my flow control meter, my backflow preventer valves, and a set of 200 Micron filters. I then level the ground by compacting the trenches, and I turn on the system for a full scale test. I monitor the standpipes I have installed at the beginning and end of the laterals to check for blockage, and when satisfied that there is good flow, I tie off these standpipes but leave them intact for future use if required.

At this point, my irrigation grid is in place and ready to operate. My costs have been as follows:

1. 2,200' of 5/8" diameter Leaky Pipe @ $.30/foot=	$660
2. 2' centers will require approximately 20 Tee connectors @ $.50 =	$ 10
3. 40' of 2" PVC Header Pipe @ $.25/foot =	$ 10
4. Two 200 Micron line filters @ $15/each =	$ 30
5. One 2" Header Line flow meter @	$ 50
6. Materials For Leaky Pipe installer @	$150
7. 20 each plugs & standpipes @ $1 each =	$ 20
8. Miscellaneous (backflow preventer valves etc.)	$ 50

My total costs at this point have been $980. I am probably going to want to add another couple of items to my field, but these are refinements to the basic system.

The first option I will want to add is a Nutrient Feeding Pump, placed in line between the Flow meter and the filters, at a cost of $100 for an efficient unit.

I will also want to add a passive solar heat sink, located on the low point of the grid

— probably in the center of the far side of the laterals grid. I will build this heat sink by excavating a trench approximately 10' by 6' by 6' deep. Into this trench I will lay a 6 mil poly liner, and two grids of pipe — the first is a heat input grid, and the second is a heat outtake grid. Once the grids are laid in and secure, I will fill the trench with crushed rock, average diameter 1–2". When the trench is filled, a poly liner is laid over the top of the rock, and the passive solar hot air collectors are connected to the heat input grid as shown. The pump which will move hot air from the collectors to the crushed rock sink, will also move the heat from the rock sink into the Leaky Pipe grid when needed. In this system I will want to move my hot air to all parts of the field at approximately equal temperatures, which means I cannot simply feed heat direct from my sink into the front of the grid. If I did, the progressive heat loss as the air moved into the grid would mean that the back parts of the field would get little if any benefit. Consequently, I will be adding several Header Heat-carrying laterals parallel to my Leaky Pipe laterals to efficiently transport my heat to each sector of the field, so as not to develop too great a temperature gradient across my field. In a larger field, I might have to space several heat sink/solar panel units at strategic locations around the perimeter of the field.

The approximate cost of this single unit Passive solar installation is:

1. 40 Cubic Yards Crushed Rock @ $2/Yard =	$ 80
2. One Solar Hot Air Panel @	$150
3. Air Pump & controller mechanisms @	$200
4. Poly Liner @	$ 50
5. Miscellaneous @	$100

Total cost of the Solar Season Extension system is approximately $580. With this system I will be able to selectively bleed hot air to the root zones of my field when even the ambient air temperature over the field falls below 50 degrees F. By mixing outside air with the hot air from the sink I will be able to control the temperature of the air moving in the grid, and thus will be able to keep the plant root zone at optimum heat levels even during severe cold.

With this + or – $1,500 investment, a grower in any productive area will be able to produce an excellent marijuana crop, or any other crop desired, with great efficiency and predictable results. Of course, the major problem in growing a unit this size is the potential loss of the crop, plus the legal hassles associated with even personal marijuana growing in most places today. I am presenting this large-scale growing option out of respect for the diverse interests of my readers; however, I seriously recommend that one consider growing small, personal-size rather than commercial scale crops, and then only in areas which recognize the issues of individual liberty, at least to a degree. With a small plot of marijuana intended for personal, private consumption, the issue is truly one of personal liberty; with a large plot, it is an issue of whether or not you are free to deal.

If one is interested in finding out more about the applications of Leaky Pipe to conventional growing situations, or would like information on the various types of growing kits which are available, write directly to the manufacturer:

Entek Corporation
Department CM
P.O. Box 879
Grapevine, Texas 76051

Just one thing — please don't write asking these folks any questions about marijuana cultivation using their product.

Grafting
with
Cannabis

Multiple
Tops
Graft

165

New ideas in marijuana cultivation had the impact of the Warmke Hops-Hemp grafting experiments reported in the earlier editions of the *Handbook*. Although my early beliefs in the source of the potency of the plant produced by these grafts were in error, nevertheless the idea of grafting with marijuana has proved successful in many ways.

This chapter arises out of a great deal of research, as well as personal observation and experience. I present the information in the spirit of inquiry, which I trust is apparent throughout the *Handbook*, rather than as a definitive description of all workable Cannabis grafts. There's lots of interesting work yet to be done.

Grafting is not a difficult operation, provided the plants used are compatible both in tissue structure and biochemical makeup. A third requisite is that both gross and minor fluid-carrying tissue match up closely enough that a maximum flow of fluids through the graft is permitted.

Cultivators have discovered that grafting makes sense when you want to work with combinations of plant characteristics. For instance, one might desire a very potent plant that is very squat in profile. Or one might wish to combine one plant, not terribly potent but with a very strong stem and deep root system, with another plant from a strain notable for the potency of its flowering tops. In fact, in just about any closed breeding situation where one or more of the desirable features are on each of two plants, the grafting approach is preferable to any of the more complex manipulations that can be performed.

Perhaps the most useful (as well as most difficult) grafts is one which allows a cultivator to grow several strains of marijuana on a single stem — the multiple tops graft.

Failure of this graft is most often due to mismatching the fluid-carrying tissues of the young top being grafted and the older host plant. Nevertheless, this graft is not too hard to perform and a success rate of about one out of three attempts can be achieved. This graft has the advantage of not involving the main stem of the host plant in trauma.

The host plant should be of sturdy parentage, such as Hawaiian, Thai, or Panamanian (Lowland Colombian). Out of a dozen or so of these plants which you have started, applying the usual selection criteria, you will have identified the most vigorous and healthy plant by the sixth week.

Somewhere along about the fourth or fifth week of the host plant's life, start the first of your batches of donor plants; that is, the seedlings whose tops are going to be grafted onto the older plants. Stagger the beginnings of these batches of donor seedlings about 10 days apart. It is good to have 10 days between grafting sessions, so the host plant can fully recover its internal hormonal equilibrium.

To perform the graft, take a six to eight-week-old host plant and locate a vigorous branch about ⅔ of the way up the stem. Trim this branch off at the stem, leaving about ½ inch protruding. The branch should be just slightly larger in diameter at the cut than the diameter of the stem of the seedling donor. Trim away a bit of the inside of this split end to make a receptacle area for the donor top (as illustrated). Now take the healthiest of your seedling batch, which should be two to three weeks old at this point, and sever the top just above the place where the first true leaves appeared. These leaves may or may not still be attached to the stem. If not, and for some reason you cannot locate the node where they were attached, simply cut off the top of the plant one-half to one inch below the first major canopy of leaves you come to going up the stem from the ground.

Split the protruding branch stub of the host plant horizontally down to the stem, but do not cut into the stem. Shape the cut end of the donor top in line with the exposed fluid-carrying tissues of the wedge-shaped cutout you performed on the host branch. A minute portion of the cut end of the donor top should protrude beyond the end of the host branch stub, once the donor is inserted into the host.

The split branch should now be tied with cotton thread or raffia; or a bit of self-sealing rubber (available as a grafting substance) could be pinched around the wound to hold the split ends shut and support the donor top.

Some cultivators who are working with this graft and variations of it report increased success if they pinch off the growing tip of the host plant after the graft is complete. This apparently removes the principal source of growth hormones for the host plant and forces her to divert growth energies to her

lateral branches, especially those in the top ⅓ of the stem. Thus, the newly grafted top must benefit from the altered hormonal patterns of the host plant.

It's not a bad idea to fit a sleeve of lightweight plastic over the little grafted top, attaching the sleeve to the main stem of the host plant and leaving it in place for five to seven days, or until the donor shows signs of vigorously taking to the graft. A graft which has failed should be removed, the location sealed with wax, and the wound left alone. It is never a good idea to try to re-make a graft on an old site.

About 10 days after the first graft, the host plant will be ready for another go. There is theoretically no limit to the number of different strains of tops which can be grafted to a single host. There is a lot of room for experimentation in this area. Using this technique, a cultivator can raise the finest tops from around the world on one or two plants in a corner of the room.

(Step one) The host plant should be 6-8 weeks old. Locate a healthy side branch about ⅔ up the plant.
(Step two) Trim branch with razor blade leaving ½ inch protruding.
(Step three) Split host plant branch. Insert trimmed donor top, tie firmly and seal with grafting wax.

A modification of this technique practically guarantees minimal graft failure, if you are interested in going through a little more trouble.

The first objective in this experiment is to create a multi-stemmed plant, which is done by pinching off the growing tip of a selected plant, beginning anytime after the second week. Pinching off the tip (the little unfolding bud at the very top of the plant) creates a rapidly healing wound site and removes the major source of plant growth hormones, as mentioned above. Just below the wound, on opposite sides of the stem, tiny bright-green lateral shoots will try to grow out, go around the old wound and upwards toward the light. Each of these shoots will develop at least one canopy of leaves within several days, and will itself have a growing tip.

Meanwhile, further down the stem, many of the lateral branches will be engorged with growth energies. Much of the energy shunted away from the growing tip in response to the trauma there surges into the upper branches as repairs are being carried out above.

It is two of these branches which we will want to encourage to become twin main stems of the plant. We do this by consistently clipping away the growing tips of the topmost tiny laterals trying desperately to grow anew from below the wounded site. Depending on the strain of the plant and the growth environment, within a couple of weeks, two mid-canopy lateral branches will, in young plants, already have begun to form themselves into twin principle stems rather than simple laterals. They will quickly climb to the vertical and rise above the wound center. These vigorous twins will reach for the sun on bright-green wings.

If we now take these new twin shoots, after they have established themselves, and perform a cotyledon wedge-graft on each of the two tops, using a donor from a different potent strain on each one, we will achieve a twin-stalked, dual-strain plant growing to lush maturity with a different head on both sides. To perform this graft, wait until the twin stems are rising well above the wound site of the original growing tip (where you have continued to pinch off the little shoots struggling to rise out of the area below the wound) and have continued in the original direction of growth. As soon as the twin stems have achieved a triple canopy (three layers of leaves) remove the top two canopies, leaving ¼ to ⅜ inches of stem protruding above the first canopy. Then, split the protruding end of each stem so that the split reaches a point between the branches of the first canopy, which will be on opposite sides of the stem. Do not split the stem below this point. Now cut off the top of your two- to three-week-old donor, severing the stem just below the first true leaves. Shape it into a wedge. Slip the wedge into the split stem, one grafted top on each of the twin stems, and bind the site with cotton thread, raffia, sealing rubber, etc. Seal with wax or petroleum jelly. You're done.

If you are in a dry environment, you may want to slip a plastic sleeve over the grafted tops, tying it shut top and bottom, to prevent excess water respiration and water loss. If you do use a sleeve, remove it as soon as the tops seem well established, or after five to seven days. Whichever is first. And open it to air the limb at least twice a day.

Creating a dual-stem host plant. (A) Pinch off growing tip. (B and C) New twin stems to receive donors. Tie and seal grafts.

Begin by raising two batches of seedlings in pots, one from a lush, tropical, lowland strain of seed and one from an airy, brilliant high-altitude strain. Apply the usual selection criteria at four weeks keeping perhaps three of the best in each batch. At eight weeks, either choose the best in each group or, if they all look good, keep all three in each group.

Take the high-altitude plant. Selecting a very sharp, clean blade, make a diagonal, upward slanting cut at a point about ⅔ of the way to the top. Cut a little over halfway through the stem. Make the cut halfway between nodes.

Now take a plant of the sturdy, potent lowland strain. Make a diagonal, downward slanting wedge cut into its stem, barely cutting into the pithy (or sometimes hollow) center. Make this cut about halfway up the stem, about halfway between two sets of branches, or nodal points. Remove a little thin wedge of tissue to open the cut.

Now slip the upper lip of the highland plant into the cut in the stem of the lowland plant, tilting the highland plant sideways and supporting the pot on a stack of bricks, or whatever. It's a bit of an art to make slices in each stalk so that they match up right, at the proper tilting angle for this graft. Perhaps you should practice on some weeds before cutting into the precious plants. It doesn't really matter what weeds you practice on so long as their stems are not woody and are of the same general size as your Cannabis plants. You are practicing *positioning* of the cuts, not the whole graft procedure (which, once the cuts are made, is very easy).

Once the two plants are joined, they will need to be tied together or otherwise secured with cotton thread, raffia, tape, or any other flat tying material. If you care to, you can seal the wound with wax or

petroleum jelly. This procedure does not call for it, but it's never a bad idea to dab a little something on to keep the inside in and the outside out.

Don't hesitate to bend away the lower portion of the highland plant to make good contact. Several times I've seen nearly mature marijuana plants bent over at the ground, their stems cracked, seemingly crushed, but obviously with complete growth energy still flowing through to the green tops. In one case, several weeks after heavy rain and winds, a group of eight big Mexican females, still lying on the ground, were alive and well, and were being harvested of their flowering tops on a rotating pruning basis. They *still* showed no signs of distress. So, a little judicious bending of the lower stem of the highland plant isn't likely to hurt its adjustment any.

After about a week, perhaps a bit longer depending on a lot of factors, the lower ⅔ of the donor plant can be cut away, and the wound site sealed with wax. At this point the grafted head will show vigorous growth, which will project it out a bit to clear the space of the existing head. This is why you angle the plant in the first place, to help the grafted head grow clear of the growth space of the original head. Clearing this space, the new head will begin strong vertical growth. Whether or not to prune and try to develop a bushy profile on the grafted head is an individual decision. Lastly, though I've never seen it done, there is no reason why one couldn't graft a second head, of a different strain, onto the stem of the original host plant, probably a few inches above the first graft, or perhaps in the next node.

It is quite feasible to continue to raise the donor plant for, with reasonable care and handling, what has been done amounts to nothing more than a radical pruning. Assuming that the whole plant has prospered during the period of jointure

170

Rooting and
Grafting
Cannabis

The
Hops-Cannabis
Graft

between the two complete plants, a likely result after severance is that a twin-stemmed beauty will arise, with one set of top laterals becoming new heads. Such a plant can be grown as itself or can be used for further grafting work.

Taking a cutting from a marijuana plant is easy and it's an excellent way for friends to share with each other.

Slice off a vigorous lateral branch, with several leaf clusters, at the stem. Then bury most of the stalk of the branch in wet vermiculite, sand, or hydroponic suspension which has been treated with Rootone to encourage generation of the fine root system that will begin feeding new growth at the growing tip. These roots arise through changes in several layers of cells along the stalk of the branch buried in the Rootone-treated moisture and medium. These cells literally change form. They erupt from the surface of the stalk in little silken tendrils, which are among the most powerful of all forms of living matter. These cells at the growing tip of the fine roots generated on the stalk of the immersed Cannabis branch in turn manufacture and disperse powerful chemical messengers throughout the branch, causing it to change form, and become an individual plant.

Rooting should not be done in very hot or humid environments, as low, pure respiration is critical to life in a rooting plant. If you are concerned about water loss (if, for instance, some of the leaves are quite large, representing a large surface area for water loss) you might want to trim off the outer half of the larger leaves. The slight additional shock to the branch is negligible and cutback in water loss can be essential.

Once rooted — a process taking one to two weeks — the branch-become-plant is encouraged to produce lateral branches by snipping back the growing tip — but not severely at this stage. A gentle nip in the bud every three to five days, removing the tip itself but very little other tissue, is what's needed. Not a radical chop.

The rooting of the branch turns it into a plant. The pinching back of the growing tip encourages lateral branches, but the base of the plant retains its branch-like internal structure for an extended period, though it does swell somewhat.

For the host plant, you will want to choose a vigorous female plant less than 12 weeks old. From 20 to 40 days after rooting has begun, depending on the size of the base of the plant compared with the lateral branch site you have selected on the 10- to 12-week-old host plant, cut off the rooted plant two inches above the ground level. Form the cut end into a wedge. Sever a lateral branch on your older host plant and slice the protruding one inch stub horizontally, almost but not quite to the stem. Insert the thin wedge of the rooted plant into the slit. Seal and bind the union. And wait. If the graft takes, which it will usually do because of very good matching tissue between the two plants, you'll have a grafted clone which has already converted from being a branch to being a full head. It's no trouble to graft a branch from one plant onto another, but without fancy manipulation that branch will never be more than just a branch. By using the technique of grafting a rooted branch, this problem is effectively bypassed, in theory. This is one of those situations where I have very little research to go on, so reports from those interested in grafting will be very valuable.

You don't get Cannabis spirit in a hops body with this graft as I naively interpreted early experimental results in the first editions of this *Handbook*. I was wrong. What you do get is a plant with a heavy, somewhat dull high. The high is improved by making an alcohol tincture of the young cones and leaves and taking the dose orally. Still, the early promise of the hops-marijuana graft as a way of successfully growing an unrecognizable marijuana plant turns out to be unsupported by experience.

There remains, however, the fact that the hops plant and the Cannabis plant are each other's only close relative on earth. It is *only* between close relatives that parts can be grafted, so it remains that no serious grower should completely write off the hops graft until further thought has been given to the possibilities. Suppose the tops of marijuana could be grafted onto the hops vine, slung like clusters of ripe grapes under the climbing vine, sucking energy through the hops body and, in turn, from the sturdy Cannabis root onto which the hops has been grafted. Sheer speculation, but if possible it presents an opportunity for the grafting of dozens of young tops onto a single vine/root graft and bringing these many tops to simultaneous fruition and flower.

The donor, or Scion of Hops, is prepared by selecting a shoot which is vigorous, polyploid if possible, and which is of the same diameter at the point where it will be cut off as is the Cannabis stem at the point where it is severed, about one to two inches above ground level.

The Cannabis plant should be five to six weeks old, well established and fully healthy. The plant should not have been exposed to very rich nutrients and its photoperiod should have been steady throughout growth — no short-day experiments, etc. Over-rich nutrition works against grafting.

The Cannabis stock is prepared by splitting it for about ½ inch, after it has been severed as described. The split is spread apart and the hops plant inserted, having been trimmed to a neat wedge. The union is then tied and sealed. That's it. The graft is simple, and successful. I will welcome reports from any growers who develop interesting results using hops.

Many cultivators have been searching for a reliable source of hops for the original experiments suggested by the Warmke data, and may yet try working with hops. With the appearance of the original *Cultivator's Handbook,* the government made hops hard to get. For people who remain interested, I am happy to have located a reliable, professional source of hops. The address is:
Mellinger's
2310 West South Range Road
North Lima, Ohio 44452

Passover Graft: Tie donor plant to host as pictured. Cut away bottom of host plant after the graft sets. Seal raw end with wax.

Cultivation of Psychoactive Tobacco

For many years now there has been a
fear that marijuana, when it becomes
legal, will be taken over by the giant
corporate tobacco interests. Rumors
abound to the effect that these huge
companies have locked up all of the most
popular words as future commercial
marijuana trademarks, that they have
secret experimental farms in other
countries, and that they are heavily
involved in clandestine marijuana dealing
already.

All of this fearful, breathless speculation
overlooks at least one important point.
The tobacco companies are able to stay in
business principally because most of us
are ignorant of what true herbal tobacco
really is — what it feels like, tastes like,
and does for the mind and spirit. That is
not the case with marijuana. We know
what good marijuana is, and we have an
increasingly strong tradition of growing
our own potent, magical plants. We will
never be fooled by bogus marijuana, the
way smokers today are being duped by
the so-called tobacco in cigarettes.

The exploitative, destructive tobacco
monopoly rests on one basic fact: most of
us have no idea how easy, and how
desirable it is to grow our own supply of
tobacco, which is actually a major
psychoactive herb. Right — psychoactive!

With minimal growing skills, an assist from modern lighting technology, and the proper seeds, anyone can grow more than enough potent herbal tobacco to keep them in high supply throughout the year. Tobacco is an interesting, attractive and easily cultivated plant that grows well both in strong natural sunlight or under strong artificial light — as does marijuana. One or two plants will supply an individual for a year, for psychoactive herbal tobacco is not at all the sort of overprocessed, dosage-controlled, perfumed and chemicalized vegetable material which is stuffed in little paper tubes and called cigarettes, to be consumed twenty, forty or sixty or more a day. A couple of hits of herbal tobacco, a couple of times a day, gives more true tobacco satisfaction and more true tobacco effect, than can ever be obtained from the little wands of commerce.

There is no reason why anyone who grows personal marijuana cannot also, at the same time, grow a fine small crop of highly potent tobacco, which has the added delightful advantage of being a legal psychoactive plant. In the following pages, along with basic cultivation and curing information, I offer documentation of the amazing fact that tobacco is, and has been throughout history until the past fifty years or so, one of mankind's three principal magical and spiritual drugs. Perhaps with this knowledge, cultivators will be encouraged to restore the tobacco plant to its rightful place, and to break the hold of the tobacco monopolies and the government on at least some of our lifespace.

I used to smoke cigarettes — three packs a day. I don't anymore. Herbal tobacco was a complete surprise to me since, with the cessation of cigarette smoking, I assumed that there was nothing more of tobacco to be experienced. The first time I discovered how wrong I was came during a visit with a friend in New Mexico, when we smoked some of his Apache tobacco. With the first smoke, I knew that this was a whole different experience. We smoked a few tobacco hits solo and, as I was close to knocked-out, we switched to a mixture of

herbal tobacco and his fine mountain-grown Sinsemilla, a combination I came to much prefer. I experienced a readiness to enter into altered states of consciousness far more open and subtly inviting than is ordinarily the case with even the best marijuana, and the high was both mellow and vastly extended in time. It was clear that herbal tobacco was an important discovery, and this initial experience soon sent me off on a program of research and correspondence to find out more about the magical and spiritual properties of this psychoactive companion of Cannabis. My initial experiences with true tobacco came early in 1977 as I was beginning the writing of this revised *Cultivator's Handbook*, and so I decided to include this chapter on the cultivation of tobacco here, prior to completion of a comprehensive *Cultivator's Handbook of Psychoactive Tobacco*, on which I'm now working.

Isn't it strange that so few of us seem to be aware of the true nature of tobacco, which was surely the New World Peoples' principal gift to us, a gift in spite of the fact that we came as slayers and thieves rather than as brothers and fellow humans? What irony that modern commercial interests have discovered how to use tobacco to extract our wealth, destroy our bodies, and warp our minds even as their antique counterparts used alcohol, smallpox and the cross to do the same to the Indians who gave us tobacco, but who had the ultimate misfortune of having built their temples with gold, emeralds, and silver. And isn't it interesting that the tobacco with which we are scourged today is devoid of the properties which made it significant and great, and made it the New World's principal agent of enlightenment: its ability to induce visions and trance states, to promote religious insight, to relieve fatigue, illness and pain, and to open the doors of perception and allow intercourse with gods and spirits. Many

of us can recall, as unknowing children, laughing at stories of primitive people trading valuable goods for trinkets and mirrors, or sneering at the Indians for selling Manhattan Island for $24 worth of dimestore junk — but what were these except people duped into accepting illusion in place of substance. And what then are we who smoke cigarettes and believe that we smoke tobacco? Aren't we trading our gold for pieces of mirror? Don't the traders go home to laugh at us? Yet, are we to blame for not knowing, for being fascinated by images of ourselves?

Many of us today use drugs in a search for peace and enlightenment and spiritual values, but many more of us use drugs to deal with the negativity in our lives, though we talk a lot about fun and experimentation. Drugs are used by so many of us to counter loneliness and confusion, and the sense of loss felt by the fading of childhood's natural high. Drugs are used to stimulate adventure and self-exploration, indeed; but more often they are used out of a sense of worthlessness, self-doubt, and as desperate antidotes to the creeping fatigue, fear, pain and paralysis which can seem so strong and inevitable as to confirm our deep conviction of hopelessness. Drugs are used to petition for release, even if temporary, from the body, the personality, and the world, all of which are like a prison for most of us at one time or another; for some of us, always.

The commercially generated and sustained cigarette cult, and the cult of alcohol in most but not all of its forms, cater to, reinforce, and create so much of the negativity in our lives that it would seem a good thing if the use of such commercial products could be reduced and finally eliminated, leaving only the natural forms, with natural people coming back into our heritage and to the gifts which are ours from the heritage of the past. True, natural, herbal tobacco is a gift to us from the New World, which is now our world.

The secret of the existence of psychoactive tobacco, once revealed, ought also to make clear the absurdity of prohibition of natural drugs — though I do feel control over man-made chemicals is important with as many careless exploiters as there are inhabiting the corporate and entrepreneurial levels of the world today. Widespread personal cultivation of psychoactive tobacco would be an effective challenge to government's crazy attempt to control cultivation of natural plants, whether tobacco or marijuana, and it could forcefully make the point that drugs are not the problem, and that trying to forbid drugs to the People when the People need drugs is crazy. It is simply an ages-old tribal boss sort of reflex — forbid what you don't like, and punish those who disobey. This reflex applied to drugs derives from the ancient observation by bosses that subjects who use drugs for pleasure, escape or enlightenment are less likely to be ideal subjects, less likely to want to sweat under the sun, dig in the dirt, work in the mine, slay the animal or the enemy, and generally do what the boss and his priests want them to do, which is to work quietly and die full of faith. So today, following ancient, unworkable tradition, laws and penalties are set up, enforced by the same sort of people who have always enforced laws for the boss, people who are themselves high on the two most destructive

mind-altering agents known in history, which are power and righteousness.

I must say, I feel a little ridiculous standing up here on this soapbox (made, no doubt, by a subsidiary of some tobacco company). But the institutional ignorance and cynicism with respect to drugs is simply appalling, isn't it? Drugs and drug-using people are not the bad guys, with all those who claim, and some who really believe, that they don't use drugs as the good guys, led in their crusade by the chiefs and the priests and the self-anointed. If the vast, brilliant mind of Man were that simple, well, we would all have had this mess figured out quite a while ago, wouldn't we?

So let the government either drop its laws on marijuana, or try to outlaw psychoactive tobacco. Meanwhile, let us grow our own of whatever we choose. Let us be moderate, work to know and love ourselves and others, live free, and be blessed. Madness burns out.

"When Raleigh, in honour of whom England should have changed her name, introduced tobacco into this country, the glorious Elizabethan Age began. I know, I feel, that with the introduction of tobacco, England woke up from a long sleep. Suddenly a new zest had been given to life. The glory of existence became a thing to speak of. Men who had hitherto only concerned themselves with the narrow things of home, put a pipe into their mouths and became philosophers. Poets and dramatists smoked until all ignoble ideas were driven from them, and into their place rushed such high thoughts as the world had not known before. Petty jealousies no longer had hold of statesmen, who smoked and agreed to work together for the public weal. Soldiers and sailors felt, when engaged with a foreign foe, that they were fighting for their pipes."

Sir James Barrie
from *My Lady Nicotine*
London, 1890

First contact between tobacco and the White Man took place during the first voyage of Admiral Columbus in 1492. After touching land at San Salvador, Columbus steered south by southwest and, after a few hours, spotted a canoe in the open sea. Pulling alongside the canoe, the Europeans saw a single Carib Indian rower with a cargo of dried leaves. The Europeans were transfixed by what they saw the Indian doing.

On a long vogage at sea, the rowers of Carib merchant canoes kept a small brazier of coals going amidships. Every 30 minutes or so, a small wad of tobacco leaves was placed on the brazier and, as the smoke began to rise, the rowers would put a forked nosepipe into the fumes and draw them in. After holding the smoke for awhile, they exhaled powerfully with a shout like the breaking of a football huddle and then went back to the awesome task of rowing the fully-loaded commercial canoe over the long sea routes.

We can imagine the feelings of the Indian, alone in his canoe, on the ocean where all his ancestors had traveled as lords and sole proprietors, suddenly being appraised by strange white beings leaning over the rails of the biggest ship he had ever seen. If there was ever a time for a smoke, that must have been it.

No words were exchanged at this first contact and, of course, Columbus had no idea what he was looking at when he noted the dried leaves being carried by the Indian. He believed he was discovering a route to the East and was expecting to find representatives of the Emperor of Cathay. It would hardly do for a man on such a lofty mission to pass the time with a lowly rower, even if that rower were the first man of a whole new world.

The next landfall was the island of Hispanola where Columbus, sweeping the south side of the land mass, detected signs of an organized civilization. He anchored and sent ashore two men, one of whom could speak Italian, Spanish, Chaldean, Hebrew and Arabic, insuring that he would be able to communicate with the local deputy of the Grand Khan of Cathay.

Upon landing, this deputy and his guard were met by a party of Caribs, who came to the beach with firebrands, carrying dried herbs rolled up in a long, brown leaf. Lighting one end of this, the New World People sucked the smoke out the other end, explaining by both sign and voice that it comforted their limbs, intoxicated them, made them sleepy and lessened their weariness, and offered some to the first men of the old world. The Indians called the objects "tobacos." To the Carib, "tobaco" was not the herb, but the instrument for smoking the rolled herb. Columbus' deputy, however, took "tobaco" to be the name of the herb. History does not record whether or not he smoked.

So, we get our word tobacco from the very first official encounter between the New World and the Old, perhaps from the first word spoken; while Western man's conclusion as to what tobacco was, the first in a long series of conclusions he made in the New World, was, sure enough, a mistake.

A hundred years later, by 1590, twenty years after tobacco's introduction at Plymouth by Sir Francis Drake, tobacco was becoming well-established as a smokable herb in England. Shortly, commercial interests noted the number of people strolling unsteadily but merrily about London's streets.

Herbs and plants are an English specialty. So the merchants figured they were on to a terrific deal. Here was an herb that grew like a weed that people were paying big money for at one point, tobacco was

valued with silver, ounce for ounce), and which could be easily manufactured and sold. One can picture the rush of greed that ran through the calculating minds of English merchants at this prospect. The market for the tobacco herb was largely the so-called scum of the earth — sailors, whores, paupers, the mentally and physically ill, the rejects and outcasts, all refuse thrown up on the dark shores of England's seaports — a cursing, wailing mob bent upon drinking, fucking and brawling itself into oblivion or heaven, whichever was obtainable. Who cared what such people put into their bodies, or what it did to them? History records little concern for these victims of greed, ignorance, and a primitive social order.

But the merchants and gardeners were in for a serious disappointment with English tobacco. Tobacco is, above all else, a sun-loving plant and, while England can be jolly and is definitely old, sunny it is not. Gro-Lux had not yet been invented in the 16th century. Tobacco grew furiously in England, but it smoked very poorly.

Sir Francis Bacon wrote the effective epitaph in about 1600: "The English Tobacco hath small credit, as being too dull and earthy; nay, the Virginian Tobacco, though that be in a hotter climate, can get no credit for the same cause." He rambles on: "A trial to make tobacco more aromatical, and better concocted, here in England, were a thing of great profit."

Tobacco was not only attractive to private commercial interests at home. It was also used to advance the purposes of imperialism as Europe carved up the world through the 17th and 18th centuries.

A French Abbé reported from South Africa in 1685: "The Hollanders gradually advance into the country which they buy up with tobacco." Another Frenchman

(Below)
Seventeenth century
tobacco manufactury

observed: "For the sake of tobacco, the poor and unsophisticated Hottentut was ready to do anything. For a handful of leaves he was willing to work a whole day. Men of the Dutch Company purchased an ox or a sheep from the natives for tobacco in ropes, or coils, an inch thick by measuring with this rope from the front end of the beast to the end of the tail."

The tobacco with which the Dutch, Portuguese, English and others seduced the world was not the style of every nation and people. The crude imperial style of commercial tobacco was only suited to certain parts of the world, those parts willing to settle for what was offered, rather than what they could grow for themselves. Then, as today, some people do for themselves, others allow themselves to be done to.

Tobacco reached the Arab world around 1600 and one writer, commenting on the practices of Turks and Arabs, says that "the mild kinds of tobacco generally used by them have a very gentle effect. They calm the nervous system and, instead of stupefying, sharpen the intellect. The pleasures of Eastern society are certainly much heightened by the pipe and it affords them a cheap and sober refreshment and probably often restrains them from less innocent indulgences." The tobacco of the Arab world was grown in the Arab world, under the sun of those hard blue skies. It was not the tobacco of the seaports of England or Europe, not the blight from white exploiter's hands. Grown in Persia and the land of the Turk, it emerged as a gentle herb, a plant of high order, a prince and fit companion for their own ancient prince, Qunnab, whom we know as Cannabis. It was lovingly sown alongside Qunnab under the hot sun.

(My own limited research to date indicates that Persian and certain Turkish tobacco plants are the best choices for personal cultivation — small, aromatic, and attractive, they contrast with the giant, rank *Nicotiana tabacum*, plant of commerce and industry, and with the harsh, potent New World varieties of *Nicotiana rustica*, the original North American Indian favorite.)

Tobacco quickly escaped from the hands of Europeans on the coasts of the world and raced inland. Within a few years of its arrival at the western and eastern coasts of Africa, it was being grown by people in the interior. The tobacco plants were given a most favored position in African villages — upon the rubbish heap. Only Cannabis and certain food plants such as the yam received such a privilege. The peoples of Africa recognized tobacco as a rightful prince as soon as they saw and experienced it.

Among the Bushongo in southwest Africa, tobacco became an important instrument of peace, as it had been for so many New World peoples. The Bushongo say, "When you have had a quarrel with your brother, you may wish to kill him; sit down and smoke a pipe. By the time this is finished, you will think that death is too great a punishment for your brother's offense, and you will decide to let him off with a thrashing. Relight your pipe, smoke on. As the smoke curls upward, you will think that a few harsh words would serve instead of blows. Light your pipe once more and when the bowl is empty, you will be ready to go to your brother and forgive him."

The African was ingenious in discovering new rituals and uses for the new herb. Porters all over the continent discovered that you could allow a small, stubbly, moustache to grow, fill it with snuff, and with a curl of the lip, serve up a nose-hit without taking your hands off the load on your head or back.

An anthropologist describes how, on the Zambezi River, near Victoria Falls, they smoke the earth. They scrape together "a quantity of moistened red earth to form a mound three inches in diameter and one inch high. The under-surface is flat because of its attachment to the ground, and the upper surface is convex. A duct representing the stem of the pipe was formed by withdrawing a hollow grass stem which had been imbedded in a wet mass of clay surrounding the bowl. The pipe would be ready for almost immediate use owing to the quick drying action of the sun. The hollow bowl of such a pipe is formed when the clay is wet and the shaft of a spear may be used to support the wet earth of the tube until it has hardened."

Such pipes are used to smoke hemp and tobacco together all over East and South Africa. Among the Bechuana, a pit is dug in the soil. A duct is made to lead to the surface by boring through the soil with a stick. "The smoker then extends himself prone on the ground in order to apply his mouth to the surface hole. Sometimes he may use a double pit, connected by a tunnel which is made to contain water." Sort of an earth bong.

It may be that the world owes the practice of hemp smoking, that is, marijuana smoking, to the introduction of the practice with tobacco. Berthold Laufer, an early anthropologist, writes that "there is no historical evidence for the opinion that hemp smoking preceded tobacco smoking. Not for ancient India, where the use of hemp as a narcotic originated, nor for the Islamic world do we have a single account of hemp smoking in times anterior to tobacco. It is quite certain that the smoking of hemp from a pipe came into vogue only as an imitation of tobacco smoking, while, in earlier times, hemp preparations were merely taken internally, either in the form of pills or liquid."

The Chinese, with their extensive herbal medicine system and knowledge of the properties of plants, saw the smoke of the tobacco plant as therapeutic very early on. An early herbalist notes that "the human alimentary and muscle systems are aided in their smooth operation as the smoke goes directly from mouth to stomach and passed from within to outside, circulating around the four limbs and the hundred bones of the body."

The plant was known in China from the 1600's onwards. It took hold rapidly, for within ten years after its entrance, the tobacco experience was firmly established. The tobacco available to these early Chinese people was first-quality and the processing was minimal. The Chinese called tobacco "smoke-wine" because it was, like wine, capable of intoxicating people gently or stuporously. The Chinese say they "eat" or "sip" or "inhale" the smoke, while the Japanese and Tibetans "drink" their smoke.

In southern Asia, tobacco has been called "the herb of yearning and affection because he who once tasted it cannot forget it and constantly hankers after it."

Tobacco is also known as the Herb of Amicability, "on account of the affectionate feelings entertained toward one another by all classes of mankind since its use became general."

Tobacco is also called "soul-reviving smoke because a puff has the power of reviving the energies of the melancholy and the wearied," and the very ancient and secret Heaven and Earth Society in China smoke their tobacco with a ritual pipe known as The Vast Bamboo.

In an unstoppable, glowing, red cloud of fire and smoke, tobacco swept across the Old World after being liberated by Columbus from the New. The powerful attraction of tobacco for the White, Black and Yellow Peoples of the earth aroused vicious opposition. Several countries imposed the death penalty for tobacco possession. In much of the Middle East, anyone caught with tobacco had their nose removed from their face for the first offense and their face, along with the rest of their head, removed for the second. In the 16th and 17th centuries, most governments condemned tobacco strongly — yet the herb spread swiftly throughout the world. No herb has been better documented than tobacco, and from the very first, tobacco joined with Cannabis as a primo psychoactive agent of the human race, far exceeding alcohol in both consumption and psychic impact.

A French writer in 1687 tells us of the fury of the Sultan of Constantinople.

"It was chiefly for tobacco that he made many heads fly. He caused two men in one day to be beheaded in the streets because they were smoking tobacco. He had prohibited it some days before because, as it was said, the smoke had got up into his nose. But I rather think that it was in imitation of his uncle Sultan Amurat (1623-40), who did all he could to hinder it as long as he lived. He caused some to be hanged with a pipe through their nose, others with tobacco hanging around their neck, and never pardoned any. I believe that the chief reason that Sultan Amurat prohibited tobacco was because of the fires, that do so much mischief in Constantinople when they happen, which most commonly are occasioned by people that fall asleep with a pipe in their mouth. He used all the arts he could to discover those who sold tobacco, and went to those places where he was informed they did, where having offered money for a pound of tobacco, made great entreaty, and promised secrecy; if they let him have it, he drew out a sword under his vest and cut off the shopkeeper's head."

As anti-smoking campaigns go, this was serious, yet the Turks and the rest of the world kept right on smoking.

What happened? Where did psychoactive tobacco go? What are all these little paper tubes that so many of us are sucking on at the rate of 20, 40 and more a day? How come nobody seems to know the magical, spiritual, visionary and euphoric uses of native, herbal tobacco? And where did this idea come from that growing tobacco was a complicated and tricky business, better left to experts, who then sell it to us in little, expensive packages. In much of the world today, tobacco is home-grown and used for trance-state induction, for magical and religious rites, for pleasure and relief from hunger and fatigue, for minor profit sold to neighbors or at the marketplace, and for use as an herbal remedy as well as psychoactive agent. So why don't Americans and Europeans know about the true potential of this plant?

If the best way to hide an idea is to make it obvious, then the secret that tobacco is a highly psychoactive plant with a long and involved history of magical, spiritual, ritualistic, and purely hedonistic usage has been effectively obscured by the universal assumption that cigarettes are tobacco and that to have smoked cigarettes is to have experienced tobacco. The commercial product called "tobacco" is as close to true herbal tobacco as rubbing alcohol is to fine chateau wine. Cigarette tobacco is ultra-processed, dosage-controlled vegetable material harvested from plants which have been specifically bred to eliminate the psychoactive properties and to conform to industrial processing requirements. This "stuff" has passed through over 100 treatments and processes with dozens of additives and chemicals to assure a uniform, long shelf-life, highly profitable drug product with only one function — to ensnare and maintain an addicted clientele, willing to trade lung disease for a cowboy/cool chic image.

Note the Surgeon General's warning: it is against cigarette smoking, not tobacco:

WARNING - The U.S. Surgeon General has determined that cigarette smoking is dangerous to your health.

On the other hand, true herbal tobacco can be very potent and if misused, dangerous. Most native American Indian people cut their tobacco with other herbs in a ratio of two parts herbal mixture to one part tobacco. The following account is from an American Indian tribe which smoked, on most occasions, only the pure, potent plant.

"He feels good over all his meat when he takes it into his lungs. Sometimes he rolls up his eyes. And sometimes he falls over, backward he falls over backward. He puts his pipe quickly on the ground, then he falls over. Then they laugh at him, they all laugh at him. Nobody takes heed, when one faints from smoking, but if he faints because he is sick, then they throw water on him. When it is from tobacco that he faints, he does not lie there stiff long.

"Sometimes when the tobacco is strong, the man himself when he smokes does not know when he faints away. Sometimes he falls to the ground and does not know it. Somebody else says: 'Look, he is fainting.' They see his hands shake.

"They say that some old men have to walk with a cane, when they have finished smoking, they feel it over their whole meat. He feels good for a long time after he smokes, if he likes to smoke, he feels good for a long while. Sometimes he falls on the ground, he feels faint. I used to see them, the old men. It was strong tobacco, that was what they liked. They fall on the ground. They come to again. They always laugh at the old men. When they smoke they talk in the sweathouse. All at once one man quits talking.

"That is the way they used to do in the old times. They used to like the tobacco so well. They used to like the tobacco strong. Whenever they faint from tobacco, they always get ashamed. They used to do that way, get stunned. Sometimes one fellow will have so strong tobacco that nobody can stand it without fainting, it is so strong. He feels proud of his strong tobacco.

"Some were fainters when they smoked, others never did faint. Some faint when the tobacco gets strong from them, and others do not. Vaskak was a fainter when he smoked. Everybody knew that Vaskak was a fainter. Vaskak used to faint, but he liked it.

"When he first starts to smoke he does not fall. It is when he finishes smoking a pipeful of tobacco that he falls; it is then that as it gets strong for him he falls."

Charles Millspaugh, a homeopathic physician and writer of the 19th century classic, *Medicinal Herbs*, wrote:

"As an habitual narcotic, the uses of tobacco are many. I place them here in the order of their harmfulness: Chewing without expectorating, inhalation of the smoke, chewing and expectorating, and insufflation of snuff. It is prepared for smoking through processes which tend slightly to meliorate against the poisonous properties, in the form of twists soaked in molasses or licorice for chewing, called plugs; shredded leaves more or less pure for chewing or smoking called fine-cut; finely-broken leaves, sometimes bleached, for smoking called granulated tobacco; rolled into cylinders, either pure or saturated with nitre as cigars or cheroots; rolled into small cylinders and wrapped in paper, as cigarettes; pulverized and kept dry or damp for insufflation or chewing, as snuff; and many other forms of use."

For hundreds of years farmers, chemists, and business people have sweated and fretted, producing tobacco with the characteristics demanded by the market of the day. Commercial tobacco growing has never been much fun. In 18th century Europe, colored and perfumed snuffs were the rage. New World growers were kept crazed trying to adapt their plants to the tastes of the fickle French court and its imitators. Cultivation and processing for aroma, taste, and appearance has been the theme of tobacco growers and merchants. Rarely has tobacco been cultivated for its psychoactive properties, since these properties are achieved through intoxication, through the selective poisoning of the human body.

Tobacco is poisonous. No doubt about it. The poisonous agent is nicotine which, in commercial cigarettes, is kept at a minimum per cigarette through intense plant breeding and extensive processing. Of course, a smoker of two or three packs a day will be taking in a lot more nicotine than someone who smokes a joint or two of home-grown, about all anyone would need.

But the tobacco experience is not confined to the achievement of a toxic state. All aboriginal and natural people know plenty of plants that poison. They regard most of these plants as extreme medicines, at best. But tobacco, with the deadly nicotine shining on its leaves, is eagerly and routinely smoked and snorted, today as yesterday by millions of Third World people.

If intoxification were all there was to herbal tobacco, then it would lie apart, in the obscure places of human knowledge in the realm of Shamans and medicine men.

And if all tobacco did was poison, there are plenty of plants that poison, most of them better, all known to the American Indian. The Indians loved tobacco, worshipped it, made peace with it, knew oneness through it. The Indians used tobacco with respect for its toxicity.

Indian peoples of North, Central and South America were uniformly familiar with the plant and prized its use in opening the doors of perception, curing bodily disease and infirmity, reducing the impact of life's twin afflictions, hunger and fatigue, and for its role in deepening and broadening human relationships on both the personal and community level. As an early enthnologist remarked, while considering the Indian people he was studying:

"It is a curious fact that while the whites took over the material tobacco from the Indians, they took with it no fragment of the world that accompanied it, nor were they at first aware that there was such a world, and again, that after all the generations which have elapsed since its introduction among the whites, it has

woven itself scarcely at all into their psychology and mythology. Lady Nicotine is enshrined among the Whites only as a drug, as a taste, as a habit, along with the seeking after mild and tasty forms, while the Karuk make tobacco a heritage from the gods, a strange path which juts into this world and leads to the very ends of magic."

There are vast amounts of fascinating information on the uses of tobacco by people all across the face of the planet. This brief chapter is not the place to present lengthy evidence of the herb's universal appeal and its deep involvement, on many levels, with the human family. In the *Cultivator's Handbook of Psychoactive Tobacco* which is in process, such matters will receive thorough attention.

There are over 100 varieties of the tobacco plant, all of which contain the psychoactive principle, Nicotia ($C_{10}H_{14}O_2$), though in varying degrees of concentration in the leaves. As with marijuana, potency itself is genetically determined, but environment and cultivation make a substantial difference in the quality of the final product.

Besides true Virginia tobacco, *Nicotiana tabacum,* for which the genus was composed, the following species and varieties are of interest: *Nicotiana rustica,* a species with green-yellow leaves, cultivated in Mexico, India, the Middle East, Turkey, and found native and escaped in many parts of the United States; *Nicotiana palmeri,* in Arizona; *Nicotiana clevelandi,* in California; *Nicotiana fructicosa,* a beautiful plant with sharply pointed capsules; *Nicotiana persica,* a fragrant plant cultivated in Persia and the best of the psychoactive breeds; *Nicotiana rapanda,* a wild tropical tobacco, producer of fine Cuban smoke; *Nicotiana quadrivalvus,* cultivated by Indians from the Northwest through the Mississippi Valley; *Nicotiana chinensis,* cultivated and wild in China and Japan; *Nicotiana trigonophylla,* a highly potent species growing wild in Southern California, Arizona, Utah, and New Mexico; *Yaqui tobacco,* cultivated in Arizona; and *Nicotiana petiolata,* which is found throughout the United States in an escaped state.

Tobacco belongs to the elite order of dark knights, the Solanaceae. It's a plant to be respected as potent and toxic. The darkness of the Solanacae is illustrated by the three princes who share the order with tobacco:

First: black henbane, (*Hyoscyamus niger* also called *Hyoscyamus lethalis*). Deadly if barely misused, often lethal anyway. A lot of lives have been taken by this plant, through both deliberate misuse and through mistaken use as a salad herb.

Next there is *Solanum nigerum,* or deadly nightshade. A very painful, messy death. Even if you changed heart halfway down, jumping from a bridge would probably be easier than taking this black prince to heart.

Finally, there is *Datura stramonium,* jimson weed. It won't kill you but it will snuff out the bright part of your lights. A common adulterant in street grass, jimson weed grows wild in vast patches, especially in the South. Unscrupulous marijuana dealers send temporary paid labor gangs out to harvest tons of the stuff. It gets dried, chopped, mixed with seeds and shake, bagged all pretty and manicured, and sold. It gets you off, but then so does automobile exhaust. (Another good reason for growing your own marijuana, tobacco, mushrooms, or other discoveries from anywhere on the planet. But if you must buy marijuana rather than growing it, please avoid "manicured" lids at all costs.)

Cultivators will discover that herbal tobacco, especially the top leaves, is a very different smoke from what they may have experienced with cigarettes, cigars, or pipes. For one thing, the smoke from home-grown, air-cured plants will usually be much more harsh than commercial tobacco (except for the mild, potent and tasty Persian species). This is to be expected. The home cultivator will not have gone through the elaborate processing and addition of chemicals to the tobacco which characterize commercial preparations. Then, also, tobacco is a plant subject to wild variability. Tobacco growers know that among plants in a row, even among leaves on a plant, there will be a great variation in quality of taste, aroma, and potency. Elasticity, taste, color, aroma, texture, and burning properties are all highly variable between plants of the same genetic background. The position of the leaves on the stalk also creates variables. Tobacco growers divide the plant into quarters when talking about quality, taste, and so forth.

The harsh qualities of most home-grown tobacco dictate that, in most cases, herbal tobacco is best smoked in a waterpipe rather than as a cigarette. This will depend, to a large extent, on the individual plant and where on the plant the leaf being smoked was located. Tobacco should never, under any circumstances, be eaten, nor its juice swallowed, nor should it be used as a suppository. Such use is lethal.

In the *Cultivator's Handbook of Psychoactive Tobacco*, I will present a number of alternative curing methods for mellowing the smoke. The sweet minty taste of good home-grown marijuana does a nice job of smoothing tobacco's harshness, as attested to by the tens of millions of Third World smokers who smoke just such a mixture daily, and by my own experiences.

Many people will no doubt be alarmed by the idea of psychoactive tobacco, primarily, they will say, because such tobacco is poisonous.

Well, all tobacco is poisonous. But, evidently, as long as people are dosed with a little poison at a time, in a lot of cigarettes daily, with profit to private enterprise and taxes to public enterprise (also known as government), then it's OK for people to take poison. There is a warning by the Surgeon General, but cigarettes are still legal. However, if people begin taking psychoactively effective hits of home-grown tobacco a few times a day, who gets the profits? Who collects taxes? When one herbal tobacco joint replaces 30 to 50 cigarettes, what then?

Ahh: Then we will certainly hear that tobacco is poison and should not be smoked in its natural form, certainly not the unblended top leaves because of the concentration of poison. However, in all the ages that tobacco has been known, most of the smoking has been with home-grown, herbal tobacco. Modern commercial monopolies notwithstanding, most of the tobacco smoked in the world today, especially when it is combined with Cannabis is smoked by poor peoples in countries far from America and Europe. They smoke the original herb.

A cultivator who is basically healthy and combines moderation with an appreciation of the potentials and the dangers of the herbal high, need have no fear of tobacco. Needless to say, perhaps, that it should *absolutely* be kept away from children and pets.

Herbal tobacco is an easily cultivated plant. Of the three major species, *Nicotiana tabacum, Nicotiana rustica* and *Nicotiana persica,* only *N. persica* is really well-suited to indoor cultivation. Only *N. persica* is small and pleasantly

Selection of
Soil and Site

To Obtain
Tobacco
Seed

Starting the
Tobacco
Plant

189

aromatic. The other two varieties are quite large and get downright rank near maturity, especially *N. tabacum*. Cultivators who are interested in gathering wild strains of herbal tobacco for seed will find extensive literature in ethnobotanical studies to guide them to field sites.

Choose a soil which is porous, well-drained and rich in organic matter. Soil which is good for Cannabis is also very good for tobacco, though tobacco often harbors viruses which are harmful to Cannabis, so there should be a distance between fields. The Cannabis should be uphill and upwind of the tobacco. The land should be as sheltered from the wind as possible, and the soil should be well-prepared and free from all other plant life. Every week to ten days during the entire growth cycle, you will want to top-dress the soil around each plant with a complete, water-soluable fertilizer. Tobacco is an extremely exhausting plant, and soil nutrients require much attention. Quite often, both in commercial fields and in native herbal tobacco cultivation, mound planting is used very effectively. A single tobacco plant set in the middle of a two foot diameter mound about 12 inches high will have all the earth support it needs for full growth. Mounds are easier than levelled ground to keep weed-free and loosened, and they give some protection from excess water build-up. If possible the land should have southern exposure and should have an elevation which gives it maximum exposure to the sun from sunrise to sunset.

It's difficult at present to track down exotic tobacco-strain seeds. In some parts of the South, State Universities have experimental programs, as in North Carolina and Tennessee, and county extension agents can often supply or turn you on to sources of the huge commercial varieties. I am in the process of establishing sources of special strains for

home cultivation, and refer interested readers to the Cultivator's Research Service Section at the end of the book.

Nicotiana rustica or *Nicotiana persica* are the preferred varieties for indoor and outdoor cultivators of psychoactive tobacco. Both are effectively started from seed. Tobacco seed is unusually virile and there is rarely any problem with germination. Also, tobacco seed is quite small. One ounce is enough to set three or four acres.

An early book describes the basic beginning steps in tobacco culture:

"The seed is usually set in beds of made soil, comprising the most unctuous native earth, enriched with wood-ashes, and other manures. March or early in April is the period chosen for placing the seed in the beds, where the young plants remain till May or June, carefully protected against frosts; when the leaves have grown to the size of a dollar and four or five appear, they are then transplanted into the tobacco field, a day of warm rain being chosen for the purpose. The field is hoed into rectangular hollows, with small raised hillocks between each. The young plants are then drawn from their native bed, and brought in baskets to the field, one being laid on the top of each mound of earth. The planter then makes a hole in the centre of each hillock with his fingers, and having adjusted the tobacco-plant in its natural position, presses the earth gently around the roots with the hand. The field requires constant care to prevent growth of weeds; and the plant in its early stages is liable to injury from the attacks of the horn worm, or tobacco-worm; a caterpiller which, if left to grow, will increase to the size of a man's finger and commit great devastation in the crops. It is ultimately transformed into a large brown moth, with variegated wings, measuring about 4½ inches from the

190

Transplanting
Seedlings

Care of
the Plant

Topping
the Plant

Removing the
New Shoots

extreme of each tip, the body having dull red patches on it. It is popularly termed the Tobacco-Hawk. It is the only insect that feeds upon the plant. No animal will touch it."

Another early writer lamented:

"In the animal kingdom there are three creatures, and three only, to whom tobacco is not poisonous – man, a goat found among the Andes, and the tobacco worm. This last is a long, smooth-skinned worm, its body formed of successive knobs or rings, each furnished with a pair of legs, large prominent eyes, and is in color as green as the leaf upon which it feeds. It is found only on the underside of the leaves, every one of which must be carefully lifted and examined for its presence. When caught, the worm is pulled apart between the thumb and the forefingers, for crushing it on the soft earth of the carefully cultivated field is impossible."

Seedlings, started in beds 6 to 10 weeks before transplanting, usually take best on a cloudy, somewhat moist day in early May. The earth should be carefully prepared and mounded. With the index finger, poke a hole in the earth and set in a seedling. Plants are never set in the earth deeper than they were set in the starting bed. To do so invites almost immediate stem rot. Likewise, take care not to bend the root in the hole, but to position it straight and to pat the earth lightly but firmly around it.

Approximately nine weeks after transplanting, the tobacco plants will have grown so that they shade the ground underneath them pretty well. Until then, at the least, the cultivator should be careful to remove all weeds, blades of grass and so forth, as soon as they appear. Several feet to either side of the plant, the earth should be kept well-aerated by working it once a week.

About six weeks after transplanting, when the plants are 18 to 24 inches high, and the tobacco plant has acquired 8 to ten leaves on a stalk, the time has come for topping. This consists of the removal of the bud at the top of the stalk. This prevents the plant from running up to seed, as the development of the flowering spike is called. At the time the plant is topped, any leaves that are damaged from rubbing on the ground can be removed.

Within days after topping, the tobacco plant will attempt to put out new shoots, or suckers. If this new growth is allowed to develop, a strain will be put on the plant and the quality of its leaves will greatly diminish. For all of its seeming strength, and it is one of the world's most versatile plants, tobacco is extremely delicate when it comes to growing a plant that will satisfy man's desires and needs.

Suckers can appear in several places on the plant after topping. They spring from the roots, in the earth alongside the plant. And they spring forth at the top of the stalk, just below where the topping took place. In addition, any leaves that begin to turn prematurely yellow or become deformed must be removed along with the suckers. Upon occasion, new growth may attempt to spring forth elsewhere on the plant, where it should be pinched off.

"Fertile soil and land beyond the reach of inundations are selected for the successful culture of the plant. To produce a luxurious growth, the farmer will trench his fields deeply, and will manure them with beancake. Manure of vegetable origin is preferred to cattle dung, which has a tendency to impart to the leaves a rather disagreeable flavor. In the spring, the seeds are sown in a well-cultivated bed, and in those provinces where the nights of the spring season are cold, the seedbeds are carefully covered with straw or mats. The fields into which the seedlings are to

The
Time of
Harvesting

(Below)
Early plantation

191

be transplanted are formed into narrow ridges, each about two feet wide and a few inches apart. The seedlings are carefully removed from the seedbed by means of small spades, great pains being taken not to shake the earth from the roots and are set in holes previously dug in the field. The plants are arranged in two rows at a distance of sixteen inches from one another. The farmers endeavor to keep the field clean of weeds which would greatly interfere with the growth of the crop. The soil between the plants is loosened at frequent intervals. A few plants are set aside and allowed to blossom for the purpose of setting seeds. The beds of all other plants are removed, so that the leaves may 'gather all their strength, grow thick, and improve their flavor.' The leaves which occupy the lower parts of the stem are plucked, so that those which cluster around the upper parts may have a chance to expand. The bunch of leaves which grows in the crown of the plant is regarded as especially fine and aromatic, and the tobacco from such leaves is known as kai-lu (covered with dew). The stems grow to a height of four to five feet, each producing from ten to twenty leaves."

In another early book on tobacco culture in the South, the following advice is given the farmer:

"During very rainy seasons, and in some kinds of unfavorable soil, the plant is subject to a malady called 'firing.' It is a kind of blight produced by the moist state of the atmosphere, or of the ground in which the plant grows; it is also liable to the opposite extreme of heat or drought. The injury is much dreaded by the planter, as it spots the leaf with a hard brown spot, which perishes, and produces holes fatal to the value of the crop. The leaves as they ripen, become rougher and thicker, assume a tint of yellowish green and are sometimes mottled with yellowish spots. The crop

being ready for gathering, the planter is careful to secure it before any autumnal frosts occur; for the plant is among the first to feel its injurious influence. Judgment is also required in cutting the plants, and this operation is consigned to the best and most judicious hands employed in the culture. Each person so employed, being provided with a strong sharp knife, proceeds along the respective rows of plants, and selects only such plants as appear fully ripe, leaving the rest a short time longer.

"The stem of each plant is severed as near as possible to the ground, and such plants as have thick stems are divided longitudinally, to admit the air and dry them quicker. The plant is then laid gently on the ground, so that the leaves be not damaged, and is allowed to remain exposed to the rays of the sun throughout the day, or until the leaves are entirely 'wilted,' as it is termed; that is, till they are flaccid, and will bend any way without breaking." The plant is then taken into a shady, open spot to continue drying.

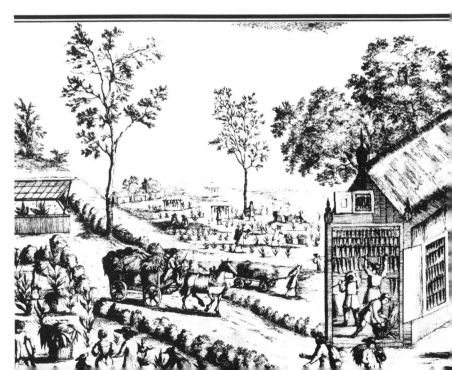

192

Drying
the
Crop

Indoor
Cultivation
of Tobacco

The most commonly employed methods of drying tobacco require good air circulation around the leaves, a temperature of between 70-85° F., and a small degree of moisture in the atmosphere to help the leaves retain pliability and aroma. Since tobacco is raised all over the world, there are countless methods of drying and curing the leaves. In *Cultivator's Handbook of Psychoactive Tobacco*, I will cover a number of methods, which I am now researching, on effective personal preparation of tobacco for snuff, chewing and smoking.

The basic shade-drying method used in much of the West requires that the plants, harvested by accepted methods, are placed on a wooden platform in the shade and kept from blowing around by means of planks laid across the stems. Flopping around in the breeze tends to bruise or tear the leaves. The temperature of the air is important. "A dry hot sunny day may cure too fast, not allowing sufficient time for that rich yellow colour to establish itself, which would be produced by a slower process of evaporation and desiccation," one expert remarks. "Four or five days drying is usually sufficient, and the plants are carefully transferred to a well-ventilated and well-lighted house. Here they are hung up and facilities afforded for admitting plenty of light and air, until the tobacco is perfectly cured, after which the house is closed. The first four or five days after putting in a great measure determine the colour. The earlier, too a planter can cut, the better curing weather will be obtained. Early autumnal frosts are fatal to a tobacco farm."

Shade-drying of tobacco (actually, drying by indirect sun) was the ancient way, and it is still practiced in much of the world. Around 1800, fire-curing was invented in an attempt to create new, more marketable styles of tobacco. Flue-curing was invented around 1840. This had the advantage over fire-curing by affording temperature and moisture control. These controls were vital for the production of multiple grades of commercial tobacco.

The home cultivator of tobacco need not be concerned at first about the various fancy methods of curing tobacco. He can stick to shade-drying and air-curing as the simplest approaches to yielding top-quality tobacco. Plenty of well-circulating air and steady moderate heat are all that's needed for excellent drying and curing, and if the drying period is relatively dry, warm weather, the cultivator will find drying a painless operation.

Since tobacco is not cultivated at present for its psychoactive properties, it is difficult to find information on indoor cultivation of small crops of herbal tobacco and I'm just beginning my own experimental program. I am hoping that interested readers will share your growing experiences with others.

Apparently the only really critical factor in indoor cultivation of tobacco, other than the problem of odor in certain varieties, is that tobacco loves light even more than Cannabis. But as of yet, there are very few indications of how much of what kind of light is needed for effective psychoactive tobacco culture.

A researcher at North Carolina State has raised tobacco plants indoors with great success using a 275 watt Lucalox lamp with an equal wattage of mercury vapor lamps.* This lamp setup is ideal for indoor cultivation of marijuana as well. The drawback is that it runs $100-$200 for a minimal Lucalox-mercury vapor lighting system. It is interesting that the research at NCSU concludes that for tobacco, and other flowering plants, Lucalox alone or metal-halide alone or mercury vapor alone is not sufficient to

---

Light and Plants by Dr. R. J. Davies, USDA

Native
American   Herbal
Curing   Mixtures

Top Leaf
Potency, Aroma
and Taste   193

grow a good plant, but that the Lucalox combined with either of the others produces excellent all-around growing environment.

The Indian customarily devoted very little effort to either the cultivation or the curing of tobacco. This plant was a great gift of the Gods of the earth, the sky and the air, rather than an article of commerce to be made into desirable tastes and colors for consumption. In most places the extent of the attention paid to the plant was that the soil was prepared with working-in of hardwood ash and kitchen scraps, the site was consecrated, the seeds scattered just before a storm, and the plant harvested when grown. After harvesting, the leaves were stripped, laid out to partially dry in the sun, taken into partial shade to cure a bit until, after several days, they were pliable and of a suitable color, at which point they were chopped up and placed in a consecrated container.

As was pointed out earlier, many different herbs have been traditionally mixed with herbal tobacco to reduce its harsh qualities. The New World Indian did not know of Cannabis — and it's interesting to speculate on the course of history had these great civilizations known the divine herb — but after the introduction of tobacco to the Old World, a mixture of two parts Cannabis to one part herbal tobacco seems to have been spontaneously decided upon in most of the world.

Native American Indians, according to the reports of various early explorers, anthropologists, and others who have studied their use of tobacco, mixed in such diverse herbs and substances as dogwood leaves and flowers, laurel, arrow root, bark, sumac leaves, red osier dogwood leaves, liquidambar, waahoo, ironwood leaves, squaw huckleberry leaf and bark, *Lobelia inflata* leaves (known as Indian tobacco), jimson weed leaves,

black birch bark, oil from muskrat glands, cherry bark, cornsilk, mullein leaves, ashes of scorpions, spiders and certain larvae, bearberry leaves, willow bark, manzanita leaves, and various dried mosses. It is obvious from the diversity of the list that many New World people chose not to take their natural herbal tobacco straight, and most of us who may grow our own tobacco and simply air-cure it in the ancient way will no doubt want to mellow the smoke a bit with an herbal companion — marijuana, of course, being my strong recommendation. Careful readers may notice a number of powerful poisons among the traditional additives listed above, and anyone considering cutting their tobacco with anything but marijuana would do well to talk with an expert herbalist before doing so.

In an older book on tobacco, we find confirmation of the importance of the top leaves of the tobacco plant as the source of the most potent smoke. "It has already been remarked that the finest leaf is the top one on the stalk, and no one knows this better than the peasants employed on the tobacco farms and warehouses in Macedonia. If not carefully supervised, these leaves will be extracted for home consumption. Special watch has to be maintained to prevent what would otherwise be an irreparable loss. Throughout the big hotels and shops of London and the provinces, the English-made Turkish cigarettes are noted and many of the hotels on the Continent, despite the high tariffs erected against these luxuries, will have no other kind."

"The top leaves are so small there is no reason to deprive them of their midribs. They are cut either by hand or machinery. Hand labour is a distinctive feature in the making of Turkish cigarettes. The blending process is an interesting sight: the operator selects

handfuls from baskets containing various kinds of leaf and showers them on the floor in order to secure as thorough a mixture as possible. A slight quantity of water is sprinkled upon the mass of fallen leaves, just sufficient to produce pliability and the heap is left all night. By the following morning, the dry leaves have absorbed the water sprinkling, and so become pliable, and the whole is ready for the cutting machine. No heat is employed as in the case of Virginia tobacco; otherwise, the delicate aroma of a Turkish leaf would be lost."

The Virginia tobacco referred to is *N. tabacum,* and the Turkish a variety of *N. rustica.*

All it takes to grow simple tobacco is good dirt, strong sun, and some seed. Fine tobacco has more meticulous requirements. The following poetic appreciation of the plant makes clear what it takes to produce fine tobacco in a world without artificial light. In the world of today, of course, artificial light and controlled indoor environments can make all the difference.

"There are comparatively few spots on this globe where Nature has put forth her very best efforts to grow tobacco, and one of these favoured sun-kissed places is the land of the peach and plum. Just as the Vuelto-Abajo produces the world renowned tobacco for the cigar, so the mountainous districts of Macedonia bring forth the richly-prized tobacco for the cigarette. Professors may talk, chemists may test, farmers may plant, but no tobacco ever can be grown that is equal to the modest little plant culled by the peasants of the Levant. It is a desideratum that in all tobacco culture there must be a happy conjunction of natural circumstances in the workshop of Nature to produce the finest product. The failure of one of these dovetailing forces simply means missing the acme of

perfection as surely as the tiniest speck on the petal impeaches the absolute beauty of the rose. Too much or little sun at the eventful moment, an adventitious shower or inopportune wind bruising the delicate tissues of a highly-matured plant, a capricious variation of atmospheric conditions just sufficient to prevent the unfolding of the fullest luxuriance of the aromatic herb — these are factors against which man can but pray, but whose absence results in an unimpeachable faultlessness and success. Such Turkish tobacco in its purity, fragrance and sweetness, possesses that subtle and delicious aroma that places it like a god amóngst men. Cigarettes made of this enchanting herb have no rival. They stand on the topmost pinnacle — incomparable and alone."
From *Field Museum of Natural History* Leaflet #18 Chicago, 1924.

The cultivation of a few fine tobacco plants for personal use makes a lot of sense, and my own few plants so far are fine, interesting beings. There's really no reason for any more of our wealth to go to companies for an herb we can so easily, and satisfyingly grow for ourselves.

The Elizabethan age was the first lifespan during which European peoples were fully involved with the use of tobacco, the New World's great psychoactive agent. The psychodrama of tobacco's rush through the societies of the Old World can be more fully appreciated if, for a moment, we remember the levels of awareness and perception which were at work in those days, four hundred years before our own lifespan.

The New World from which tobacco came was dominated in its central and southern regions by several highly evolved, brilliant but rigid, high civilizations, and in the north by a rich fabric of tribes and nations whose

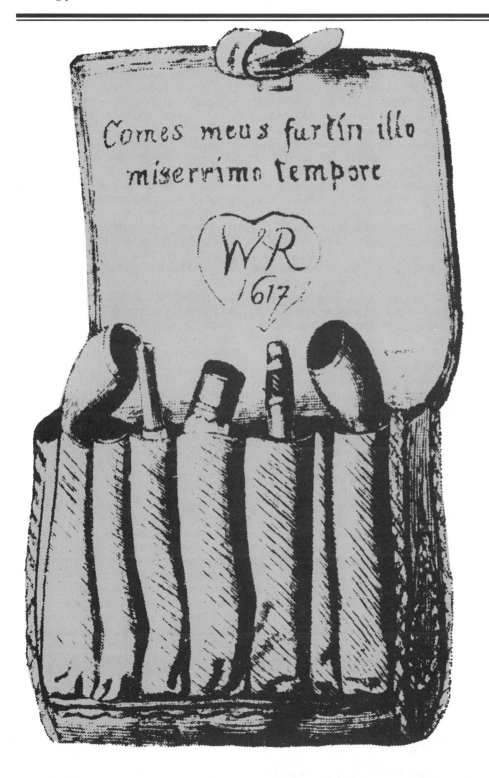

spiritual consciousness was raised as high as the snowy peaks, and whose humanism and earth-sense was often as broad as the vast plains of their continental home. But all Indian societies of the New World were vulnerable in the same way — none had ever been exposed to any but basically their own kind. None had ever been invaded by another kind of human, none had ever been truly challenged on a broad spiritual or technological plane by an absolutely alien culture, as had the civilizations of Europe, the Middle East, and Asia throughout their 10,000-year history of development alongside each other time and time again. The New World was new because it was, and had been, totally isolated from the Old, and the New World fell to the Old because it was wholly dependent upon that isolation for continuity.

When the Spanish, with all of the strength and formidable characteristics of the cockroach came foraging into the jungles of Central America they found El Dorado, guarded by the highly organized, enormously strong, but fatally rigid ant-societies of the brilliant, tragic Indians. The ant-soldiers were powerless against the cockroach-soldiers. The collective body of Spanish mercenaries and fighters, priests, whores, and merchants were for the Indian, the embodiment of Quetzalcoatl, the feathered serpent, whose return was expected. They were the hairy white-ones in whose image the coming of Quetzalcoatl had long been foretold, and the date of Cortez' landing on the coast at Veracruz corresponded exactly with the date of the ancient Quetzalcoatl's prediction of his return, in the form of white men with bearded faces, coming in wooden ships bearing the sign of the cross from the direction of the rising sun. This prediction, graven into rock two thousand years earlier by Quetzalcoatl himself, had been kept clean and true by a hundred generations of priests through

the rise and fall of several great Indian cultures. When the white men finally appeared on Good Friday, the Indian people of the central and southern regions, for all practical purposes, knew that their time was at an end. Only in the north was the coming of the White man resisted, bravely, but in vain, for here there was no such living legend. For more than three hundred years the glorious Maya, the noble Inca, and the mystical Aztec peoples have been gone, dead. The cockroaches found gold and silver, and the ants were instantly doomed. In the north, the process took much longer, principally because the land was more vast, and the riches of another kind, requiring generations to appreciate and exploit. But in both cases, the Indian had no real defense, neither technological, which mattered little, nor spiritual, which was the crack through which doom was poured.

In Europe, the age of Elizabeth was a lifespan which saw an enormous, deep, painful opening of many levels of awareness for every person, from the dullest to the most sensitive. While Quetzalcoatl was raging through the New World, plucking out the throbbing red and gold heart of his Indian peoples, the magic herb of this New World was wrenching the dark heart and mind of the European into the light. Life in Europe was brutal and miserable for almost all men, women and children when tobacco first appeared. In the harsh yet somehow soothing, heavy but somehow enlightening rush of this gifted smoke these people, for the first time in their own lives and for the first time ever in the long chain of their ancestors, experienced inspiration — literally breathing in a higher state of being. Writers on the history of tobacco don't dwell on the conditions of ordinary life in the late 1500's in Europe, but if one does reflect on how most people lived then, it becomes clear that tobacco's relief of suffering and transformation of

197

consciousness introduced into European civilization perhaps its greatest evolutionary boost. It's only now, in the late twentieth century, that marijuana has come to have anything like the impact of tobacco in those days, and the difference is still enormous.

On top of that great sea of dark, miserable, dreary lives floated the states of Europe, the military and civil institutions, a few wealthy individuals, and of course the various great arks bearing the various images of one called God. Down in the sea of life things smelled bad, felt bad, were dull and totally routine, hurt, and were dangerous. To those awakening, life in the sea must have been terrifying for all but the most poetic and creative. One can see in the almanacs of the period, which were what the newly awakening people were attracted to read, elaborate forecasts and visions of the awful tides of the coming year — life was to consist of terrible tempests, monstrous births, bloody snows, great floods and destruction, and convulsions in the heart of the earth.

Printing was brand new, and so therefore was reading, and judging by what the late 16th century was learning from the almanacs in an almost exclusive diet of terror and foreboding, they must have been as thrilled by the prospect of the terrible and the mystical as we today are thrilled by assault and death on television, and by madness and pain in the daily lives of our fellow creatures brought to us live on the news.

The awakening of Europe was as painful as the dying of the New World, and the dance of death and life was simultaneous and intertwined. That tobacco played a central role is undeniable; it certainly was not the only central influence upon the European steps in the dance, but its role has been hidden from most of us in our contemporary education, due largely to a lack of appreciation on the part of

our educators and masters for the true role of psychoactive drugs in the evolution of consciousness on the planet. My desire in this chapter, and in my work, is to offer for others to consider a point of view too often ignored, to perhaps point to a path which intertwines with the other great paths along which people have arisen since time beyond memory, and along which we will probably be traveling for a long time to come, in hope that by seeing more clearly where we have come from, we might discern more clearly where it is that we are privileged to be going.

(Below) Cystolith trichomes;
upper surface of Cannabis leaf
(X 450)

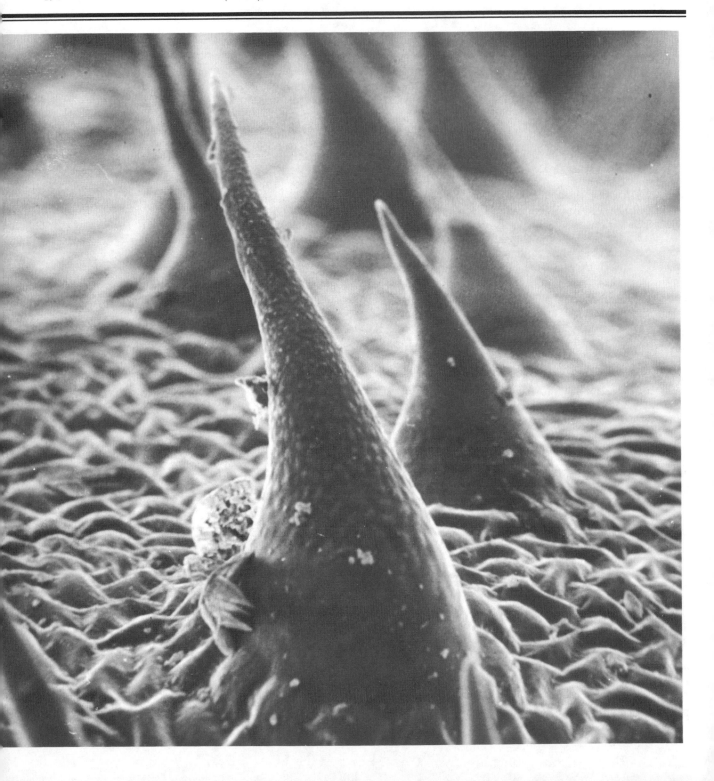

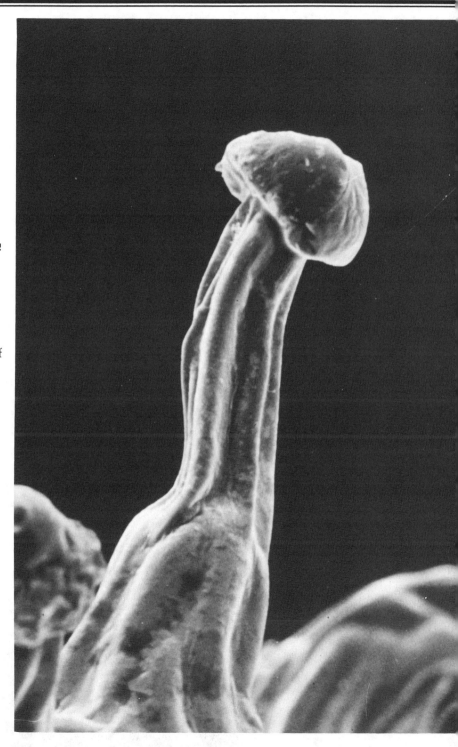

(Below)
Stalked glandular trichome;
bracteole lower surface (x310)

Cultivation and Enhanced Awareness

Plants Be just as Humans Be; each individual, whether plant or animal, is a Being. Between all Beings, and especially between high-order Beings such as Cannabis plants and Humans, there is reciprocity on many levels. You or I cannot long remain in the presence of another Being, whether plant or animal without experiencing, perhaps unconsciously, a swirling, crackling exchange of water vapor, gasses, radiations, vibrations, subtle electricity, chromatics, images and other mental and physical phenomena.

All Beings are interrelated with all other Beings, but particularly with those in the immediate physical vicinity, by field phenomena and processes. Among high-order Beings the phenomenon of intentionality of Mind is added to the ordinary natural field processes. Once intentionality of Mind is added to the field, the forms and patterns of interaction between Beings become evolutionary in potential far beyond the ordinary, organic processes by which life evolved on the planet before Mind.

People who are close with plants have long recognized the value of directing conscious, warm, positive attention toward these old, green Beings. There is really no special secret to the success of "green thumbs" other than their ability to achieve rapport with the plant Being, giving relaxed, undivided attention and caring treatment to each plant. Cannabis in particular is so responsive that almost any form of friendly attention paid to these plants will be reciprocated by lush, potent growth and generation of high molecular structures.

For many of us, the marijuana plant is the great contemporary herbal sacrament and a primary source of illumination. The richness of any sacrament lies in the attitude of the person who takes in the physical form of the sacrament, and in whose mind the sacrament takes new form. The biology and ecological relationships of the marijuana plant yield subtle and complex metaphors for understanding one's own relationship with the Earth, Sun, Air and Water, and finally with the great Mind. When we set out to bring the seed of the plant to life by bathing it in the waters, placing it in the earth, enabling it to unfold into the air and the light, if we contemplate our own coming to life as we work to bring the plant to life, we see that as we do with the plant, so was done with each of us. Isn't it curious how seeds, when bathed in water, come to life? They have been elsewhere, and the waters bring them to life. They *come* to life. Isn't that most curious? To gain full appreciation of the Being of another, it is necessary to be able to clearly *see* the other, to become fully aware of the complete nature of the

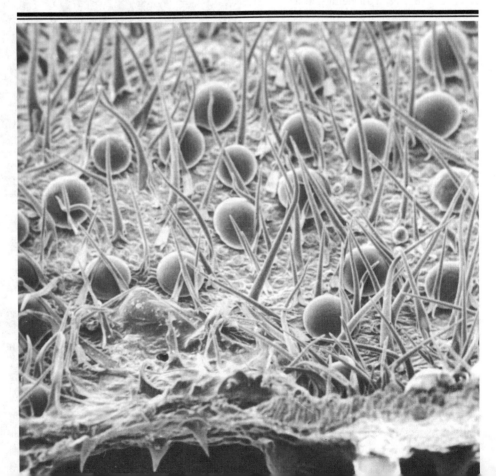

(Right) End-view of sessile glands and covering trichomes on lower surface of Cannabis leaf; cystolith trichomes of upper surface visible at bottom of the figure. (X 115)

other. Most of us are trapped by habituated, patterned, acculturated sensory and mental machinery. We literally do not have available to us the requisite neurophysiological pathways for seeing in its full sense. These pathways are developed only by actual experience, just as muscles are developed only by use. Neurological pathways in the brain for full seeing, for the realization of our potential for broad and deep awareness, exist only as possibility until and unless we develop them. For effective use of awareness in cultivation, we must train our mental and sensory capacities for the work we wish to do. Exercises which de-program habitual ways of not-seeing, ways of interacting with an illusory world built up from concepts into

neurological structures which are only partly congruent with the world of actual Being, where all plants and creatures live, are needed by cultivators who want to explore the uses of expanded awareness as a cultivation tool.

The *Cultivator's Handbook* presents here a simple technique which has served myself and others well. The technique is called Three-Dimensional Strobe Viewing. It is a technique which reveals the extraordinary in the ordinary. The basic exercise was developed by Jean Houston, a great teacher and Seer, who isn't especially interested in drugs and the Mind any more, but who gets appreciative credit for the inspiration for this exercise anyway.

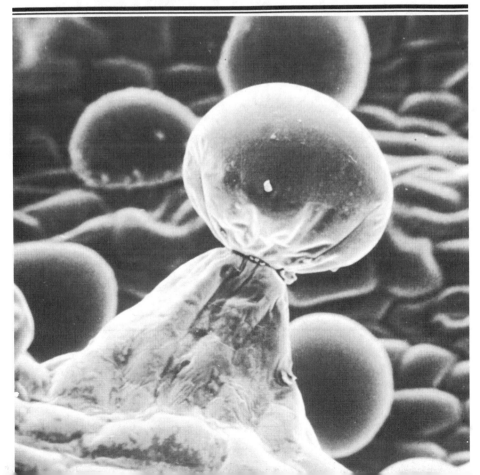

(Left) Stalked glandular trichome with spherical head, Cannabis Sativa (X 400)

(Below) Sessile gland

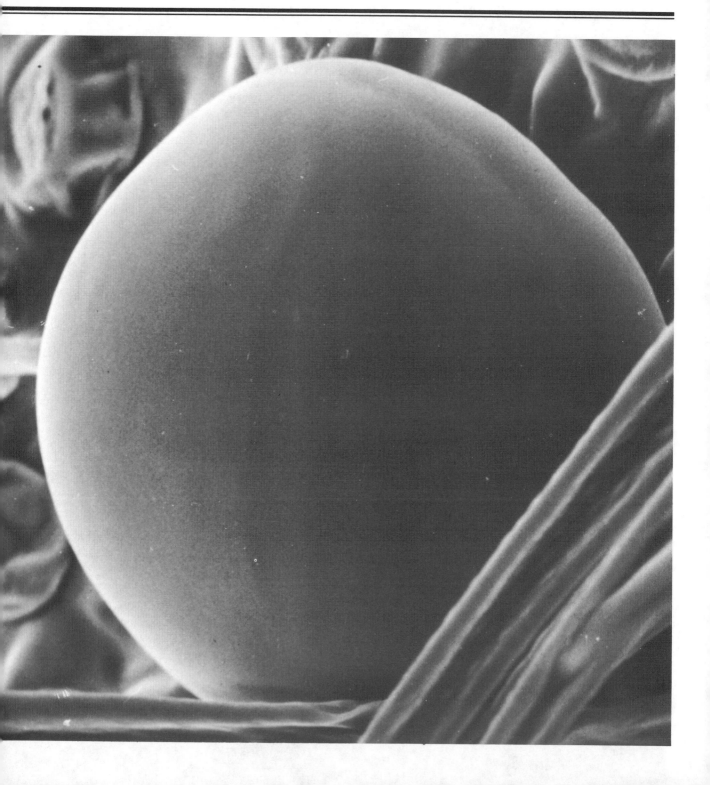

To begin, go or be led into the presence of your plants with your eyes closed, and make yourself comfortable. Take any position, standing, sitting, kneeling or lying, but be facing one of your plants, and be near to it. Now with your eyes remaining closed, allow your attention to travel over your whole body, and to explore the spaces around your body, and to go into the spaces within your body. Pay attention to what is going on between the surfaces of your skin and the plant in whose presence you rest, and note the relationship between your subtle muscle orientation and the plant. Pay attention to your body cavities — ears, nose, and mouth. Note whether or not there is an awareness of the plant within these cavities. If warm and even sensual thoughts and images want to come into awareness, allow them to do so. Extend your awareness to the wind, the light, to the fields of phenomena which surround and penetrate your Being and that of the plant. At what points, and in what ways, are these fields enmeshed with each other? Allow your traditional senses to come to bear. What sounds, smells, taste and other sense impressions come to you? Gradually relax, and allow yourself to Be, in the presence of the Plant Being.

After a few minutes of relaxed attention to as many levels of perception as come into your awareness, move your face very close to your plant. If you have a helper, he or she can position your head; if not, use your sense of touch and get close to the plant, but keep your eyes closed at all times. Aim your head directly at some part of the plant — it doesn't really matter which part, it only matters that if your eyes were open, you would be able to see some aspect of the plant — a leaf cluster, a flower head, the base, a branch, a growing tip. Once you are in position, be still for a minute or so and allow your awareness of the plant to settle down, allowing the disturbance of thought and motion to subside. Breathe deeply, quietly, naturally and calmly.

Now, simply blink your eyes open and shut once. Do not hold your eyes open; a simple blink is what is needed. After you blink and are once more with your eyes closed, slightly re-position your point of view. Waiting ten seconds or so, blink again once. Experiment with the best frequency of blinking for yourself. Never blink twice from the same position, and don't be concerned with the nature or quality of what you see when you blink, or with the afterimage you retain, simply allow the impressions you will receive to enter into your awareness. Proceed with the strobe-blinking from as many angles and perspectives as you care to achieve. There is no need to be concerned with losing orientation to the plant, because your internal mechanisms will keep you oriented. Don't hesitate to go into contortions to achieve unusual perspectives. Maintain silence. Allow awareness to open to the total interchange between yourself and the plant, not just to the visual input and its effects.

There is no particular set of "results" to be expected from this exercise. To be expectant is to be like too many folks who, the first time they try marijuana, ask their more experienced friends — "When is it going to happen?" Of course all that anyone guiding such a friend can say is that "IT" has probably already happened. "IT", is simply a matter of seeing, in new ways.

(Below) Premature female
flowers forming
at a leaf node

Often with this exercise people experience surprise, delight and excitement. Memories of the world's vivid nature in childhood come shimmering into awareness. A description of the exercise might be that it is a form of communion, which is a powerful form of communication which goes two ways and is full of deep-level content. Often there is felt to be a strong, new link established between the viewer and the natural world, not simply between the viewer and the particular plant which is the focus of awareness. Strobe-viewing will, if practiced regularly over a week or two, place you in a whole new relationship with the plants which you are raising. If you are cultivating a number of plants together, you may want to Strobe on a different plant each time, or to concentrate on only one plant. Either way is OK.

From the shift in perspective gained through this simple exercise, it is but a natural move into altered states of consciousness with respect to the Plant Being which you are cultivating. You will become aware of the deep processes of the Being which is held in your awareness. The breathing Being, for instance, with its great tides of gas and vapor drawn in through the skin, sluiced through the tissues, processed in cellular workshops, stripped of molecules and atoms, mixed with the metabolic wastes, pumped once again to the leaf surfaces, and expelled into the atmosphere by powerful bladders, becomes real to you as you raise your awareness of the plant through the focussing of attention promoted by this exercise.

Many such experiences and realizations come to the cultivator who practices Three-Dimensional Strobe Viewing. In appreciation of the fundamental place of Mind and Intent in the emergence of new levels of energy and form, the cultivator pays respect to the elemental world. Since the beginning of life on the planet, the dance of the plant has been with the physical elements, and only recently in geological time has the element of conscious Mind entered upon the dancing ground in the form of Man and his Brain and Body. Through our caring for plants, we rediscover our relationship with the natural world. Our blood is of the ancient seas; is not our consciousness of the ancient forms? The legends of ancient high civilizations which trace through our shrouded memories like fine golden threads never reveal the forms of these forgotten civilizations. It is not necessary to have elaborated brain physiology like Humans in order to experience Being. Perhaps it's not unreasonable to sense that Human Beings are the inheritors of the profound dreams of ancient fish, bird, reptile, and other creature civilizations. Just as our body goes through the physiological experience of full evolutionary history in its embryonic stages, may not our psyche bear within its nature the experience of all the high forms which have gone before? It may be that not only is our body that of many previous creatures, but that much of our ordinary and familiar human experience derives directly from the experience of a dominant fish species in some ancient sea, or from the memories of an advanced bird who flew in ancient skies.

As we raise our plants, let us be aware of the old forms with which we engage. Through the use of enhanced awareness techniques such as Three-Dimensional Strobe Viewing, we can work to see that the caring which we direct toward the plants also washes over ourselves, those we love, and the community about us. In the states of expanded consciousness and awareness created by such exercises, there should be no doubt that this work is nurturing not just to the plant. In plants as well as in creatures love is the key element in growth, and it is through awareness that love is given and received.

With such insight, let each of us move onwards, along with Robert Crumb's little Guru, into the Fog. One closes the eyes and the Fog is there. The eyes flash open, then shut again, and in the afterimage of focussed awareness there burns an inner light. Another flash, and the Fog is burned away in another corner of the inner field of vision. Another flash, and there is clarity in another place. Thus we can bring ourselves to *seeing*.

The search for clarity and interior vision in the foggy lands of normal, habitual, time-bound consciousness is a search for a most precious gem. Every one of us remembers having seen this gem at one place or another in our life. Each of us remembers one or several such moments when everything seemed special, clear, vivid, peaceful, tangible and intensely intelligent. Memories of these times can be painful, because of the poignant contrast with our accustomed lives, our ordinary ways of seeing and being. Yet we treasure these times when we have glimpsed the gem of illumination. If we can but realize that such moments are not lost to us, nor are the secrets forbidden to us, but that the place and the knowledge may be revealed through the doing of certain deeds, then we may live our lives with present joy, and may pursue our daily activities in the certain knowledge that illumination may be chosen and received.

We who love the marijuana plant may work to vitalize those capacities of mind and body which generate rapport with the plant, and will thus experience not only the benefits of directed attention in creating a higher more illuminating plant for our ultimate use, but will also experience the validity of such directedness of mind in the raising of our own consciousness and capacities in other ways, for other purposes. In this respect, Three-Dimensional Strobe

Viewing is simply an easy, readily
available experience open to cultivators
which can lead on to other, broader,
deeper realization and practices. Any
cultivator who practices regular viewing
with one or many plants several times a
week will not only create a higher
experience when the plant is ultimately
consumed, but will also create a higher
state of mind in which to enjoy and
benefit from that experience, and others.

With that promise, dear Reader, it
becomes time to close this *Handbook.*
For some, we may already have gone
beyond the strict limits of marijuana
cultivation. Thank you for joining me in
this botannical and spiritual inquiry into
the nature of our ancient friend,
companion and teacher, *Cannabis sativa.*

Marijuana Bibliography

*essential for cultivators

Abel, Ernest, ed.; *Behavioral and Social Effects of Marijuana*, MSS Information Corp., N.Y., 1973.

*Abel, Ernest, ed.; *The Scientific Study of Marijuana*, Nelson-Hall, Chicago, 1976.

Anderson, L. C.; *A Study of Systematic Wood Anatomy in Cannabis*, Botanical Museum Leaflets, Harvard, 24(2) 29-36, 1974.

Andreoli, Vittorino; *Marijuana-Dimensione Clinica & Giuridica*, Milan, Tamburini, 1974. (In Italian)

Anson, E.; (in) *Journal of the Dublany Agricultural Experimental Station*, Vol. II, No. 2, 1913; pp 50-68.

W. Armstrong & J. Parscandola; *American Concern Over Marijuana in the 1930's*, Journal of Pharmacological History 14(1) 25-35, 1972.

Arnoux, M.; *Effect of Photoperiod & Nitrogen Supply*, Journal of Amelior Plantes 16, 259, 1966. (In French)

Arnoux, M.; *Influence of Environment on Sexual Expression in Hemp; Effect of Nitrogen Nutrition*, Annual of Amelior Plantes, 16(123), 1966. (In French)

Arutinyantz, S. M.; *Chemical Investigation of Indian Hemp*, St. Petersburg, 1881. (In Russian)

Attice, J.; *A Case of Poisoning by Cannabis Indica*, British Medical Journal, London, 1896; p 948.

Auide, J.; *Studies in Therapeutics; Cannabis Indica*, Therapeutics Gazette, Vol. 6, Detroit, 1890; pp 523-526.

*George Avery & Elizabeth Johnson; *Hormones and Horticulture*, New York, 1947; pp 282-300.

Bailey, L. H.; *Cyclopedia of American Agriculture*, Vol. II, London, 1907; pp 377-380.

Banal; *Note Sur Les Extraits de Cannabis Indica*, Montpelier Med., Vol. 15, 1890; pp 461-465. (In French)

*Battaglia, B.; *Sul hascisch et sua azione nell' organismo umano*, Psichiatria, #5, Naples, 1887; pp 1-38. (In Italian)

Beane, F. D.; *An Experience with Cannabis Indica*, Buffalo Medicine and Science Journal, Vol. 23, 1883-84; pp 445-451.

Bentlif, P. B.; *A Case of Poisoning by Extract of Cannabis Indica*, Clinical Sketches, London, 1896.

Berke, Joseph; *The Cannabis Experience*, Peter Owen, London, 1974.

Berkman, Anton; *Seedling Anatomy of Cannabis Sativa*, Chicago (Ph.D. Thesis), 1939.

Bertherand, E.; *A propos de la prohibition du haschisch en Turquie*, Journal of Medicine and Pharmacy of Algeria, Algiers, 1896. (In French)

Berthier; *Le Haschisch administré comme hypnotique*, Bulletin of the Society of Medical Practicioners, Paris, 1867. (In French)

Birch, E.; *The Use of Indian Hemp in the Treatment of Chronic Chloral and Chronic Opium Poisoning*, Lancet, London, 1889.

Bloomquist, E., *Marijuana—The Sacred Trip*, Glencoe, Beverly Hills, 1971.

*Bonnie, Richard; *The Marijuana Conviction: A History of Prohibition in the U.S.*, Univ. of Virginia Press. 1974.

Borthwick & Scolly; *Photoperiodic Responses in Hemp*, Botannical Gazette, Vol. 116, 1954; p 14.

Bridwell, Raymond; *Hydroponic Gardening*, Woodbridge Press, Santa Barbara, 1974.

Brooklyn Botannical Garden; *Handbook On Biological Control of Plant Pests*, Brooklyn, New York.

Browne, E. G.; *A Chapter from the History of Cannabis Indica*, St. Bartholomews Hospital Journal, London, Vol. IV, 1896-97; pp 81-86.

Brue, Ronald; *The Pot Report*, Award Books, N.Y., 1971

Buchwald, A.; *Ueber Cannabis Praparate*, Breslau, 1885. (In German)

Bureau of Plant Industry; *The Cultivation of Hemp in the United States*, Cir. #57, 1910.

*Burgess, A. H.; *Hops-Botany, Cultivation and Utilization*, New York, 1964.

Burroughs, H.; *Le Chanvre Indien (Cannabis Indica)*, Lyons, St. Etienne, 1896. (In French)

Caldwell, J. & Sever, P.; *History, Structural Chemistry, Pharmacology & Metabolism of Cannabis*, Clinical Pharmacology & Therapy 16(6), 1974; pp 989-1013.

Cano Puerta, Guillermo; *Marijuana: Yerba Maldita*, Medellin, Brazil, 1967. (In Spanish)

Central Africa Journal of Medicine, *Dagga Smoking in Rhodesia*, 12(11), 1966; pp 215-16.

Vera Charles & A. Jenkins; *A Fungous Disease of Hemp*, (in) Journal of Agricultural Research, USDA, Vol. III, No. 1, Oct., 1914; pp 81-85.

Christison, A.; *On the Natural History, Action, and Uses of Indian Hemp*, Monthly Journal of the Medical Society, London & Edinburgh, Vol. 13, 1851.

Ciba Study Group #21, *Hashish—Its Chemistry & Pharmacology*, Boston, Little Brown, 1965.

*Coffman, C. & Gentner, W., *Effects of Drying Time and Temperature on Cannabinoid Profile of Stored Leaf Tissue*, Bulletin of Narcotics, (26)1, 1974; pp 67-70.

Comfort, L.; *An Overdose of Cannabis Indica*, Milwaukee Journal, Vol. III, 1895; p 370.

Cook, A. B.; *Poisoning by Cannabis Indica; Two Drams of Herrings English Extract of Indian Hemp being taken without Suicidal Intent*, The American Practitioner, Louisville, Ky., Vol. XXX, 1884; pp 25-30.

Coutselinis, A. & Miras, C.; *Effects of the Smoking Process on Cannibinols*, UN Document # ST/SOA/SER.S/23, 1973.

*DeCourtive, E.; *Haschish—Etude Historique et Physiologique*, Paris, 1848. (In French)

De Pasquale, A.; *Ultrastructure of the Cannabis Sativa Glands*, Planta Medica, 25, 1974; p 238.

Dewey, Lyster; *The Hemp Industry in the United States*, (in) USDA Yearbook, Vol. 118, 1901; pp 541-555, illus.

D'Ippolito, G.; (in) *State Agricultural Bulletin of Italy*, Vol. 45, No. 4, 1912; pp 302-320.

D'Lima, C.; *Indian Hemp Fiber*, (in) Agricultural Journal of India, Vol. II, No. 1, 1916; pp 31-41.

Dodge, Charles; *Cultivation of Hemp and Jute*, (in) Fiber Investigations #8, USDA, 1898; pp 5-23.

Dodge, Charles; *Culture of Hemp in Europe*, (in) Fiber Investigations #11, USDA, 1898; pp 5-28.

Dodge, Charles; *Fiber Investigations #9*, USDA, 1897; pp 106-110.

Dodge, Charles; *Hemp Culture* (in) USDA Yearbook, Vol. 74, 1895; pp 215-22.

Dodge, Charles; *The Hemp Industry in France* (in) Fiber Investigations #1, USDA, 1892, pp 27-31; pp 64-74.

Doorenbos, N.; *Address before the American Pharmacist Academy*, Academy of Pharmacological Sciences 117th Annual Meeting, Washington, D.C., April 12-17, 1970; p 77.

Doorenbos, N. et al; *Cultivation, Extraction, & Analysis of Cannabis Sativa*, Annual N.Y. Academy of Science, 191, 1971; pp 3-14.

*Douglas, James; *Advanced Guide to Hydroponics*, New York, Drake Publishing, 1976.

*Duvel, J. W. T.; *The Vitality and Germination of Seeds*, Ph.D. Dissertation, Univ. of Michigan, 1902.

Edes, R. T. ; *Cannabis Indica*, Boston Medical & Scientific Journal, 1893.

Eyre, J. V. et al; (in) *Journal of the Royal Agricultural Society of England*, Vol. 74, 1913; pp 127-172.

Fairbairn, J. W.; *Cannabinoid Content of Some English Reefers*, Nature, Vol. 249, No. 5454, 1974; pp 276-78.

*Fairbairn, J. W.; *The Trichomes and Glands of Cannabis Sativa L.*, UN Bulletin on Narcotics 24(4), 1972; p 29.

Fisher, H.; *Case of Cannabis Poisoning*, Cincinnati Lancet-Clinic, Vol. 37, 1896; p 405.

Fishlowitz, G. G.; *Poisoning by Cannabis Indica*, Medical Record, New York, Vol. 50, 1896; p 280.

Fleming, Dave; *Complete Guide to Growing Marijuana*, Los Angeles, Peace Press, 1969.

Frazier, Jack; *The Marijuana Farmers: Hemp Cults and Cultures*, New Orleans, Solar Age Press, 1974.

Fristedt, R. F.; *Hemp from a Medical View*, Upsala, 1969-70.

*Fullerton, D. & Kurzman, M.; *Identification and Misidentification of Marijuana*, Contemporary Drug Problems 3, 1974; pp 291-344.

*Garner, Robert; *The Grafters Handbook*, New York, 1958.

*Garner, W. & Allard, H.; *Effect of the Relative Length of Day and Night and Other Factors of the Environment of Growth and Reproduction in Plants*, (in) Journal of Agricultural Research, USDA, Vol. 18, 1928; pp 553-606.

*Garner, W. & Allard, H.; *Flowering and Fruiting of Plants as Controlled by the Length of Day*, (in) USDA Yearbook, 1920; pp 377-400.

*Garner, W. & Allard, H.; *Further Studies in Photoperiodism*, (in) Journal of Agricultural Research, USDA, 1923; pp 871-920, illus.

Geiser, M.; *Poisoning by Cannabis Indica*, Medical Record, New York, Vol. 50, 1896; p 519.

Gill, N. & Vear, K.; *Agricultural Botany*, London, 1958; pp 204-205.

Giraud, J.; *L'art de faire varier les effects du hachich*, Encephale, Paris, 1881; pp 418-425. (In French)

Githens, Thomas; *Drug Plants of Africa*, Philadelphia, 1949.

Gley, E. & Richet, C.; *Notes sur le hachich*, Bulletin of the Society of Psychology and Physiology, Paris, 1886; pp 1-13. (In French)

Godard, E.; *Egypte et Palestine*, Paris, 1867; pp 343-357. (In French)

Goode, Erich (ed.); *Marijuana*, Atherton Press, 1969.

Goode, Erich; *The Marijuana Smokers*, Basic Books, N.Y., 1970.

Gould, Robert (ed.); *Symposium of Gibberellins*, No. 28, Advances in Chemistry Series, Washington, D.C., 1961.

Grimaux, E.; *Du hachisch, ou chanvre indien*, Paris, 1865. (In French)

*Grinspoon, Lester; *Marijuana Reconsidered*, Harvard University Press, 1971.

*Grupp, Stanley; *The Marijuana Muddle*, Kendall-Hunt Pub., Dubuque, Iowa, 1976.

Hamaker, W.; *A Case of Overdose of Cannabis Indica*, Therapeutics Gazette, Detroit, 1891; p 808.

Hammond, C. & Mahlberg, P.; *Morphology of Glandular Hairs of Cannabis Sativa from Scanning Electron Microscopy*, American Journal of Botany, 60, 1973; p 524.

Haney, A. & Kutschied, B.; *Quantitative Variations in the Chemical Constituents of Marijuana*, Economic Botany 27(2), 1973; pp 193-203.

Hare, H.; *Clinical and Physiological Notes on the Action of Cannabis Indica*, Therapeutics Gazette, Detroit, Vol. 3, 1887; pp 225-228.

Harris, Dudley; *Hydroponics: Growing Without Soil*, North Pomfret, Dudley & Charles Publishers, 1975.

*Hartman, Hudson; *Plant Propagation: Principles and Practices*, Prentice-Hall, Englewood Cliffs, N.J., 1975.

Havas, G.; (cited in) *Agricultural Botany*, USDA, Vol. 36, 1917.

*Hayward, Herman; *The Structure of Economic Plants*, New York, 1938; pp 214-245.

Hellman, Arthur; *Laws Against Marijuana—The Price We Pay*, Univ. of Illinois Press, Urbana, 1975.

Henkel, Alice; *Weeds Used in Medicine*, Bureau of Plant Industry, USDA, 1904, Farmers Bulletin #188.

Henkel, Alice; *Wild Medicinal Plants of the United States*, Bureau of Plant Industry, USDA, 1906, Bulletin #89.

*Heslop-Harrison; *Auxins and Sexuality in Cannabis Sativa*, Physiology of Plants, Vol. 9, 1956; p 588.

Heslop-Harrison; *The Experimental Modification of Sex Expression in Flowering Plants*, Biological Reviews, Vol. 32, 1957; p 38.

*Heslop-Harrison; *The Sexuality of Flowers*, New Biology, Vol. 23, 1957; p 9.

Heslop-Harrison; *Growth Substances and Flower Morphogenesis*, Journal of the Linnaen Society, London, Vol. 56, 1959; p 269.

*Heslop-Harrison; *The Modification of Sex Expression in Cannabis Sativa by Carbon Monoxide*, Proceedings of the Royal Society of Edinburgh, (Sec. B), Vol. 66, 1957; p 424.

Heslop-Harrison; *Leaf-shape Changes Associated with Flowering and Sex Differentiation in Cannabis Sativa*, Proceedings of the Royal Irish Academy (Sec. B), Vol. 59, 1958; p 257.

Heslop-Harrison; *Effects of Gibberellic Acid on Flowering and the Secondary Sexual Difference in Stature in Cannabis Sativa*, Proceedings of the Royal Academy (Sec. B), Vol. 61, 1961; p 219.

Heslop-Harrison & Woods; *Temperature-Induced Meristic and other Variation in Cannabis Sativa*, Journal of the Linnaer Society of London, Vol. 55, 1959; p 290.

*Heslop-Harrison; *Cannabis Sativa*, (in) Evan's *The Induction of Flowering*, Cornell Univ. Press, 1969; pp 205-226.

Hirata, K., *Sex Determination in Hemp*, Journal of Genetics, Vol. XIX, 1927-28; pp 65-79.

Hochman, Joel; *Marijuana and Social Evolution*, Prentice-Hall, 1972.

Hood, L. V. S.; *Headspace Volatiles of Marijuana*, Nature 242(5397), 1973; pp 402-03.

Hungerford, M.; *An Overdose of Hasheesh*, Popular Science Monthly, New York, Vol. 24, 1883-84; pp 509-515.

Identifying & Controlling Wild Hemp, Agricultural Experimental Station Bulletin #555, Kansas State University, 1972.

Ireland, T.; *Insanity from the Abuse of Indian Hemp*, Alienist and Neurologist, St. Louis, Mo., Vol. XIV, 1893; pp 622-630.

Johnson, L.; *A Manual of the Medical Botany of North America*, New York, 1884; pp 245-46.

Johnson, D. W. & Gunn, J. W.; *Dangerous Drugs: Adulterants, Dilutents and Deception in Street Samples*, J. Forensic Sciences, 17, 629, 1972.

Jones, H. L.; *Note on Cannabis Indica as a Narcotic*, Practicioner, London, Vol. XXXV, 1885; p 251.

Jones, Ralph; *Marijuana*, Endicott, N.Y., 1938.

*Joyce, C. R. B. & Curry, S. H. (eds.); *The Botany and Chemistry of Cannabis*, J & A Churchill, London, 1970.

*Kamstra, Jerry; *Weed: Adventures of a Dope Smuggler*, Harper & Row, 1974.

Kebler, L. F.; *Habit Forming Agents*, Farmers Bulletin #393, Bureau of Plant Industry, USDA; pp 3-19.

Kelly, W.; *Cannabis Indica*, British Medical Journal, London, 1883; p 1281.

*Kirby, R. H.; *Vegetable Fibers*, New York, 1963; pp 46-61.

*Korte, F. et al; *New Results of Hashish-Specific Constituents*, UN Bulletin on Narcotics 17, 35, 1965.

Kraemer, Henry; *Botany and Pharmacognesy*, Philadelphia, 1902; pp 226-27, 275, 351-353.

Kubena, R. K. et al; *A 43 Year Old USP Fluidextract of Cannabis*, Journal Pharmacological Science 61(1), 1972; pp 144-45.

Lailler, A.; *Therapeutique: du chanvre indien*, Annual Med.—Psychologie, Paris, Vol. XII, 1890; pp 78-83. (In French)

*Lallemand, C. F.; *Le Hachych*, Paris, 1843. (In French)

Lapin, L.; *Ein Beitrag zur Kenntniss der Cannabis Indica*, 8, Jurjew, 1894. (In German)

Lees, M. C.; *Cannabis Sativa sen Indica: Indian Hemp*, British Medical Journal, London, Vol. XI, 1888; pp 95-98.

*Lepinske, Harry; *Jamaican Ganja*, Exposition Press, N.Y., 1973.

Lewis, Barbara; *The Sexual Power of Marijuana*, P. H. Wyden, N.Y., 1970.

Lord, Jess; *Marijuana and Personality Changes*, Health Lexington Books, Lexington, Mass., 1971.

Mackensie, S.; *On Some Classes of Cases in which Indian Hemp is of Special Service*, Medical Weekly, Paris, Vol. II, 1894; p 457.

Marijuana—An Annotated Bibliography, Macmillan Information, N.Y., 1956.

MaHinson, J. B.; *Cannabis Indica as an Anodyne and Hypnotic*, St. Louis Medical & Scientific Journal, Vol. LXI, 1891; pp 265-71.

Margolis, Jack; *A Child's Garden of Grass*, Price/Stern/Sloan, Los Angeles, 1969.

Marshall, C. R.; *The Active Principle of Indian Hemp*, Lancet, London, 1897; pp 235-39.

*Masood, A. N. & Doorenbos, N. J.; *Effects of Gibberellic Acid & Indoleacetic Acid on Cannabis Sativa*, Journal of Pharmacological Science, 62(2), 1973; pp 316-18.

McGlothlin, William; *Marijuana—Analysis of Use, Distribution & Control*, US BNDD, 1971.

*McPhee, Hugh; *The Influence of Environment on Sex in Hemp, Cannabis Sativa L.*, (in) Journal of Agricultural Research, Vol. XXVIII, No. 11, USDA, 1924; pp 1067-83.

*Mechoulam, Ralph (ed.);
Marijuana—Chemistry, Pharmacology,
Metabolism and Clinical Effects,
Academic Press, N.Y., 1974.

* Merlin, Mark; Man and
Marijuana—Their Ancient Relationship,
Farleigh Dickinson Univ. Press, New
Jersey, 1972.

*The Methods For Identification of
Cannabis Used by Authorities in USA,
United Nations Document
ST/SOA/SER.S/3.

Miller, Loren, (ed.); Marijuana—Effects
on Human Behavior, Academic Press,
N.Y., 1974.

Mittleider, J. R.; Food for Everyone,
Woodbridge Press, Santa Barbara, 1975.

Moore, Laurence; Marihuana (Cannabis)
Bibliography, Bruin Humanist Forum,
L.A., 1969.

Nahas, Gabriel; Marijuana, Deceptive
Weed, New York, Raven Press, 1975.

Nelhans, Bertil; Cannabis: Afrika,
Uppsala, Sweden, 1972. (In Swedish)

*Nelson, Clarence; Growth Responses of
Hemp to Differential Soil and Air
Temperatures, (in) Journal of Plant
Physiology, 1936, pp 294-309, illus.

Ochse, Soule and Dijkman; Tropical and
Sub-Tropical Agriculture, Vol. 2, 1966, pp
1161-65.

Oertel, T. E.; Observations on the Effect
of Cannabis Indica in Large Doses,
American Medical-Surgical Bulletin, New
York, Vol. 8, 1895; pp 365-68.

Oliver, J.; On the Action of Cannabis
Indica, British Medical Journal, London,
1883.

The Facts of Light About Indoor
Gardening, Ortho Chemicals, Chevron
Oil Company, San Francisco, 1975.

O'Shaughnessy, W. B.; On the
Preparations of the Indian Hemp,
Gunjah (Cannabis Indica), Their Effects
on the Animal System in Health, and
Their Utility in Treatment of Tetanus
and Other Convulsive Disorders,
Calcutta, 1839.

*Oster, Maggie (ed.); The Green Pages,
Ballentine Books, New York, 1977.

Phillips, R. et al; Seasonal Variations in
Cannabinolic Content of Indiana
Marijuana, Journal of Forensic Sciences,
15, 1970; p 191.

*Preliminary Study of the Occurrence of
Cannabis Components in the Various
Parts of the Plant, United Nations
Document ST/SOA/SER.S/26.

Prentiss, D. W.; Case of intoxication
from a comparatively small dose of
Cannabis Indica, Therapeutic Gazette,
Detroit, Vol. VIII, 1892; p 104.

Pritchard, F.; Change of Sex in Hemp, (in)
Journal of Heredity, Vol. 7, 1916; pp
325-29.

*Quimby, M. W. et al; Mississippi-Grown
Cannabis: Cultivation & Observed
Morphological Variations, Economic
Botany, 27, 1973; pp 117-27.

Ram, H. Y. & Jaiswal, U.S.; Induction of
Female Flowers on Male Plants of
Cannabis Sativa, Experientia 26(2), 1970;
pp 214-16.

Ram, H. Y. & Nath, R.; Morphology and
Embryology of Cannabis Sativa,
Phytomorphology, 14, 1964; pp 414-29.

Ramnek, G.; (in) Journal of Experimental
Agronomy, (USSR), Vol. II, No. 6, 1910;
pp 865-66.

Renz, G. A.; *My Experiment with Cannabis Indica*, Northwestern Lancet, St. Paul, Minn., Vol. V, 1885-86; p 203.

Review of Recent Research on Synthesis, Analysis, Metabolism & Pharmacology of Marijuana, Canadian Journal of Pharmaceutical Science, 9(1), 1974; pp 1-7.

Reynolds, J. R.; *On the Therapeutic Uses and Toxic Effects of Cannabis Indica*, Lancet, London, 1890; p 637.

Richet, C.; *Poisons of the Intelligence: Hasheesh*, Popular Science Monthly, N.Y., 1878; pp 482-86.

Robertson, R.; *Toxic Symptoms from the Tincture of Indian Hemp in Official Doses*, Medical Times and Gazette, London, pp 817-19.

Rochebrune, A.; *Toxicologie Africaine*, Paris, 1897. (In French)

Rodale, J. I. (ed.); *The Complete Book of Composting*, Rodale Press, Emmaus, Penn., 1968.

Rodale, J. I.; *The Organic Way to Plant Protection*, Rodale Press, Emmaus, Penn., 1966.

Rosevear, John; *Pot, A Handbook of Marijuana*, New York, 1967.

Rowell, Earl; *On the Trail of Marijuana: The Weed of Madness*, Pacific Press, Mountain View, Calif., 1939.

Rubin, Vera (ed.); *Cannabis and Culture*, The Hague, Mouton, 1971.

*Rubin, Vera (ed.); *Ganja In Jamaica*, The Hague, Mouton, 1975.

Russell, George; *Marijuana Today*, Myrin Institute, 1975.

Saltman, Jules; *Marijuana and Your Child*, Grosset & Dunlap, N.Y., 1970.

*Schaffner, J.; *Complete Reversal of Sex in Hemp*, Science, Vol. 50, 1919; pp 311-13.

Schaffner, J.; *The Influence of Environment on Sexual Expression in Hemp*, (in) Botanical Gazette, 1921; pp 197-219.

*Schaffner, J.; *Influence of the Relative Length of Daylight on the Reversal of Sex in Hemp*, Ecology, Vol. IV, 1923; pp 323-34.

*Schaffner, J.; *Rejuvenations in Hemp*, Ecology, 1927; pp 315-25.

*Schaffner, J.; *Further Experiments in Rejuvenation*, American Journal of Botany, Jan., 1928; pp 77-85.

*Schaffner, J.; *Sex Reversal and Photoperiodivity*, American Journal of Botany, June, 1931; pp 424-30.

Singer, Arnold (ed.); *Marijuana: Chemistry, Pharmacology, Metabolism and Clinical Effects*, New York Academy of Sciences, 1971.

Sinnott, Edmund; *Plant Morphogenesis*, New York, 1960; pp 221, 317, 399, 430.

Small, E. & Beckstead, H.; *Common Phenotypes in 350 Stocks of Cannabis*, Lloydia, 36, 1973; p 144.

Snyder, Soloman; *Uses of Marijuana*, Oxford Univ. Press, N.Y., 1971.

Stepanian, Michael; *Pot Shots (Drawings by R. Crumb)*, Delacorte Press, 1972.

Stevens, Murphy; *How to Grow Marijuana Indoors Under Lights*, Sun Magic Publishing Co., Seattle, Wash., 1973.

Stimson, Mary Drake; *Marijuana Mystery*, Dorrance & Co., Philadelphia, Penn., 1940.

Stockberger, W. W.; (in) *Production of Drug-Plant Crops in the United States*, Bureau of Plant Industry, USDA Yearbook, 1917; pp 169-176.

Stockberger, W. W.; *Drug Plants Under Cultivation*, Farmers Bulletin #663, Bureau of Plant Industry, USDA, 1915.

Stromberg, L.; *Minor Components of Cannabis Resin I*, Journal of Chromatography, 63, 1971; p 391.

Stromberg, L.; *Minor Components of Cannabis Resin II*, Journal of Chromatography 68, 1972; p 248.

Stromberg, L.; *Minor Components of Cannabis Resin III*, Journal of Chromatography, 68, 1972; p 253.

Suckling, W.; *On the Therapeutic Value of Indian Hemp*, British Medical Journal, London, 1891; p 12.

*Talley, Paul; *Carbohydrate-Nitrogen Ratios with Respect to the Sexual Expression of Hemp*, (in) Journal of Plant Physiology, 1934; pp 731-748.

Tart, Charles; *On Being Stoned*, Science and Behavior Books, Palo Alto, 1971.

*Sister Mary Etienne Tibeau; *Time Factor in Utilization of Mineral Nutrients by Hemp*, (in) Journal of Plant Physiology, 1933; pp 731-47.

Tinklenberg, Jared (ed.); *Marijuana and Health Hazards-Current Research*, Academic Press, N.Y., 1976.

Toth, L.; *Grimault et Compagnie cigarettes indiennes au Cannabis Indica*, Budapest, 1881. (In French)

Truitt, E. B.; *Biological Disposition of Tetrahydrocannibinols*, Pharmacological Review, 23, 1971; p 273.

Tukey, H. B.; *Plant Regulators in Agriculture*, New York, 1954.

*Turner, et al; *Stability of Cannabinoids in Stored Plant Material (Cannabis)*, Journal of Pharmacological Science 62(10) 1973; pp 1601-05.

Valle, J. R., et al; *Study of Male and Female Plants*, Journal of Pharmacology, 20, 1968; p 798.

*Van Der Veen, R. & Meijer, G.; *Light and Plant Growth*, London, 1959, pp 41, 52, 65, 78-9, 83-93, 119-154.

Walsh, J. H. T.; *Hemp Drugs and Insanity*, Journal of Mental Science, Vol. XL, London, 1894; pp 21-36.

Warden & Waddeil; *The Active Principle of Indian Hemp*, Indian Medical Gazette, Vol. XIX, Calcutta, 1884; pp 259, 354.

*Warmke, H. & Davidson, H.; *Polyploidy Investigations*, (in) Carnegie Institute of Washington Yearbook, No. 41, 1941-42.

*Warmke, H. & Davidson, H.; *Polyploidy Investigations*, (in) Carnegie Institute of Washington Yearbook, No. 42, 1942-43.

*Warmke, H. & Davidson, H.; *Polyploidy Investigations*, (in) Carnegie Institute of Washington Yearbook, No. 43, 1943-44.

Wood, H. C.; *On the Medical Activity of the Hemp Plant as Grown in North America*, Proceedings of the American Philosophical Society, Philadelphia, Penn., Vol. XI, 1869; pp 227-33.

*Yanda, Bill & Fisher, Rick; *Food & Heat Producing Solar Greenhouse Design, Construction, & Operation*, John Muir Publications, Santa Fe, N.M., 1976.

Index

Please believe me — most of us know nothing of the reality behind commercial cigarettes and other such products. Yes, it is known that 350,000 people die each year from smoking cigarettes. Yes, it is known that the cigarette companies make tremendous profits from this death and destruction and that use of cigarettes and other so-called "tobacco" products is harmful for humans even if there weren't constant reminders of the fact by the Surgeon General, the American Medical Association, and countless other surrogate parents. But as with most evils, it is what is not known, combined with the certainty that what is known is the whole story, that is making victims of millions of people.

The same government which will put a person in jail for holding or growing even a small amount of marijuana is allowing a vast criminal conspiracy to kill and cripple hundreds of thousands each year. This conspiracy involves billions in tax revenues for its government, hundreds of thousands of lucrative bureaucratic jobs, and political influence which reaches into and effectively controls even the smallest communities in the country.

It is a classic example of a successful conspiracy, in that its participants and its victims are mutually deceived and misled. The levels of operation within this conspiracy are so convoluted that they almost defy description. However, I would like to take this brief space in the *Cultivator's Handbook* to alert those of you who care to what is going on, and to ask you to be alert to opportunities within your own community to confront this conspiracy, to work against its influence, and to do what you can to ultimately reveal and defeat it. If concerned citizens will get involved in this public debate over the role of government and the cigarette industry in the deaths of millions, it may

be possible to bring a measure of sanity not only to the anti-drug hysteria now sweeping this country, but also to countermand the reality of the truly criminal behavior of our own government and of many of the major corporations in the country. Perhaps in this way we will all come to see the day when we are not only free to pursue our own particular vision of inner reality, but are also free of the tyranny imposed by self-annointed officials and self-serving industries seeking profit and power from exploitation of carefully crafted illusion and ignorance.

The basic problem with confronting this conspiracy is that its surface appears so mundane, so ordinary, that it is almost impossible on first glance to appreciate the depth of its influence on our lives, and the venality of its motivation. The conspiracy is between the American government and the cigarette industry, and involves all types of tobacco products — which are not only familiar to all, but about which the public also feels it knows all there is to know.

I will simply outline the major dimensions of this conspiracy, without editorializing, and hope that what is read here will prompt people to take action at their local level. Every community in America today is involved to some degree in the controversy of non-smokers' rights, and in the debate over the harmfulness of passive smoking.

The principal facts involved in the murder of cigarette smokers and so many others are these:

Cigarettes and other tobacco products manufactured in the U.S. and elsewhere for sale in the European Economic Community (EEC) market are subject to stringent regulation by EEC government health authorities with regard to pesticide

residue content. This regulatory environment is based on qualified scientific and medical assessment of the added, increased risk to public health presented by pesticide residues in tobacco products. U.S. government agencies, including U.S.D.A. and U.S. Department of Commerce, participate in the preparation and enforcement of standards for U.S. tobacco growers in production of tobacco meeting these EEC regulations.

All cigarettes and all other tobacco products sold in the United States contain residues of a wide range of pesticides and other potent agrichemicals (some radioactive) applied during agricultural production and subsequently during storage. The bulk of these pesticide residues occur on tobacco of foreign origin, which comprise over 40% of the tobacco in average U.S. cigarettes (1982), up from 6% in 1970. There is considerable evidence of overapplication and mis-application of these chemicals. Many of these agrichemicals are banned for any application in the U.S., and their presence in any regulated Food, Drug or Cosmetic product is banned. Tobacco products sold in the U.S., however, are specifically exempt from inspection for, or regulation of, pesticide residue content, by any agency of government at any level.

Many of these chemical contaminants and additives in cigarettes and other tobacco industry products are known to be extremely dangerous to human health in minute concentrations, such as those found in secondary smoke. The health effects of these chemicals in chronic, minute doses includes genetic damage; damage to fetuses; respiratory, neurological, circulatory system, and reproductive system damage; and other damage, primarily irreversible in nature and cumulative in effect. The health effects of breathing secondary tobacco smoke are not debatable, as implied in tobacco industry advertising, because the health effects of inhaling the known chemical contaminants in tobacco industry products are well established by irrefutable scientific evidence.

The health effects of the pesticide residues present in tobacco products have not been studied by any U.S. government agency for their health effects on humans when consumed by smoking, and the scientific/medical literature in this area is very thin. EPA–mandated product safety data sheets on many of these pesticides, however, warn specifically against respiratory exposure: and against smoking in any environment in which they are present. In addition, there has been extensive EPA study of the combustion of pesticides and the resulting by-products, which has resulted in published warnings concerning exposure to such combustion as causing danger to human health.

The economic arguments for weakening most proposed anti-smoking ordinances are based on the idea that since nobody has actually proven that secondary tobacco smoke, or passive smoking is harmful, it is unreasonable to go overboard in restricting public smoking behavior. The issue is presented as a disagreement between equally reasonable positions — those who claim smoking as a personal liberty and privilege, and those who object to breathing the smoke of others as a matter of personal liberty and privilege. The fact is that the issue of breathing secondary cigarette smoke has very little to do with the issue of breathing *tobacco* smoke. In addition to the established presence of harmful contaminants and additives, as detailed above, the fact is that many brands of cigarettes contain little real

tobacco, but are constructed of synthetic smoking materials made from tobacco scrap and industrial waste, saturated with chemicals designed to provide taste, aroma, nicotine effect, and unpleasant effects if the smoker tries to switch brands. A comprehensive anti-smoking ordinance would provide protection to the public from the smoke of cigarettes made from a wide range of synthetic materials, none of which have ever been investigated for their health effects when consumed in this way. The tobacco industry has established itself as exempt from inspection and regulation by virtue of tobacco being classified as neither a food nor a drug, and has proceeded to use this total exemption to manufacture products which have little or nothing at all to do with tobacco, but which are equally exempt from scrutiny by any agency charged with protection of public health.

It can be shown by reference to extensive technical and industry literature that tobacco manufacturers have known of the presence of these pesticide residues in their products for many years, and that qualified industry scientists have raised the issue of the potential for negative human health effects of these pesticides in a wide variety of technical and scientific literature. It can be shown that the tobacco manufacturing industry has been in a position to know of the established negative health impact of these pesticide residues for many years, and that in no instance has it taken ameliorative action with regard to products intended for the U.S. market, while taking extensive ameliorative action with products intended for the EEC market.

Much of the evidence for the assertions just made can be found in published scientific and industrial literature, but nowhere is the trail of guilt more clear than in the patent literature. Here is

where we find the hard core bottom line evidence of cigarette industry liability for knowingly manufacturing for profit products which kill people.

Patent # 4,079,742
March 21, 1978
Assignee: Philip Morris
This patent deals with a new process for manufacture of synthetic smoking materials. Pages 1–5 contain an excellent summary of the existing patent literature devoted to development of synthetic smoking materials, showing a long-term trend in this direction in the industry. The patent discusses the wide range of cellulosic materials, primarily industrial and agricultural waste materials, used in development of synthetic smoking materials.

Patent # 3,332,428
July 25, 1967
Assignee: Liggett & Myers
    also
Patent # 3,419,543
December 31, 1968
Assignee: Liggett & Myers
These patents discuss the use of phosgene (military nerve gas) to produce flavoring compounds for smoking materials (page 2). This demonstrates clearly the effect of the absence of regulation, as well as the lengths to which such unregulated scientific research will go.

Patent # 3,920,026
November 18, 1975
Assignee: Liggett & Myers
Discusses methods of masking the undesirable taste and aroma characteristics of poor quality tobacco, and tobacco waste, allowing these materials to be used in manufacturing cigarette products. Shows industry trend toward use of trash materials.

Patent # 3,720,214
March 13, 1973
Assignee: Liggett & Myers
States that "the smoke components responsible for biological activity are formed in the pyrolysis zone of the cigarette cone," and proposes mixing zinc oxide in with the smoking materials as a way to reduce delivery of these components to the smoker. Shows awareness of biological activity (an industry buzzword for disease).

Patent # 4,319,585
March 16, 1982
Assignee: Liggett Group, Inc.
Discusses development of synthetic flavoring agents. Makes several very important statements. "It is well known, as far as the ultimate consumer is concerned, that flavor and aroma are perhaps the largest factors in his selection of a smokable tobacco product." "The term 'tobacco,' as used throughout this specification, is intended to mean any composition intended for use by smoking or otherwise, whether composed of tobacco plant parts or substitute materials, or both." In addition, this patent refers to toxicity studies done on several of the synthetic flavoring components under discussion — indicating that such studies are carried out by industry, and should be available through subpœna process.

Patent # 3,529,602
September 22, 1970
Assignee: Philip Morris
Discussion of the development of a tobacco substitute, with very significant comments showing industry awareness of the biologically damaging properties of regular tobacco (especially pages 1, 2, 8, and 9). Refutes industry contention that nobody has shown tobacco itself to be harmful.

Patent # 4,243,056
January 6, 1981
Assignee: Philip Morris
Discusses a method of impregnating smoking materials with flavorant agents. A very significant discussion of the difficulties of removing residual solvents used in such impregnation. Such solvents include acetone, cyclohexane, and benzene — all identified as carcinogens long before the date of issuance of this patent. Establishes that industry continued using such solvents after their danger was well known.

Patent # 3,964,496
June 22, 1976
Assignee: R. J. Reynolds
Discusses the use of puffed rice as a synthetic tobacco smoking material. Makes several very significant statements concerning industry use of additives. "The burning rate, flavor, and other properties of non-tobacco smoking products can be altered by incorporating with the puffed rice suitable additives such as flavorants, tobacco extracts, nicotine, humectants, ash improving additives, etc." "The materials which are used with the puffed rice to form smoking products are employed in amounts depending upon the effects desired."

This brief appendix merely outlines some of the major reasons why the government and the tobacco industry are responsible for the most massive atrocity in history. I hope that people will read between and behind the lines, and will go from there into active involvement in the debate over smoking in their own community.